Value for Money in Health Services

A Comparative Study

Brian Abel-Smith

Professor of Social Administration
London School of Economics and Political Science

HEINEMANN
LONDON

Heinemann Educational Books Ltd
LONDON EDINBURGH MELBOURNE AUCKLAND TORONTO
HONG KONG SINGAPORE KUALA LUMPUR
IBADAN NAIROBI JOHANNESBURG LUSAKA
NEW DELHI KINGSTON

ISBN 0 435 82005 2
Paperback ISBN 0 435 82006 0

Published by Heinemann Educational Books Ltd
48 Charles Street, London W1X 8AH
Printed Offset Litho and bound in Great Britain by
Cox & Wyman Ltd, London, Fakenham and Reading

VALUE FOR MONEY IN
HEALTH SERVICES

Preface

All over the world more is being spent on health services and a higher proportion of the cost is being paid by taxation or social insurance. Increasingly access to health services has come to be regarded as a right: the modern state is seen to have a duty to ensure that all can use them, whether they can afford to purchase them or not.

But how useful are health services in promoting health? On what principles should health services be organized and financed? How can the services be improved? How is it possible to ensure that a full range of services is available wherever they are needed? How is it possible to ensure that value for money is obtained for health services? Can the professions be left to promote both quality and efficiency? How far is professional freedom compatible with the accountability for public funds? These questions are being asked in both poorer and richer countries.

This book is written on the assumption that there are lessons to be learnt about the organization and financing of health services from studying both the market for health services and the experience of the way that market operates in different cultures and at different levels of development. Thus much of this book is about health economics in its widest sense. But much also is about public administration and the sociology of medicine. The problems of organizing and financing health services cannot be resolved by any value-free theory. I have not hesitated to allow my own values to intrude towards the latter part of the book.

In the first part of the book, the context is set by an attempt to describe the historical evolution of the organization and financing of health services in different countries. Inevitably the description is limited by the availability of literature in the English language. But the aim is to indicate the contrasts between different cultures and political systems. There is a great opportunity for future research workers to improve on my tentative attempt to sketch the history of world health services and make comparisons between different countries and different continents. And I fully expect that further research will show that my bold attempt at a general description is inadequate and possibly misleading on a number of points. Moreover, a description of this kind can never be up-to-date. The references indicate the dates at which statements were true.

I then attempt to come to grips with some of the fundamental questions. What is the case for free or subsidized health services? Why and in what ways is the medical market regulated? I then turn to some parts of health services which require separate discussion both in theory and from study of the experience of different countries. What are the effects of different ways of paying doctors? What are the effects of the operations of the world pharmaceutical industry and how are countries attempting to regulate the industry? What are the underlying economics of the provision of hospital services?

Next I discuss the underlying criteria for health planning. What contribution do health services make to human welfare and can it be measured? What is the relation between health and socio-economic development? I then consider separately planning in the more developed countries and in the developing countries. Finally I discuss education and training.

The suggestion that I should attempt to write such an ambitious book came from my friend Dr Archie Cockrane – in a ski-lift at Davos, Switzerland. Originally we hoped it would be a joint work, but pressure of other responsibilities made it impossible for him to participate as joint-author. But his ideas – particularly those expressed in his penetrating book *Effectiveness and Efficiency*[1] – have greatly influenced my thinking and I owe a great debt to him for all he has taught me as well as for his comments on an earlier draft of this manuscript.

Others who kindly read this book in draft are: Mrs Ida Merriam, Mr David Piachaud, Miss Jennifer Roberts, Mrs Rosemary Stevens and Mrs Dorothy Rice and her colleagues in the Department of Health, Education and Welfare (United States). I am grateful to all of them for extremely valuable comments, suggestions and references which have enormously improved the book as it has progressed.

1. A. L. Cockrane, *Effectiveness and Efficiency*, N.P.H.T., 1972.

PREFACE

Almost the whole of the book was compiled before I joined the Department of Health and Social Security as a Special Advisor to the Secretary of State in March 1974. The work that I have done on it since has been mainly of an editorial and revisionary character. The views expressed are of course entirely my own and have not been affected by my access to official information in the past months.

Brian Abel-Smith

Contents

		page
Preface		v
1	Charity, Government and Voluntary Insurance	1
2	Compulsory Health Insurance and National Health Services	13
3	The Money Barrier	32
4	The Medical Market	45
5	Tradesman or Priest: the Payment of the Doctor	58
6	The Pharmaceutical Industry	77
7	The Efficient Use of Hospitals	101
8	The Search for Priorities	121
9	Health and Economic Development	138
10	Planning in More Developed Countries	154
11	Planning in Developing Countries	177
12	Education and Training	198
13	Conclusion	217
	Index	223

CHAPTER 1

Charity, Government and Voluntary Insurance

Modern scientific medicine has a history of not much more than two hundred years. Indeed it has often been said that it was not until this century that the average patient who consulted the average doctor was likely to derive benefit from the encounter. Nevertheless effective remedies for illnesses were developed during the nineteenth century and earlier and some preventive actions came to be taken, if not always from a correct understanding of the process by which illness spread.

One of the most remarkable medical discoveries was that of vaccination against smallpox by Jenner in 1798. It is this and this alone which made it possible virtually to eliminate smallpox from much of Western Europe and North America by the end of the nineteenth century and has made it practicable for WHO to make a concerted effort to eliminate it from the world. The effective medicines developed in the nineteenth century, other than laxatives which were used in excess, included morphine, quinine, strychnine and atropine and later codeine and cocaine. It was not until the end of the century that X-ray and pathology came to be used as diagnostic tools.

Until the development of anaesthetics in the eighteen-eighties only quick and superficial surgery could be practised – the cutting out of stones in the gall bladder, the lancing of boils, the removal of cataracts, and amputations. Moreover all surgery was very dangerous before the development of aseptic techniques. After the development of asepsis and anaesthetics, there was a rapid expansion of surgery, and thus of hospitals, from the late nineteenth century onwards.

Judged in terms of mortality rates there were dramatic improvements in health in the richer countries of the world during the

1

nineteenth century. But these were mainly due to higher standards of nutrition and personal hygiene and the introduction of clean water and sewage disposal in cities. Improved environmental health services removed the scourges which had killed the young and middle-aged for centuries. Personal hygiene, sanitation and improved nutrition, rather than the isolation of cases in hospitals, conquered cholera, typhoid and the plague in Europe and North America. Maternal and infant mortality fell as hygienic and nutritional standards rose, despite the excessive use of forceps and other implements to 'assist' childbirth.

As modern scientific medicine gradually proved its value it gradually replaced the traditional medicine which had evolved in Europe as it had evolved in other countries of the world and in other cultural traditions. Virtually all societies have developed healers and traditional remedies for sickness. In many societies healing has been closely associated with religion. This was true of Europe before the age of scientific medicine and it is still true of many countries today. In primitive society the medicine man was and still is sorcerer, priest and physician in one.[1] Still today in many societies Western scientific medicine is in active competition with traditional medicine. Many people seek help from both or only use Western medicine when traditional medicine has failed to produce results.

Though there was little medical care of proven value in Europe until the end of the nineteenth century, those who could afford it consulted doctors when they were ill and were purged, bled and provided with a range of distasteful medicines either by the doctor or by the chemist. In all societies there seems to be an urge to intervene in sickness – even when there is no evidence to suggest what intervention will be beneficial. Down through the centuries, the common law of Europe and America recognized the maintenance of the common health as one of the great tasks of society. To secure his right to practise the doctor had to prove his knowledge, his integrity and his skill. He was not free to select or to reject his patients at will. He had a social duty parallel to that of the priest.

As one who follows a common calling he held himself ready to serve all in need to the limit of his capacity. Nor was inability to pay a valid excuse for the refusal of his service. The law recognized him as a kind of unofficial servant of the community and exempted him of the ordinary rules of the market. . . . To insure adequacy

2

of service, a special rule of law was decreed for the physician: he was permitted to charge different fees to patients differently situated. ... It elevated medicine above commerce, broke the pecuniary connection between the doctor's service and his reward, and gave legal recognition to the principle that persons were to be served according to their needs, that charges were to be assessed in terms of ability to pay.[2]

The Development of Hospitals

Those who had comfortable homes, stayed at home when they were sick. But hospitals came to be provided in many different cultures. They were found in the Indian culture, in the huge Arab Kingdom which spread across Southern Europe as well as in the early Christian Church. Hospitals became part of monasteries and convents and various Sisterhoods and Brotherhoods had duties to care for the sick. During the thirteenth century there were some 19,000 hospital units or annexes in Europe.[3]

Hospitals served the sick who were without families or servants – the poor, travellers and those working away from home. Special provision was often made for soldiers and sailors for whom government accepted a duty of care. But a further need, increasingly recognized during the nineteenth century, was to isolate those with infectious diseases although the precise method by which infection spread was little understood. Thus hospitals were created for cases of smallpox, cholera and typhoid. During the nineteenth century special public hospitals were established in Sweden to treat cases of venereal disease in hospital and in Norway to isolate lepers. Hospitals were also set up to confine mental patients of all social classes who were seen as a danger either to themselves or others, or both.

Gradually, or suddenly in the case of the French Revolution, many continental European hospitals were transferred from control by the Catholic Church to control by public authorities because of either mismanagement, misappropriation of funds, anti-clericalism or just the absence of adequate financial backing.[4] In Spain and Portugal and their colonies in Latin America, however, the Catholic Church retained a major role in the provision of hospitals until well into the twentieth century.

In both Denmark and Sweden it had, by 1870, been made the duty of local authorities to provide hospitals.[5] Thus, in Scandinavia, the hospitals were developed largely as a public service. Indeed the Swedish hospitals were separated from the poor law during the eighteenth century and came to be regarded early on as a service provided for the whole community. They were originally provided by the smallest units of government (the parishes) and financed by a head tax. From 1862 the hospitals were handed over to the newly-formed counties and financed from taxes on spirits and charges to patients.[6]

In Britain, after Henry VIII had suppressed the monasteries, hospitals became secular institutions. Charitable bodies provided the bulk of hospitals for acute cases until the National Health Service was started in 1948. But this private sector was gradually supplemented by public provision for the mentally ill, the chronic sick and cases of infectious diseases. And where the provision for the acute sick by charitable effort was inadequate to provide for all who needed care, an acute sector of hospital care was gradually developed by local authorities. While, from the nineteenth century, the majority of the physically sick in institutional care in Britain were in publicly-owned institutions,[7] until 1948 the main teaching hospitals and the most prestigious hospitals for the acute sick were provided by charity. The main criterion for admission to both charity and local authority hospitals was medical need. The question of payment was not normally raised until after the patient had been admitted and charges were only made to better-off patients. It was accepted that most patients were unable to pay for hospital care. Patients' direct payment unaided by insurance never contributed much to the running costs of hospitals in Britain: it was not until 1881 that any major hospital accommodated any paying patients at all. And even in 1938, paying patients were substantially less than 5 per cent of all hospital patients.

The British system of voluntary hospitals was extended to North America. Most large hospitals in North America which survive today were established by public subscription and wealthy industrialists, though some originated in the poor law such as Bellevue Hospital in New York. But there was also a long tradition of small private hospitals set up by physicians or surgeons for their own patients,[8] and some early hospitals were established to provide clinical instruction for medical students.[9] While some of the early voluntary non-profit hospitals were open to all regardless of economic status, race, colour or creed, many others were provided by and for particular

4

religious groups: the construction of a Catholic hospital would lead to a rival hospital for Protestants and occasionally of a further hospital for the Jewish community. Early on hospitals in the United States took a much more substantial proportion of paying patients. By 1893 the majority of hospital beds were occupied by paying patients: the management would authorize a stated number of beds for the use of free patients, and this number could not be exceeded.[10] At the turn of the century paying patients contributed about one third of the running costs of hospitals.[11]

The extensive development of government and charity hospitals in Europe for those who could not afford to pay led to the appointment of doctors to work in them – generally for a full-time or part-time salary. Thus there emerged a separate class of paid doctors with hospital appointments. In Britain, the division between doctors working in the main voluntary hospitals and doctors working outside corresponded with an ancient class distinction within the profession between Fellows of the Royal Colleges of Medicine and Surgery and what were originally the apothecaries. Similar traditional distinctions can be found in France, Sweden and Italy. The higher class of doctors obtained a virtual monopoly of the principal hospital appointments which provided them with the opportunity to specialize. But they undertook their voluntary hospital work for virtually no direct payment and supported themselves by private consultation, for which they charged about ten times more than a general practitioner. It increasingly became medical etiquette for specialists to confine themselves to cases referred by general practitioners. The referral system and the higher charges of specialists preserved a fairly sharp distinction between specialists and general practitioners in the main towns.[12] It also meant that specialist services to those who were not wealthy were given at hospital out-patient departments rather than in the specialists' private offices. Thus in Britain not only free in-patient care but also out-patient specialist services were made available to the poorest section of the population almost as a right. Similarly in Sweden extensive out-patient departments were developed at the local authority hospitals.

Out-of-Hospital Services

As part of the development of 'poor law' or public assistance services in a number of European countries, doctors were paid to give medical care to the poor either on a part-time or full-time salaried basis – particularly in the more remote areas. In Norway, salaried services for the poor have a history of over 350 years[13] and a similar system was to be found in the more isolated parts of Switzerland. These rural salaried doctors were given responsibilities for the general supervision of the public health. Under the Poor Relief (Ireland) Act 1851 dispensary doctors were employed to provide free services to the poor throughout Ireland. The dispensary doctor was paid a salary but also allowed to engage in private practice.[14] Only in very recent years has this system been abandoned.[15] The dispensary system was also used in London for a period during the nineteenth century. A system of dispensary doctors was extensively developed in Poland as well.

In the German Duchy of Nassau, doctors were appointed as civil servants in 1818 to provide a complete system of public medicine. Each one of the twenty-eight districts had a physician-in-chief (Medizinalrat) with two assistant physicians and one or two assistant surgeons.[16] The system was abandoned in 1861 when Nassau became a province of Prussia. Similarly, in 1864, medical care was made a public service in the rural districts of Russia. The local district assembly (zemstvo) built hospitals and medical stations and appointed physicians and other medical personnel as government officials to provide health services to the local population. Physicians were paid salaries, very often had free living quarters, were paid travelling expenses and entitled to a pension when they retired.[17] The system of medical stations or polyclinics staffed by salaried doctors was extended to cover the whole country after the communist revolution when compulsory insurance was introduced. It was similarly used in Czechoslovakia during the nineteen-twenties in very different political circumstances.[18]

In Britain, home nursing was started as a separate charitable movement from 1859[19] and in time came to be heavily subsidized by and gradually transferred to local authorities. Midwifery developed in Britain, the Netherlands, France, Belgium[20] and some other countries as a separate, independent profession to take a major responsibility for normal home confinements. Salaried midwives also came to be employed by local authorities. In Britain, the registration of midwives as an independent, free-standing profession was bitterly opposed by the British Medical Association, but eventually established by the Midwives Registration Act (1902).

6

In the United States, medical opposition to this development was successful.

Developments in the Colonies

In Latin America one of the first initiatives of the colonizers was to provide a high standard of hospitals for the armed forces and later for the police. These separate hospitals for those who administered 'law and order' have generally survived until the present day. In addition both the Spanish and the Portuguese endowed a limited number of Catholic hospitals (beneficencia or sanitas casas) which were supported by the wealthy from a sense of *noblesse oblige* to relieve distress among the poor. Small payments were made to the medical staff for their part-time services. In some countries (e.g. Peru), those patients who could make some payment were provided with slightly more comfortable and private facilities, and full-cost private rooms were established for the well-to-do.[21] As the cost of providing hospital services increased many of the hospitals received grants from government to augment their incomes from charitable sources.

The Catholic hospitals were later supplemented by Government hospitals, health centres and medical posts staffed by part-time salaried doctors to serve the poor – particularly where there was no charity hospital. Government hospitals played a particularly large part in Mexico which had few charity hospitals. When employers established large enterprises far from the towns, to exploit natural resources (mines and plantations) they also established health services – both health centres and hospitals. Later, laws were passed to require large-scale employers of labour, who were operating far from organized services, to establish specified health services. Such a law was enacted in Peru in 1924.

When Europeans developed colonies in Asia and Africa, environmental public health services were started and campaigns were run to combat the main infectious diseases. Originally, as in Latin America, hospitals and other health services were provided only for the army and for the colonists. In the same way as armed forces take with them their medical services, so did the colonial services. In time, these services were extended to provide a limited service to the indigenous population, mainly in the urban centres. The government hospital services were supplemented in some countries (e.g. India)

7

by indigenous charitable effort and by mission hospitals – particularly in Africa. As in Latin America when large mines and plantations were established far from the towns, employers began to provide medical services and legislation was often introduced to require services to be provided.

Voluntary Insurance for Doctors' Services

Meanwhile, a strong voluntary health insurance movement developed in Europe, out of which compulsory health insurance was later to develop. Organizations of working men, often developing out of earlier guilds, pioneered the system. Mutual benefit societies, sickness funds and friendly societies were established from the late eighteenth century as industry developed and a class of working people, separated from the land, formed in the towns and cities. The sickness insurance movement was often run by local working people for their mutual benefit and tended to be strongest among the more skilled workers. Contributions were generally on the same basis for all members though there were variations in the benefits for which members could subscribe.

In 1804, about thirty years before the British Medical Association was founded, there were about a million members of friendly societies in Britain, though systematic information about their activities is not available. Originally they provided cash benefits in sickness. Later on doctors were engaged to certify illness and provide treatment. By 1900, there were, in Britain, seven million members of friendly societies – most of them entitled to invalidity cash benefits, the services of a doctor, and the drugs he prescribed.

The voluntary sickness insurance movement was also extensively developed in Austria, Germany, Switzerland and Scandinavia during the nineteenth century, though in continental Europe it was often on an occupational basis and was encouraged by government.[22] It spread later to Australia and New Zealand though on a smaller scale. In the earlier schemes, it was common for doctors to be paid by capitation or salary as this simplified budgeting and administration for these somewhat amateur organizations which depended, during their early years, on the voluntary work undertaken by their members. The voluntary health insurance societies generally provided cash benefits and then later health services in kind. In Sweden and France, however, cash benefits were also normally provided to reimburse patients for part of their medical bills.

8

Thus in these countries the consumers of medical care came to be organized before the doctors were effectively organized and they were in a position to dictate the terms of service of the doctors whom they engaged to provide services. From being master, doctors found themselves servants of the funds. There were many aspects of these terms of service which caused resentment. The societies tended to appoint some doctors and not others to work for the funds: those doctors who were excluded found that many of their patients were induced to transfer to doctors who had been appointed.[23] Disciplinary matters were often handled by lay committees which in effect decided professional matters. And, finally, the level of remuneration fixed by the societies was regarded by the profession as grossly inadequate. The societies were accused of exploiting their quasi-monopolistic position in each area. The resentment of doctors led to the development of new medical organizations and the strengthening of existing organizations to fight the societies.[24]

Parallel to this consumer-sponsored health insurance, there also developed doctor-sponsored health insurance in some European countries. To protect themselves from bad debts, doctors persuaded their patients to make regular payments while they were well so that they could be looked after if they became sick. This was developed most extensively in Holland where most of the sick funds were originally founded by doctors. It is probably for this reason that there has never been so much friction between the funds and the profession in Holland as in many other countries. Doctor-sponsored pre-payment was also started in Spain[25] and on a small scale among middle-class patients in Germany and Britain.

The insurance of doctors' services came to Northern Europe before hospital insurance. This was partly because there was much less use of hospitals than is the case today and partly because both charity and public hospitals were already providing extensive free services to those who could not afford to pay.

Voluntary insurance was also started in Argentina, Brazil and Uruguay though later and on a much smaller scale than in Europe. In Latin America its function was to secure better services for immigrants of particular nationalities than was available for the indigenous population. In the case of Brazil, for example, medical societies owning their own hospitals were established to serve well-to-do families of Portuguese extraction. In the United States consumer-sponsored friendly societies to provide for doctors'

9

services on the European pattern became established in some urban communities including the East Side of New York in the early years of the twentieth century but ceased to function when County Medical Societies ruled that it was unethical for a doctor to contract his services with an organization of this kind. From 1929 a few consumer cooperatives employing salaried doctors even started in the rural Western States despite strong opposition from the organized profession. By 1949 there were over a hundred cooperatives but after a further ten years only a handful were still active.[26] Two large urban cooperatives in Washington, D.C., in 1937 and Seattle, Washington, in 1946 faced determined opposition from the profession. After a long legal battle the A.M.A. and the local medical society were found guilty of restraint of trade.[27]

In Israel a mutual sick fund (Kupat Holim) was established in 1911 by 150 Jewish agricultural pioneers and steadily expanded among the growing Jewish community during the period when the settlers lacked the sovereign power of statehood. The sick fund developed its own hospitals, convalescent homes, pharmacies, laboratories and mother and child centres. Doctors were employed on a salaried basis to staff the hospitals and other institutions and to provide out-of-hospital services for polyclinics served by the fund. One-third of the hospital beds in Israel today are still owned by the fund which covers 70 per cent of the country and population.

Conclusions

In terms of health improvement, the main achievements of the nineteenth century were in the field of environmental health. The measures proved to be remarkably effective and provided immense benefits to all social classes at relatively low cost.

Compared to these steps to promote collective health, the development of services to promote individual health was more expensive and less effective. As more techniques of treatment were developed, different societies began to evolve a variety of mechanisms to make them available to those who were unable to purchase them on the open market. In some countries medical charities became widely developed. In others, governments took the initiative to provide some minimum of service to the poor and those living in remote communities which could not support a doctor. At the same time workers and doctors evolved simple insurance schemes to enable those who were well to pay in advance for services which they would need to purchase if they became sick.

Governments intervened to an extent varying in different countries to try and solve the particular problems which they regarded as important – special types of disease or the needs of particular sections of society. Provision was made when no other suitable mechanism existed to do the job. When governments set up services they generally hired doctors on salary to provide them just as judges, teachers or policemen were employed. Where premises were needed for them to practise, they provided them. It was not until the twentieth century that some medical associations began to assert that doctors were in a special position which required them to avoid a salaried relation with government or other 'third parties' and fight for the retention of independent practice. Moreover in some countries, the role of the doctor gradually changed. He saw himself less as a priest giving service to the community and more as a professional practitioner who provided his services only to those who could purchase them.

NOTES

1. H. E. Sigerist, *Medicine and Human Welfare*, Yale U.P., 1941, p. 109.

2. W. Berg, 'Justice and the Future of Medicine', *Public Health Reports*, Vol. 60, No. 1, 5 January 1945.

3. Commission on Hospital Care, *Hospital Care in the United States*, The Commonwealth Fund, New York, 1947, p. 426.

4. H. C. Burdett, *Hospitals and Asylums of the World*, Vol. 3, Churchill, London, 1893, pp. 76, 423, 454, 618.

5. ibid., pp. 448–57, 662.

6. O. W. Anderson, *Health Care: can there be equity?*, Wiley, 1972, pp. 39, 42.

7. B. Abel-Smith, *The Hospitals 1800–1948*, Heinemann 1964.

8. Commission on Hospital Care, *op. cit.*, 1947, p. 434.

9. ibid., p. 442.

10. Burdett, op. cit., p. 56.

11. Anderson, op. cit., p. 50.

12. B. Abel-Smith, op. cit., pp. 101–18.

13. K. Evang and K. E. Thorvaldsen, 'The Organization and Financing of Health Services in Norway', B.M.A., *Health Services Financing*, 1969, p. 497.

14. A. Duncan, 'The Organization and Financing of Medical Care in Ireland', B.M.A., op. cit., pp. 422–3.

15. B. Hensey, *The Health Services of Ireland*, Institute of Public Administration, Dublin, 1972.

16. H. E. Sigerist, op. cit., p. 142.

17. Sir Arthur Newsholme, *International Studies on the Relations between the Private and Official Practice of Medicine*, London, Vol. 2, Allen and Unwin, 1931, p. 241.

18. ibid., p. 241.

19. Mary Stocks, *A Hundred Years of District Nursing*, London, Allen and Unwin, 1960.

20. Sir Arthur Newsholme, op. cit., Vol. 2, pp. 26, 57.

21. M. I. Roemer, *Medical Care in Latin America*, Studies and Monographs III, Pan-American Union, Washington, D.C., 1963, p. 14.

22. See pp. 13–14 below.

23. J. Hogarth, *The Payment of the General Practitioner*, London, Pergamon, 1963, p. 211.

24. B. Abel-Smith, 'Paying the Family Doctor', *Medical Care*, Vol. 1, 1963, p. 20.

25. Sir Arthur Newsholme, op. cit., Vol. 1, p. 24.

26. Herman and Anne Somers, *Doctors, Patients and Health Insurance*, Washington D.C., Brookings, p. 348.

27. ibid., p. 349

CHAPTER 2

Compulsory Health Insurance and National Health Services

While friendly societies of the British type developed in Germany[1] on a smaller scale and at a later period, the main development of health insurance in the different states of what later became Germany was on an occupational basis. Much of it came into being as a result of government encouragement and later legislation.

Sickness insurance evolved in the mines as early as the thirteenth century and in the guilds during the fourteenth and fifteenth centuries. In the eighteenth century there was a sporadic development of sickness insurance for groups such as domestic servants who were outside the guild system. The major emphasis in the early period was on provision for cash benefits in sickness rather than medical treatment.

Compulsory health insurance was pioneered in several states of Germany in the eighteenth century to provide for the sickness and old age of civil servants. But the most important precedent for the development of compulsory insurance was in the mining industry. During the sixteenth century the miners in several states were provided with both cash benefits in sickness and medical treatment. Some owners employed their own doctors and provided their own hospitals. The miner contributed to the health insurance fund, either a weekly flat-rate contribution or a contribution related to earnings. Employers generally contributed a percentage of profits. Increasingly these schemes for miners became regulated by laws which specified the obligations of employers and made contributions compulsory.

By the early nineteenth century, Prussia had laws which not only regulated provisions for miners and civil servants but which specified that domestic servants had to be retained and paid wages during sickness and after accidents. In 1845 mutual assistance was made compulsory for journeymen and apprentices. And after the revolutionary year 1848, a law was passed in 1849 which allowed the municipal authorities to order workers to join mutual welfare funds providing medical care, drugs, sickness and other cash benefits. Employers could be asked to contribute up to 50 per cent of their workers' contributions and in return were granted the right to participate in the administration of the fund. In 1854, a further law made it possible for municipalities to require employers to contribute and this legislation was extended to the North German Federation in 1866 and later with minor amendments to Bavaria, Württemberg, Baden and Hesse. By 1868, there were over 170,000 members of 78 miners' funds in Prussia alone and in addition over half a million members of nearly 4,000 other funds.

Thus the enactment of national compulsory insurance in Germany in 1883 and in Austria five years later built upon extensive precedents of compulsory health insurance at the local level and the schemes for miners and civil servants. The feudal obligation of the employer to his work-people was given legislative force in a society developing national markets where the employer without an obligation to pay to a sick fund might undercut the employer who had such an obligation. One political motive for this initiative was to reduce the cost of poor relief. But much more important was the desire to contain socialist and revolutionary activity by creating a new loyalty of the worker to his employer and the State. Moreover the employers obtained representation in the administration of the insurance funds which had previously been exclusively controlled by workers.

The administration of compulsory health insurance was left in the hands of the numerous local sick funds. All low-income workers were eventually required to join a sick fund and the funds were required to operate under legislative regulations. And it was not long before governments became involved in disputes between the sick funds and the profession concerning levels and methods of remuneration, disciplinary sanctions and other matters. There were major protests from doctors about the 'closed panels' restrictions operated by the funds and the profession demanded the right for any doctor to work for health insurance. The substitution of payment for case and later fee-for-service systems of payment for capitation or salary, which the German profession fought for and eventually won, was a means of establishing open competition between all doctors who wished to take part in the health insurance scheme.

In Britain, compulsory health insurance also involved the extension of an existing system – the friendly societies some of which had by this time become powerful national organizations. While Lloyd George, the architect of the scheme, had studied Germany's experience, his motives for introducing it were political in a narrower sense than those of Bismarck in Germany. He was concerned about the health of workers, particularly after the low standards of fitness revealed at the time of the Boer War. He was also keen to rescue workers from the unpopular poor law, lower the cost of poor relief, and secure employers' contributions towards sickness insurance. But perhaps his main concern was to introduce a measure which would be popular with the working class and thus win greater support for the Liberal Party at the expense of the growing Labour Party.

The announcement of his scheme galvanized the doctors into united action and the British Medical Association, which had long been critical of the terms and conditions offered by the friendly societies, specified the terms upon which it would support the scheme. Its main demands were to secure higher remuneration than the friendly societies had been prepared to pay and to secure participation in the administration of the scheme. Lloyd George eventually offered a higher capitation than he had first suggested and the scheme became administered at the local level by insurance committees, composed of representatives of the doctors, the friendly societies and members appointed by the government.[2] The principle was accepted from the start that every doctor could participate in the scheme who chose to do so. The capitation system of payment was retained and continued to have the support of the profession. This might not have happened if the right of every doctor to join the scheme had not been conceded at the beginning. In a sense, the intervention of government in Britain had the effect of rescuing general practitioners from the control of friendly societies, while in Germany it initially enhanced the power which sick funds could exercise over the profession.

The capitation system and the closed panels which were originally associated with it, were gradually eliminated in Norway as well as in Germany, and their role was substantially reduced in Denmark, Italy and Austria. In Austria, payment per three-monthly case became the most common way of paying the practitioners.[3] Where fee-for-service systems of paying doctors under compulsory insurance were introduced, they generally had the effect of fragmenting the delivery of medical care between episodes of illness. The patient could 'shop around' among different doctors according to the patient's own diagnosis of his need. Fewer patients had one personal doctor who knew their whole medical history or most of it from continuing participation in its management. Increasingly patients went direct to specialists, and general practitioners were left with a declining share of the market. This process did not however occur in those parts of Denmark where doctors came to be paid on a fee-for-service basis owing to the entrenched tradition of referral from general practitioners to specialists, which was incorporated in the compulsory insurance regulations.[4] But capitation was still used in much of Denmark and in the rural areas of Italy and in Spain, the Netherlands and Britain. Where capitation payment was retained, it had the effect of protecting, promoting and crystallizing the concept of the general practitioner as the doctor to whom the patient went first for medical care.

Social insurance was originally established for the employed population and compulsory membership was often confined to those with earnings below a defined limit. There was, however, no income limit in Italy and Belgium and the limit was later abandoned in some other countries. But it was retained in Germany and Holland where the medical profession has fought to retain private practice among the better off, with strong support in recent years from commercial insurance companies which have developed considerable voluntary insurance among the higher income groups. During the nineteen-fifties various categories of self-employed were brought into social security in Western Europe and coverage was extended to retired workers, students, the unemployed and handicapped under special arrangements.

All the early compulsory insurance schemes provided service benefits. In other words, the scheme paid the doctor directly for the services he provided to insured persons. This was the pattern of health insurance introduced in Japan in 1927: the Japanese government had modelled their medical education on the German pattern and similarly copied the German social security scheme.[5] There had been no tradition of voluntary health insurance in Japan though some employers provided health services for their employees. Health insurance was developed on an occupational basis, originally covering manual workers earning below an income limit in firms with five or more employees in specified industries. The scheme was gradually extended until the whole population was covered by 1961.[6] Thus health insurance came to be provided by over three thousand organizations offering varying benefits.

In Western Europe and Japan the doctor remained an independent contractor and normally practised from premises which he owned. In the U.S.S.R., as mentioned earlier, insurance doctors were paid salaries and practised from government-owned polyclinics. This was the pattern adopted when Chile introduced health insurance in 1924 for workers but not for their dependents. Existing government and private clinics were taken over and expanded to provide the service. In the more remote parts of Chile there were extremely few private practitioners who could have participated in the scheme if it had been established on the Western European pattern.

Pharmaceutical benefits were normally included in compulsory insurance and public health service schemes. While many doctors dispensed their own medicines, it gradually became more common for the mixing to be undertaken by the pharmacist in his shop. As a result of the vast range of effective drugs produced by the pharmaceutical industry from the middle nineteen-thirties onwards, more and more preparations became factory-made. Normally these were obtained from local pharmacists' shops, and either the pharmacist or the patient claimed reimbursement from the sick fund or government scheme. In Japan, however, there were few pharmacies: typically each doctor provided, and still provides, his patient with the drugs he prescribes.[7] Prices for drugs and medical consultations are fixed by the government after negotiations with the profession.

Reimbursement of Patients for their Expenditure on Doctors' Services

Countries which developed a compulsory or voluntary insurance scheme from the nineteen-thirties onwards generally adopted arrangements by which patients were reimbursed for part or all of their expenditure on health services. Lobbying by the medical profession, often accompanied by 'strikes' or threats of 'strikes' played an important role in securing that health insurance took this form. Indeed there developed an international movement among doctors for a 'free profession'. It was held that the doctor should be paid direct by the patient and not by a 'third party' – government, social security or private insurer. This movement which crystalized in France in the twenties and in French-speaking Switzerland had an important influence on the thinking of the profession in the United States at the same period.

The opposition in France to 'third parties' was essentially opposition to the German sick fund system with which the French medical profession became familiar in Alsace and Lorraine in the inter-war period.[8] Voluntary insurance had been restricted historically to cash benefits. Under the law introduced in 1920 it was intended that doctors would be paid as a service, but the opposition of the doctors led eventually to the adoption of a reimbursement plan. The doctor certified that he had received his fee without stating what it was and the patient was reimbursed 80 per cent of a standard medical fee. The actual charge levied by the doctor could, however, be larger than the standard fee.[9] The French profession's medical 'charter' of 1935 which demanded direct payment of medical fees by the patient to the doctor became adopted by the World Medical Association.[10]

Switzerland, which had little compulsory but considerable voluntary health insurance, developed service benefits in some cantons and a reimbursement system in others – representing a transitional stage in the international history of health insurance. Other countries adopting a reimbursement system were Australia for its subsidized voluntary insurance scheme from 1950, Sweden in 1956 and Finland in 1964. Many Latin American countries also introduced health insurance of this type: in these countries there was virtually no tradition of voluntary health insurance providing service benefits and the government services which employed doctors were of a very low standard and were used only by the poor. Social security was developed to enable the manual worker to obtain access to the services used by those who were well-off – particularly the doctor in independent private practice.

In many countries, governments had originally tried to institute service plans and capitation payment, but were foiled by the profession. This, for example, was the experience of New Zealand. The government introduced a capitation scheme for general practice in March 1941. This was opposed by the Medical Association and few doctors joined the scheme. In the same year the scheme was replaced by a fee-for-service plan, although a number of doctors continued under the capitation system until 1960.[11] In 1962 in Canada, the government of the Province of Saskatchewan planned to introduce compulsory insurance for doctors' services and pay doctors directly the fees for the services they had provided. After a strike the government conceded the option of reimbursement for those doctors who preferred it. There had been pioneer plans to cover doctors with health insurance services in Swift Current (Saskatchewan) from 1946 and Newfoundland from 1934. Alberta (1963) and Columbia (1965) followed with plans using existing carriers and Ontario introduced a voluntary plan run by its Department of Health in 1966. From 1968 the Federal Government of Canada offered a 50 per cent matching grant for provincial programmes which met standards which were laid down. By 1971 all the remaining provinces had started comprehensive plans.[12]

Under most reimbursement plans there is a schedule of fees. Under some plans this schedule is negotiated with the profession and represents the maximum any doctor can charge; under others doctors are free to charge patients additional sums if they wish to do so. In practice this has often meant that doctors and others have raised their fees still leaving the patient with a substantial bill to pay which is not reimbursed.[13] Under the Medicare programme in the United States which has covered the aged since 1 July 1966, there is no schedule of fees; the doctor is paid 'reasonable' charges which take into account his customary charge and the prevailing charges of other doctors in his area.

The Insurance of Hospital Services

The development of compulsory health insurance for doctors' services raised the question of whether hospital services should also be covered by the scheme. Where acceptable hospital care was provided by local government without stigma as in Sweden, Denmark or Australia or by voluntary hospitals as in Britain, health insurance excluded hospital care or only made token provision for it. In continental Western Europe, however, where hospitals normally charged and free care was only provided as part of the poor law and involved stigma, health insurance was used to provide hospital care as a right. Later supplementary voluntary insurance was developed for those who wished to obtain a right to a higher class of accommodation.

Where contributions were related to earnings and where the employer also paid substantial contributions, a much higher proportion of hospital costs was shifted on to the scheme. Thus, a substantial part of hospital costs came to be paid for by social security funds in Belgium, France, Germany and Holland. Often the government also participated in hospital financing either by making a contribution to social security funds or by meeting the deficits of hospitals. Hospital insurance helped to bolster up the finances of hospitals provided by religious organizations and enabled funds to be diverted to other religious purposes including quasi-political purposes.

In Britain, when compulsory insurance with flat-rate contributions was introduced in 1911, it was rare for in-patients to pay anything for treatment and there was no obvious crisis in hospital financing. Hospitals were therefore excluded from the scheme.[14] When the whole system of health insurance was reviewed by a Royal Commission in the middle 1920s, it was decided that neither wage earners nor employers could afford to pay higher contributions to enable hospital benefits to be included in the scheme. Potential increases in revenue from social insurance contributions were reserved for the extension of cash benefits for widows and old people. There developed instead a system of voluntary contributory schemes which did not confer any rights to hospital care. Workers were encouraged to contribute to hospital funds what they could afford on a regular basis – and the money collected was distributed among the voluntary hospitals in the locality: those who contributed were normally excluded from attempts to charge on a means-tested basis. By 1938 these schemes raised about a third of the revenue of the voluntary hospitals and covered about ten million people. Some voluntary full-cost hospital insurance did, however, develop on a small scale among those who were comfortably off in the later inter-war years.

In Canada and the United States hospital insurance came much later than in Europe and preceded the development of insurance for doctors' services. Moreover, it developed under quite different types of agency, to serve different sections of the community and to meet different objectives. 'Blue Cross' was a voluntary insurance movement which was promoted by the hospitals themselves in the early nineteen-thirties[15] in response to a crisis in hospital financing. The hospitals sought to secure a larger proportion of 'semi-private' patients as distinct from public ward patients who could pay the whole cost of the service they needed. Prepayment, therefore, began among those with better than average incomes, and spread down the income scale as the country became more affluent. Blue Cross was 'community-related': the same premium was paid by each member irrespective of age or health status. From the early 1940s, profit-making insurance companies entered the field by offering hospital insurance to those with 'good risks' at lower premiums than were charged by Blue Cross under its 'community-rated' scheme. Inevitably the Blue Cross plans were eventually forced to abandon community ratings and adopt risk-rating but too late to stop the commercial carriers from winning the major part of the business.

Compulsory health insurance was originally included in the drafts of Roosevelt's 'New Deal' social security legislation of 1935 but finally omitted as a result of intensive lobbying by the medical profession. There were initiatives to introduce a 'National Health Program' in 1939 and various attempts to introduce health insurance in separate states. From 1943 to 1957 there was a stream of bills to provide comprehensive health and medical care benefits for persons covered by the social insurance system with special arrangements to bring in those on public assistance in each state. Though these bills were acceptable to President Roosevelt and strongly supported by President Truman they were defeated as a result of extensive opposition of the medical profession which had become extremely wary of any form of government control. The main focus of political activity was then diverted to a narrower campaign (1952–65) to provide hospital insurance only for the aged. In 1960, a bill was passed to finance medical care for the aged who were indigent or 'medically indigent' through grants to the States. This led to generous provisions in States which were wealthy and no implementation of the Act in States which could not afford their share of the cost. The breakthrough which came in 1965 led to health insurance for the aged and a better but still separate system of means-tested medical care for the indigent and 'medically indigent'. The Commercial insurers were allowed to function as fiscal intermediaries for the hospital costs and medical service costs of Medicare.[16]

The debate on whether there should be a more extended health insurance scheme in the United States still continues. There are many rival approaches. Some would graft health insurance on to the social insurance scheme with part of the cost paid from general revenues. Others would pay for the whole scheme from general revenues. Still others would encourage employers to provide health insurance and provide for others as necessary with government funds channelled through private insurers. The American Medical Association has gone so far as to propose the financing of health insurance through tax credits. Premiums for health insurance could be deducted from income tax payments.[17]

Progress was made earlier in Canada where compulsory health insurance was first applied to hospitals (excluding the payment of the doctor for hospital services). The first plan was started in the province of Saskatchewan in 1947. British Columbia followed two years later and Alberta started a less extensive plan. After the federal government offered, from 1958, to pay 50 per cent of the cost of provincial schemes, the rest of Canada became covered by 1961.[18]

In Australia, a unique method of financing hospital care became established from 1950, which was, in some respects, a compromise between the arrangements in Europe and those in the United States. While there was compulsory government insurance for old age pensioners, widow pensioners and certain other categories, insurance was voluntary for the bulk of the population. Over 90 per cent of the population not covered by other schemes were covered by voluntary non-profit insurance. The government paid about half the cost of health insurance and also half the cost of government hospitals. The insured person could pay different levels of premium for care in a private ward, an intermediate ward or a public ward.[19] The same insurers reimbursed patients for doctors' services. In 1973 the government announced its intention to introduce comprehensive health insurance paid for by a levy on taxable income up to a ceiling, a levy on third-party motor insurance and on workmen's compensation.[20]

The Effect of Health Insurance on the Hospital System

In most of Europe, North America, Chile and Australasia insured persons used the existing hospitals when hospital care became covered by insurance. Existing hospitals were also generally used by the schemes established in India (1948), Burma (1954) and Tunisia (1960) which covered only small proportions of their populations.

In France, however, the advent of social security run on a reimbursement basis resulted in an expansion of small private doctor-owned hospitals or 'cliniques'.[21] Standards of amenity in government hospitals were low and those insured persons who could afford to supplement the standard rate of reimbursement for hospital care paid by the social security scheme selected the type of hospital which had previously only been used by the higher social classes. In Japan, hospitals were few when health insurance was started and charitable hospitals were fewer still. Health insurance resulted in a mushroom growth of small doctor-owned hospitals. By the nineteen-sixties, there were 30,000 doctor-owned hospitals or clinics housing in-patients and under 300 hospitals in other ownership.[22] In the United States, the advent of Medicare and Medicaid led to a mushroom growth of small privately owned nursing homes separate from the hospitals for the care of the chronic sick.

In Spain and some parts of Italy, where the standards of charitable and public hospitals were low, separate hospitals were built for social security patients. In Peru the insurance scheme for manual workers originally used the existing charity hospitals which were overcrowded and of a low standard. But dissatisfaction with these hospitals led to a policy of constructing social security hospitals of a much higher standard for members of the fund. The first 'workers' hospital which was opened in Lima in 1941 was a model for its time and attracted attention around the world. When a separate social security scheme for Peruvian white-collar workers was established in 1948, patients were allowed to choose between private hospitals and hospitals or clinics operated by the fund.[23] An even more impressive hospital than that provided by the manual workers' fund was built in Lima: its spacious marble-lined lobbies and corridors were of a magnificence 'out of proportion to any other hospital in Latin America'.[24] This precedent of establishing separate hospitals for members of different funds was followed by many other countries in Latin America. Thus, for example, Mexico, Venezuela and Argentina all built large impressive hospitals exclusively for persons covered by the different social security schemes.

In Europe voluntary insurance originated as a movement of mutual aid or 'solidarity' among the working classes: it was these schemes or similar schemes which were extended to cover most of the rest of the population. In Latin America, with the possible exception of Chile, social security became a divisive rather than a unifying force. A hierarchy of schemes was developed which reflected and reinforced the sharp social stratification of the population. Moreover social security only covered a minority of the population. The costly standards provided under social security sharpened the contrast with the meagre services provided by government and charity for the rural population and for the urban population not covered by any fund or special scheme.

National Health Services

The gradual acceptance of the citizen's right to medical care, as such care became recognized as effective, underlies a century or more of European history. Provision was made by government, social insurance and charity to an extent which varied in the different countries. Given this premise it was not wildly out of line with the arrangements made in neighbouring countries for Russia to substitute a public service plan for the insurance method of financing in 1937, and for Britain to do the same in 1948. Lest it be supposed that there was some political ideology shared by these two countries, it should be pointed out that the insurance method of financing is still retained in Poland and that in Scandinavia hospitals were provided for many years on a public service basis without adopting the grandiloquent title of a National Health Service. The transition to a public health system has often, but not always, involved the extension of existing compulsory programmes.

The establishment of Britain's National Health Service involved the transition from a compulsory health insurance scheme providing limited benefits to approximately one half of the population to a service available to the whole population. The service was organized in three separate streams. The home nursing and preventive services were provided by local authorities, the hospitals by separate non-elected public authorities created for the purpose, and further authorities were created in each area to supervise the contracts made with general practitioners, opticians, dentists and pharmacists. From the nineteen-twenties, the medical profession had demanded that the health insurance for out-of-hospital benefits which had only covered the worker should be extended to cover his wife and children. Until the early nineteen-forties, it was held by successive governments that the money could not be found to pay for this either out of taxation or out of compulsory health insurance contributions.

A further major step was taken at the same time: apart from providing services free of charge the main change was the transfer of virtually all hospitals into national ownership. Previously the main acute hospitals had been owned by voluntary bodies and other hospitals by local government. Many haphazard influences had affected the size and location of the various units, provision was uneven in different parts of the country and many hospitals were considered too small to meet the needs of modern medicine. The need for some system of hospital planning had long been recognized. Neither the voluntary hospitals nor the medical profession was prepared to accept a hospital system controlled by the local authorities. Both preferred national ownership. With the exception of the teaching hospitals which had separate Boards responsible to the Minister of Health, hospitals were planned by regional boards appointed by the Minister and were managed by local committees appointed by these boards. Thus the purpose of establishing the National Health Service was not just to make services available to the whole population without charge, but to plan the distribution of services and to plan the size, function and location of hospitals. A further important aim was to secure that both general practitioner and specialist services were made available in parts of the country which had previously been under-provided with them.

Similarly when Chile established its National Health Service in 1952, the charity hospitals (beneficencias) were taken over by the government and welded into one planned hospital service. Ambulatory care was provided by using and developing both the clinics established by the social security scheme to provide ambulatory care and the preventive clinics run by the government. The social security scheme for white-collar workers was at that stage left outside the National Health Service.

More revolutionary was the introduction of a National Health Service in Cuba. Following the political revolution in 1958, all health facilities were taken into central government ownership and practically all services were provided free of charge. Small hospitals were closed and new larger hospitals were built. By 1969, 65 per cent of the hospital beds had been built between 1958 and 1968.[25] A major aim was to extend and improve the hospital services outside the capital, Havana. Similarly, health centres staffed by salaried doctors were constructed. The proportion of all doctors working in the capital was reduced from 65 per cent to 42 per cent in 1971.[26]

Following a large exodus of doctors in the years following 1958, medical education was expanded and there were by 1970 more doctors in Cuba than in 1958. The health services are planned centrally, provincially, regionally and locally.[27]

Conclusions

The variations in the organization and financing of medical care in different countries are the product of long-established customs modified by long histories of development. But beneath these customs and histories are fundamental differences in attitudes and values. How does the medical profession see its role and how is it organized? What is the attitude to government and what are perceived to be its duties to help different sectors of the population? How powerful are institutions provided by religious groups? How important is the provision of health services thought to be?

In Europe, with the exception of Spain and Portugal, medical care has long been regarded as more of a right than in North or South America. This attitude has influenced countries colonized in Africa and Asia by the British, French and Dutch, just as the attitudes of the Spanish and Portuguese have influenced Latin America. In the United States provisions by public authorities for both the poor as a whole and for the sick poor in particular were much less developed than in Europe and voluntary hospitals never provided free services on the same scale. Several reasons can be suggested for this. First, the 'poor' were often Blacks and new immigrants with whose needs older white settlers did not really identify. Secondly, until relatively recently, land was available where it was thought the 'poor' could settle and make a living and thus poverty was widely regarded as the fault of the poor. Thirdly, the medical profession was strongly organized at the state level before health insurance, either voluntary or compulsory, became an issue. Fourthly, the Western European countries (with the possible exception of France) developed strong working class movements which became an important political force. Such a force came much later in the Americas and in the United States it was never of the same character as in Europe.

In the United States, voluntary insurance was originally started by hospitals in an attempt to relieve their financial problems but the profit-making insurance companies entered the field and secured the majority of the business. The insurers made little attempt to restrain the prices charged by the providers of services or to influence the organization of health services. Indeed, until certain unions (the Miners and later the Automobile Workers and others) became concerned about the cost and quality of health services and this interest began to spread to employers, and until the entry of Government with Medicare and Medicaid, there was virtually no countervailing power[28] to challenge the interests of providers – the hospitals and the doctors. In Europe, on the other hand, voluntary insurance developed primarily as a non-profit movement, sponsored, controlled and paid for by manual workers, who drove hard bargains with providers of services. When insurance was made compulsory and employers were made to pay part of the cost, the aim of government was political – to improve the conditions of workers without placing excessive burdens on industry.

In much of Latin America the aim of introducing social security was also political – to win and retain the support of industrial workers and their leaders by providing workers with the medical privileges of the rich and often also their leaders with the control of vast social security empires. There was less concern about the costs which fell on employers. There was thus no impetus to restrain any unreasonable demands of providers or search out the most economical way of providing health services. Some sick funds have been allowed to become powerful political entities in their own right with all the rights of patronage and privilege and the corruption which can flow from this. In many countries of Latin America, social security agencies have become virtually 'a state within a state' and governments have hesitated to impose controls in view of the close association of social security with the trade union movement. In Israel, social security became almost a state within a state before the Israeli state was established. Kupat Holim, the largest sick fund associated with the trade union movement, continued to retain its major role in the provision of health services long after the Israeli state was established.

While tradition, politics and values have all played a part in influencing the pattern by which health services are financed and organized in different countries, some governments and consumers' organizations have succeeded in altering these patterns. This intervention has been gradually extended as problems of cost, distribution and quality have become identified and solutions to these problems have been sought.

27

Attempts have often been made to classify the different methods of financing and organizing health services which are found throughout the world into constellations or systems. Any basis for classification must give predominance to one feature rather than another. For example the organization of the services provided to the bulk of the Israeli population is similar to the patterns of Eastern Europe though the Israeli services are run by voluntary insurance and those in Eastern Europe by government or social security. The pattern of services in Sweden and Britain are not dissimilar, though Sweden retains a health insurance scheme and Britain does not.

What is more helpful is to list some of the key questions which need to be asked to describe a system of organizing and financing health services:

1. Do patients have an unrestricted choice of doctor for each episode of illness, OR
    (a) are they required to enlist with a primary care doctor whom they select (and if so, how easily can they change to another doctor)
    (b) are they assigned to a primary care doctor on a geographical basis?
2. Do patients have direct access to specialists or have they to be referred by a primary care doctor?
3. Do doctors providing services outside hospitals own their own offices or practise from premises provided for them?
4. Does the patient's original doctor choose whether to be responsible for the patient's care in hospital or must he hand over responsibility to separate doctors who work primarily or exclusively in hospitals?
5. If there are separate hospital doctors are the establishments of particular specialities laid down on a regional or national basis?
6. How are doctors, dentists and other personnel paid and is it on a full-time or part-time basis? Are they allowed private practice?
7. Do patients pay their own bills for health services? If so, can they claim whole or partial reimbursement from health insurance or social security? Or does the service or social security agency pay providers of health services directly?
8. Are charges and fees regulated and if so, by whom? Are the regulated charges maxima or do they apply only to the level of

28

reimbursement of the patient so that the provider is free to charge more if he wishes?

9. What proportion of the costs of particular services does the patient ultimately have to pay other than through taxes and insurance contributions? Are there limitations on the use of particular services? When taxes are used to finance a programme, are they payroll or other earmarked taxes?

10. If there is insurance, is it compulsory or voluntary and if the latter, how far is it a condition of employment? Are special arrangements made for the low-income section of the population to provide them with equal access to medical care services?

11. How far are hospitals owned by public authorities, social security, non-profit agencies and private operators?

12. Are hospital owners or potential owners free to build new facilities or extensions without prior approval from some planning authority? How is hospital construction financed?

13. Who controls and finances medical education? How is the number of places in medical schools determined and who determines it?

14. Who controls the social services which can substitute for and support health services? How extensively are they developed?

Different patterns of provision may be provided for different sections of the population. Thus, as we have seen, health services in Latin America are generally stratified: private services for the wealthy, social security for the salaried and industrial worker, and charity and public assistance for the peasant and the poor.

While many questions need to be answered to describe a system of organization, the answers do not indicate the goals of health services as interpreted by different societies, nor the effects of the system of organization on the quantity and quality of what is provided. How adequately are medical needs met? Are services available wherever they are needed? To what extent are unnecessary services provided?

NOTES

1. The author wishes to acknowledge the help of Mrs A. Hess in interpreting and explaining the origins of health insurance in Germany.

2. R. M. Titmuss, 'Health', in M. Ginsberg (ed.), Law and Opinion in England in the Twentieth Century, London, Stevens, 1959.

3. J. Hogarth, *The Payment of the General Practitioner*, Pergamon, 1963, p. 346.

4. ibid., p. 401.

5. See F. Ohtani, *One Hundred Years of Health Progress in Japan*, I.M.F.J., Tokyo, 1971.

6. See Social Insurance Agency, *Outlines of Social Insurance in Japan*, 1972.

7. Osaka Public Health Association, *Medical Care in Japan*, Osaka, 1965, pp. 2–4.

8. R. E. Bridgman, 'Medical Care under Social Security in France': *International Journal of Health Services*, Vol. 1, No. 4, November 1971, p. 332.

9. ibid., p. 333.

10. ibid., p. 332.

11. J. T. Ward, 'Organisation and Financing of Medical Care In New Zealand', B.M.A., *Health Services Financing*, 1969, p. 475.

12. For a brief summary of development in Canada see J. E. F. Hastings 'Federal and Provincial Insurance for Hospital and Physicians' Care in Canada', *International Journal of Health Services*, Vol. 1, No. 4, November 1971, pp. 398–413.

13. J. Van Langendonck, 'The European Experience in Social Health Insurance' *Social Security Bulletin*, Vol. 36, No. 7, July 1973, p. 28.

14. A hospital benefit restricted to the treatment of tuberculosis was, however, introduced for a short period.

15. H. and Ann Somers, *Doctors, Patients and Health Insurance*, Washington, D.C., Brookings, 1961, p. 292.

16. See I. S. Falk, 'Medical Care in the U.S.A. 1932–72', *Milbank Memorial Fund Quarterly*, Vol. 51, No. 1, 1973.

17. Dorothy P. Rice, 'Financing Social Welfare: Health Care', *Encyclopedia of Social Work*, National Association of Social Workers, 1973, pp. 433–442. See also D.H.E.W. *National Health Insurance Proposals*, 1974.

18. For a brief summary of development in Canada see J. E. F. Hastings, 'Federal and Provincial Insurance for Hospitals and Physicians in Canada', *International Journal of Health Services*, Vol. 1, No. 4, November 1971, pp. 398–413.

19. See J. M. Last, 'How Australia Pays Doctors', *New Society*, 14 April 1966, p. 14, and R. B. Scotton and J. S. Deeble, 'Compulsory Health Insurance for Australia', *Australian Economic Review*, 4th Quarter, 1968, pp. 9–10. There are current plans to revise the Australian system. See *Report of the Health Insurance Planning Committee to the Minister of Social Security*, A.G.P.S., Canberra, 1973.

20. Ministry of Social Security, *Australian Health Insurance Program*, A.G.P.S., Canberra, 1973.

21. Bridgman, op. cit., pp. 336–7, 339.

22. Osaka Public Health Association, op. cit., pp. 2–4.

23. M. I. Roemer, op. cit., p. 31.

24. ibid., p. 33.

25. V. Navarro, 'Health, Health Services and Health Planning in

Cuba', *International Journal of Health Services*, Vol. 2, No. 2, August 1972, p. 412.

26. ibid., p. 413.
27. ibid., pp. 423–4.
28. State insurance commissioners have had powers to approve increases in non-profit health insurance premiums but their attempts to intervene had limited short-term effects.

CHAPTER 3

The Money Barrier

No government now leaves health entirely to the private market. The trend during this century has been for more governments to provide or to secure the provision of more services to more people either free or at nominal charge. What is the justification for providing free health services?

In the case of most goods or services people are left to decide for themselves what to buy with whatever money they retain after paying tax. Though governments may regulate or alter by tax or subsidy the prices of many goods and services on the market for a variety of reasons including the need to collect revenue, consumers are normally left to spend their money as they please. Even in centrally planned economies such as those of Eastern Europe, where the government controls the bulk of production, consumers are still largely free to decide what they will buy at the prices which are established. It is generally held that this freedom enables each individual to obtain the greatest satisfaction from what he spends – or at least more satisfaction than if spending decisions were taken by others.

Social Budget

The first reason why some health services may be provided free at time of use is because it is cheaper to provide them that way. It would be absurdly expensive for each city dweller to try and arrange for clean water to be delivered and his sewage to be collected or to install his own system of sewage disposal. The collective provision of urban water supplies and sewage disposal systems is obviously cheaper. The cost can be paid for by local taxation or, where it is economic, by charges based on water used. Similarly, it is cheaper to spray a whole area to eliminate mosquitoes than for each household to do it if and when it wishes to. Those who spray benefit not just

themselves but their neighbours. All would benefit if local mos-
quito-breeding grounds were destroyed, but it would be extremely
difficult to charge according to how much people wanted a mos-
quito-free neighbourhood. These are collective goods which are best
provided collectively and paid for by taxation.

This argument for collective goods is of narrow application. But
closely related to it is the wider argument for 'external benefits'. Our
health does not simply depend on our own actions and expenditures
but on the actions and expenditures of others. If it is left to private
choice in a private market, each individual will take into account
only the value to himself of prevention or cure – not any advantage
to others. Those who want to protect themselves from possible
assault by drug addicts, alcoholics or the mentally ill have an
interest in paying for services to care for those with these forms of
deviation. Those who want to protect their family's health have an
interest in paying for the health education of others so that levels of
personal hygiene are raised and the risk of dirty food or dirt in public
places is reduced. Those who want to be safely promiscuous have an
interest in paying for a service to prevent and cure venereal disease in
others. Those who want freedom from cholera, the plague, smallpox
and typhus have an interest in paying for immunization, eradication
and surveillance throughout the world.

Neither the sick person nor the community may be able to
distinguish communicable disease from other diseases – at least in the
early stages. Thus, where dangerous communicable diseases are
prevalent or endemic and the community has not been protected
against the risk (by vaccination or immunization) or no effective
method of protection exists, a basic health service to diagnose all
sickness may be needed to detect communicable diseases. Moreover
this service may not be used to the extent required unless treatment is
provided not only for communicable diseases but for all diseases. In
a very poor country with little or no private curative facilities outside
the main centres of population, the provision of basic curative services for all purposes may be needed to identify and treat communicable disease. For example, experience has shown that malaria
cannot be eliminated by environmental measures alone. Curative
services are an essential part of an eradication programme and they
may not be sufficiently used by malaria patients unless they are used
to help all patients.

This argument provides a justification for the provision of basic diagnostic and treatment services in countries where dangerous communicable diseases are prevalent. These are, on the whole, the poorer countries of the world. It does not, of course, follow that services of this kind should necessarily be the government's top priority in such a country. The benefits from the use of resources in this activity must be weighed against the possible benefits in other fields of economic and social development.

The 'externalities' argument applies also to medical research. Everyone may benefit if new ways or cheaper ways are found of preventing or curing disease. In some cases (e.g. pharmaceuticals) firms can recover research costs through patent rights but often patenting is impracticable. What people are prepared to give in voluntary subscriptions for research does not represent the value to society of medical research. There is therefore a case for collective subsidy.

A further case for free services is where government is using compulsory powers. If the law requires certain categories of persons to be confined against their will because of infectious disease, drug addiction, alcoholism or mental illness, it would be inequitable to require them to pay the cost unless they were held to be morally responsible for their condition. Moreover, some will be unable to pay and those who are defined by society as mentally ill cannot be expected to make rational choices. The compulsory detention of the sick shades into the compulsory detention of the criminal and there are many areas where similar considerations apply.

Thus intervention by government to provide or secure the provision of health services free or below cost is justified for certain specific services. The extent to which these services should be provided at government cost in particular countries depends on an assessment of the benefits expected from spending money in this way compared to others.

The Limitations of Private Choice

These are the justifications for government financing of certain health services. Is there a justification for more extensive provision of free services? The general argument rests on the inability of consumers to make informed choices. First, they can seldom know in advance if they will be 'needing' health services, when they will be needing them, or how much they will be needing them. Secondly, the cost of meeting this need can be wholly disproportionate to their ability to pay. Thirdly, a major health need eliminates their ability to earn. And finally they can seldom know in advance what benefits the purchase of health services will provide.

While, within limits, the health services 'needed' by a country can be predicted, no individual can predict his own need for health services – that his state of health will be such that it could be substantially improved by using health services and that without the help of the services this improvement would occur later, to a lesser extent or not at all. People know in advance how much food they expect to demand each day, month or year and can plan accordingly. They cannot plan their demand or know their need for health services in the same way. Some health needs may become regular and predictable once a diagnosis has been made: a medicine may need to be taken three times a day or dialysis may be needed three times a week. A chronic patient may get to know the important symptoms and thus be able to exercise informed choice. But at any time there can be a sudden and unexpected new need, whether caused by accident or disease. Moreover, even when the new need has been identified, neither patient nor doctor may know with certainty how much medical care will be required or when it will be required.

Unpredictable needs are not, of course, confined to health services. Cars break down, television tubes fail, and things get lost and broken. But what is peculiar to the health field is that the amount which may have to be spent per unit of time may be extremely large in relation to earnings per unit of time. The income of a year may be needed to pay for medical care during one week.[1] A year's medical care can consume a lifetime's earnings, let alone a lifetime's savings. Moreover, sickness, if severe, destroys earning capacity at the same time as it generates the desire for unplanned, exceptional expenditure. The need may turn out to be very long-lasting. The impairment caused by an accident may require intensive care for the injured person for the rest of his life. A child may be born with a physical or mental handicap, requiring life-long care. Indeed, the technical medical requirement can change over time, not only because of changes in the patient's condition, but also because of advances or assumed advances in medical knowledge. An expensive cure may be developed some time in the future for a condition which cannot be cured now.

Technical change is not peculiar to medicine. New expensive products are constantly being developed which consumers would like to be able to purchase. If they *had* known beforehand what new products would become available for purchase, they *might* have decided to save up to buy them. They become aware afterwards that they spent their money in a way which they later regretted. But lack of knowledge of the future is a dominant feature of health services. As people do not know in advance what they will want to purchase from the health market and do not know what valuable services may become available later, they are in no position to distribute their expenditure over life to the best advantage. Nor can they know in advance the size of the lifetime budget which will be available to them for allocation to different uses – not least because ill-health can destroy earning capacity. Inability to afford most goods may be remedied by saving up to buy them later on. In the case of health services, there may be no chance of earning or saving unless the illness is treated now. It is somewhat unreal to envisage a motor accident victim with multiple fractures weighing up at the hospital door his preferences for medical treatment compared with food, clothing or a new car. In such situations, money is no object.

Voluntary Insurance

The private market provides a mechanism by which people can make provision for expenditures, the need for which can be predicted in advance for groups of the population but not for individuals. This is the function of insurance. The age of death cannot be predicted for the individual, but can, within limits, be predicted for the whole population. Thus, people can buy life insurance and pension policies. Similarly people can insure their homes against the risk of fire and their cars against the risk of accidents. The insurer can offer cover with reasonable confidence because death rates do not change greatly from year to year and thus the financial commitment is broadly defined in advance. Similarly the insurer can agree in advance to pay for the damage to or loss of house or car, and to provide a defined sum per year from a specified age until death.

Insurance companies also offer policies to pay medical care bills. But, while they can predict on the basis of accumulated experience how many people are likely to make claims, they cannot know in advance how large their bills will be. What the consumer may want is a guarantee that the insurer will pay not only for him to visit the doctor whenever he wants, but for anything which the doctor may decide he needs at any stage of his life – a policy without a monetary limit of the type which is applied in life insurance, pensions and fire. The insurer is not willing to assume an unlimited risk of this kind – particularly when those who decide what expenditures are needed are not company employees under their control but independent doctors in private practice. Quite apart from this, there is the underlying problem that future changes in medical technology cannot be predicted in advance. At any time a new and expensive treatment may be developed which doctors will use on a wide scale. If insurers agreed to pay for anything any doctor ordered, they would be gambling on a limit to the costs arising from medical advances.

Thus, health insurers place careful limitations on the claims they will meet. They may place a monetary limit on claims by each individual during a year. They normally insure for a year only and do not guarantee to renew for a further year at any specified price. Or they may limit the number of days of hospital care they are prepared to pay for. Or the person covered may be required to pay for the first few days of care or a proportion of the cost of each day of care, or for the doctor's services while in hospital. By making the patient pay part of the cost, the insurer makes the risk more predictable. The services of out-of-hospital doctors may be included but not the cost of the pharmaceuticals, as this is one of the areas where there is a special risk of unpredictable increases in expenditure. (What would happen, for example, if a new, costly but effective remedy were developed for the common cold?) The exclusion of pharmaceuticals from the policy also provides an indirect restraint on the number of times patients may seek to visit their doctors, as visits usually lead to a prescription and thus to a bill for the patient.

No private insurance company is prepared to provide the full health insurance cover which people want. Where doctors themselves offer insurance they are prepared to offer more extended cover. This is because they are, to a considerable extent, able to decide how far the demands of patients should be met. They can, therefore, keep expenditure for their patients within the annual premium income from their patients, by, for example, issuing less costly prescriptions or authorizing less hospital admission. The consumer or his employer is, in effect, making an annual contract with a group of doctors to provide such health services as *they* consider the insured person needs during the year. Some social security agencies have their own hospitals and recruit doctors under a contract of employment. This puts them in a strong position to ensure that their doctor employees keep expenditure within the annual budget. This is also the economic basis of what have come to be called 'health maintenance organizations' in the United States. It is hoped that the fixed budget will lead to more services being provided on an out-of-hospital basis.

But even this pattern of organization can only meet the consumer's requirement on an annual basis. Each year there is a contract for that year and each year the price for cover is quoted by the insurer. The consumer has to pay the premium, go elsewhere, or go without. Such a system does not meet the requirements of the chronic sick. For example, a consumer pays his premium for the first year and becomes ill during it, and continues to be seriously ill when the second year's premium is due. His illness has stopped him working and he has no savings. He may be receiving a social security benefit and sick pay, but he may not be able to raise the cost of the premium out of this reduced income. Worse still, the premium he will be quoted, if a quotation is made at all, will be much higher than the previous year because he is now chronically sick.

Competitive private insurance inevitably results in risk-taking – quoting lower premiums to people who are less likely to use health services and higher premiums to those who are expected to be heavy users. Rival insurers will attempt to identify those to whom a lower price can safely be offered and those to whom it would be prudent to charge a high price – even if they do choose to take their custom elsewhere. Those wishing to be insured are, therefore, given health examinations in the attempt to identify how much medical care they are likely to need. It is known that older people use more health services than younger people. Thus, premiums are adjusted accordingly. Those who have made heavy use of particular kinds of health services in the past are more likely to be heavy users in the future.[2] And so on.

The more effective methods are discovered of predicting the individual's future need for health services, the more the premiums charged in a competitive insurance market will vary between individuals. Those with chronic illness will be quoted the cost of the services they are expected to use. Those who most 'need' insurance cover are least likely to be able to purchase it. The insurer, whether profit-making or like Blue Cross in the U.S.A. non-profit, who does not adjust his premiums to risks will be left with the bad risks, as the good risks are offered cheaper policies elsewhere. If he does not recognize this in time and raise his premiums accordingly, he will end up bankrupt. Thus, health insurance becomes less and less a system of insurance, and more and more a system of prepayment.

Thus while voluntary health insurance can meet the requirements of the healthy, it cannot provide for those who require most medical care. Moreover, healthy people with low incomes – particularly the low-paid and the aged with low pensions – will find premiums a heavy burden. Although people attach great importance to health services when they get ill, other demands may take precedence when they are well. In all societies people are under pressure to conform as far as possible with conventional standards of feeding, clothing, housing, furnishing and leisure activities. When people are relatively poor for the society they live in, the pressure to achieve the standards of that society leaves little with which to provide for the future – particularly the unexpected future. It is for this reason, quite apart from ignorance of health risks and of the magnitude of possible bills for health services or from carelessness, that many people, even in what by world standards are affluent societies, do not insure themselves for health care to the extent that insurance is available.

The extension of voluntary health insurance can be encouraged by tax concessions. These concessions are justified by the argument that premiums paid to keep the body in good repair are costs necessarily incurred to earn an income and thus logically deductible against income tax. Employers may provide voluntary health insurance as a fringe benefit. This may be an advantageous way for employers to remunerate employees if the premium is treated under the tax laws as a business expense and is not taxable on the employee. Moreover, it becomes economic for insurers to quote lower terms to cover large groups of people rather than individuals. Indeed, in the United States the premium charged in a group plan is about half that charged to an individual who insures himself. This is partly because the administrative costs of insuring a group under one policy are lower than collecting annual premiums and issuing policies to each individual. It is also because group plans involve the insurer in less sales expenditure than individual plans. In 1972, the administrative costs of group plans were 13·4 per cent compared with 47 per cent for individual plans.[3] Most of those covered by health insurance in the United States are covered under group plans. Nevertheless, even in that country, where voluntary health insurance is most developed, nearly a quarter of the civilian population have no insurance for hospital care and surgical care. For health care other than doctors and hospitals, only 5 per cent of consumer spending is met by insurance.[4]

Part of the problem is that while the rich can afford to buy health services when they want them and the not so rich can afford to buy health insurance, the poorer take the risk that they will be able to buy, should the need arise, such health services as they cannot do without or expect the government to step in and provide services for them.

Health Services and the Redistribution of Income

It is often argued that health services should be provided free at public expense because they are a necessity. But food is also a necessity yet no society regularly provides free food though many provide all or a substantial part of health services free to all or most of the population. The measures which more developed countries take to ensure that some people do not go without food are either to subsidize food or to redistribute incomes – mainly through social security schemes. Even in the richest countries many people would go short of food unless government intervened – in old age, when supporting a large family, in widowhood, unemployment, sickness and other adversities. Thus income is redistributed to meet these needs through social insurance, family allowances and public assistance programmes. It is rare for much food to be provided in kind. Similarly governments may regulate minimum wages, and encourage the provision of occupational pension schemes and sick pay schemes by tax concessions.

In poor countries food may be provided free in the crisis of a famine due to crop failure or war, but these are exceptional measures to deal with a situation which it is hoped will be temporary. In such countries it is not practicable to run social security schemes covering the whole population – urban and rural – such as are to be found in the more developed countries. Not only are such services expensive but to run a national scheme requires a large and efficient bureaucracy of trained clerks and administrators to determine eligibility for benefits – quite apart from collecting the revenue. Personnel with this education and training are not available in sufficient quantity. Nor could they be recruited to work where they would be needed. Social security requires a firm basis of individual taxation, a certain general level of literacy and the ability to establish such facts as age, paternity and marriage, to certify sickness and for certain schemes to establish income and capital. Hence social security cannot be used to redistribute income or only to a limited extent. Yet in such countries the gap between the living standards of the stable urban population and the rural population may widen as development proceeds. While standards of living in the industrialized sector rise, the peasant farmer or hired agricultural worker may be no better off than before. In such a society, health, education and other services in kind are means of enabling the benefits of development to be shared more equally – or simply for the richer to be taxed to help the poorer. Some developing countries give considerable priority to health for this among other reasons.

But income can be and is redistributed in the more developed countries by social insurance and public assistance programmes. What is the case for treating the 'need' for health services as different from the 'need' for food? Should people be left to make their own choices between expenditure on food, health insurance or payment of health bills? Is the problem of unmet 'need' for health services just part of the problem of low standards of living generally – bad housing, inadequate nutrition and low standards of clothing and heating – in short the problem of poverty? Is the remedy to raise the level of social security payments and still leave people to make their own decisions on how to spend whatever money they have? Is there a case for singling out health services for special provision – apart from those health services where the 'externalities' argument described above applies?

The key point which distinguishes health services from food services is that few people can exercise informed choice when deciding what health services to buy. The ordinary consumer cannot know the likely consequences of not receiving health services until he has taken medical advice and then he may only be informed in terms of probabilities. While he learns from experience what satisfaction he derives from eating particular food, he cannot, generally, know what perils he might avoid if he consulted a doctor. He is not in a position to exercise informed choice and may therefore go to doctors less than he would if he had this infomation.[5] It is hard to think of the consumer weighing up the possible need for medical care in 'unanticipated situations, unforeseen states of the world, unconceptualized situations'.[6] The decision process which might result in the initiation of care is often 'a game played not to maximise outcomes, but to reduce losses and to minimise losses. It is the only game in town.'[7] 'Medical care is not a good: it is a least bad'.[8]

Going to the doctor may involve loss of working time, travel costs and overcoming the fear that something serious may be found which you want to postpone knowing. Some people do not go to the doctor because, as they see it, they *cannot* afford to be ill. The family *must* have the wages. The work *must* be done on the farm or business and there is no one else to do it. The mother *cannot* be ill because there is no one else to look after the children. These are all barriers to the use of health services quite apart from any charges for it. It is not the same as buying food. Even if health services were provided free and were available without appointments or delay, there is no guarantee that all health needs would be met. The provision of free health services removes some but not all of the barriers to the use of health services.

The Right to Health Services

In the past few decades nearly all the richer countries of the world have come to regard at least the most costly health services as a right which must ultimately be provided by government to those who cannot pay and have not insured. It is regarded as unacceptable for people to be denied health services if they are *proved* to be unable to pay for them. But if the same facilities were made available free to people who did not insure, even if they could have afforded to do so, this would discourage the growth of voluntary health insurance and be unfair to those of the same income group who did pay premiums – in some cases at considerable sacrifice. For these and other reasons, the services provided for the poor are generally poor services and the process of applying for them is made stigmatizing.

Where countries ultimately underwrite the costs of medical care, the principle of voluntary health insurance becomes less viable and less equitable. The inequity of assisting financially those who have not made provision for themselves is one reason why insurance for pensions and cash benefits in widowhood, unemployment and sickness has been made compulsory in many developed countries. It is also one of the reasons why compulsory health insurance has been introduced in so many countries to pay for health services. A second reason is because compulsory health insurance can avoid the risk-rating of voluntary insurance. All covered by the scheme can be brought in on the same terms. Thirdly, one giant scheme covering a whole nation or a series of large occupational schemes can be operated at lower administrative cost simply because insurance is compulsory. Employers and employees do not have to be sold insurance, they are required by law to buy it. Fourthly, compulsory health insurance can be used to control the cost distribution and quality of all health services provided for the whole population.

Under a compulsory scheme, the concept of insurance is often stretched far beyond the principles of private insurance. Certain classes of beneficiary may be exempt from paying a premium. For example, in many continental European countries the standard rate of premium paid by the husband is regarded as covering his dependent children and dependent wife. Pensioners can be exempt from premiums as under the hospital insurance part of the Medicare programme in the U.S.A. on the theory that their social insurance premiums paid during working life covered them for health care in old age. The premium can be adjusted to take further account of the principle of ability to pay and be made earnings-related even though the higher-paid may have less need for health services over life than the low-paid. Or the premium can be paid out of general tax revenue as in some of the provinces in Canada.

But there is a limit to the extent to which the principle of social insurance can be adapted to meet social needs and still remain credible as an insurance scheme – as something different from an ear-marked tax to finance a public service. If some categories are not excluded from the rights purchased by paying the insurance contributions, it ceases to be insurance in any normal use of the term. Those excluded may be those who become chronic sick or disabled before reaching adulthood, or new immigrants, or people who have for any reason been either not employed or self-employed within the country and thus never paid any insurance contributions. Normally separate provision for these groups is made through a public assistance scheme. And usually this creates stigma of some kind. The credibility of social insurance is normally secured by penalizing in some way those outside the scheme.

Conclusion – The Right to Health Care

The governments of some countries have regarded the receipt of health services as an unsuitable area for stigmatizing anyone. Stigma, as well as charges, discourage the use made of any service and, in the case of health services, it is considered important that all should be encouraged to use them. Thus it is held that medical need alone should provide a right to medical care and that health services, like defence or the police, should be provided as a tax-financed public service to the whole population.

The removal of the money barrier does not make it necessary to nationalize health services. All that may be done is to pay patients' bills and leave doctors, dentists and others to practise from their existing offices and leave hospitals to be run by a variety of private non-profit and profit-making agencies. The reasons for regulating or controlling the supply of health services are different from the reasons for removing the money barrier. They are considered in the next chapter.

NOTES

1. For example, in Ontario a heart transplant costs $110,000: *Medical Care Review*, Vol. 29, No. 11, December 1972, p. 1259.

2. For example, under Medicare in the United States, 5½ per cent of those covered for 61–6 months used $50 or more of services every year. D.H.E.W., 'Persons Meeting SMI deductible, 1966–71', *Health Insurance Statistics*, Note No. 57.

3. Marjorie Mueller, 'Private Health Insurance in 1973', *Social Security Bulletin*, Feb. 1974, p. 37.

4. C. Kramer, 'Fragmented financing of Health Care', *Medical Care Review*, Vol. 29, No. 8, August 1972, p. 882.

5. S. E. Berki, *Hospital Economics*, Lexington, 1972, p. 127.

6. S. E. Berki, op. cit., p. 127.

7. ibid., p. 130.

8. ibid., p. 131.

CHAPTER 4

The Medical Market

Whether health services are bought privately or under a compulsory insurance or government programme, resources are used which could have met other needs. Thus individually or collectively people want value for money in terms of quality services for what they spend on health services. Is this most likely to be secured by encouraging free competition between doctors both in their role as providers and in their role as purchasing agents?

The Limitations of Consumer Choice

The case for the provision of any goods or services by private individual contractors and firms is that competition results in goods and services at a price and of a quality for which consumers are prepared to pay. Producers who provide what consumers judge to be value for money prosper and those who are less successful in achieving this do less well or fail. Few countries have laws to say that butchers or hairdressers must have passed an examination and been registered. A hairdresser whom many consumers think provides a good service can raise his price: a hairdresser whose services are less well esteemed may nevertheless attract customers *because* he is cheap, or he may go out of business. Thus, the private market is ultimately controlled by the preference of customers.

This extremely simple statement of the advantages claimed for a private market system needs, of course, to be modified in many ways. Producers try to persuade consumers to want what they did not want before or want more. They may also try to eliminate competition by controlling markets. For many types of goods there are in practice few suppliers and these suppliers may not compete in the same sense as the small farmer who takes his goods to the village market and gets the best price he can for them. The latter is, by definition, one of

45

many farmers supplying the market. The customers who buy the class of goods he sells know what they are buying and the farmer is not in a position to persuade people to want his goods more than anyone else's just because they are his. The price he gets for his goods depends on what customers want and what competing products are on the market. If his goods are of high quality he will expect to get more; if they are of poor quality, he will expect to get less. This is because customers can assess quality. They learn to do this by experience – by what they have come to prefer and are thus prepared to pay a little more to have. It is the housewife's evaluation of quality not the scientist's which determines what rewards farmers will get for particular produce.

This somewhat idealized picture of the village food market – chosen because of its untypical simplicity – can be used to make three important points which distinguish the market for health services. First, the main demand for the use of health resources comes mainly from the key provider – the doctor – rather than from consumers. Secondly, consumers are only to a very limited extent able to assess the quality of health services they are receiving or have received. Thirdly as consumers often want health services urgently, this limits the extent to which they can shop around to find the best buy.

The provision of a good or service free of charge will normally lead to an enormous increase in demand and thus either there has to be rationing or queuing will develop which is just another form of rationing. The exceptions are such goods as air and water which are in abundant supply – at least in those parts of the world where most economists work. But people do not drink as much water as they possibly can just because it is free or because the charge is the same however much is drunk. They have other ways of occupying their time and water drinking beyond a point yields little satisfaction. Similarly people do not necessarily want to spend their time talking to their doctor about their health and matters related to their health. Nor will they consume as many medicines as they can obtain just because they are free. There are some people who do visit their doctor much more than their physical health warrants and consume medicines in larger quantities than is medically necessary. But anxiety of this kind about health is itself a medical problem – difficult though it may be to treat. Moreover many people have unrealistic expectations of what health care can do for them. It cannot repair the ravages of time or reverse the impact of a lifetime of deprivation or destructive behaviour.

Though a doctor or dentist may request a patient to come for a health examination or immunization, patients normally initiate the use of resources in the health service by requesting advice or care more often than not as a response to pressure and advice from friends and relatives. This is not true of patients brought into hospital unconscious or of patients compulsorily detained in mental hospitals. Neither consciously demand health services. But once the patient has arrived, it is those working in the health services, and, in the case of more developed countries, largely doctors and to a lesser extent dentists and opticians, who decide what resources will be used. They decide how much of their time to spend on each patient, what diagnostic tests should be taken, what treatment should be provided, whether the patient should be admitted to hospital and if admitted how long he should stay. Thus it is doctors and other health personnel rather than patients who requisition and distribute the main health resources of a nation by deciding what response to make to the demands of each patient and the extent to which steps should be taken to seek out patients who might benefit from particular services but are making no demands. The patient who is known to be hypochondriac can either be brushed off if this is considered to be in his best interests or the causes of his anxiety about his health can be explored. Water cannot stop itself being wasted, but a doctor can stop a patient wasting his time if he decides to do so or has an incentive to do so.

The patient is not in a position to know how much of the doctor's time he needs – what examinations should be undertaken, what questions should be asked and answered or what features of his medical history may be relevant. Nor does he know what preventive and curative actions can improve his health. Indeed, he is usually going to the doctor to discover what is wrong with him and how it can be cured or prevented. He is trusting the doctor to perform two roles *on his behalf.* The first is the diagnosis of what is required and the second is the provision of the necessary services by himself or others. It is because there is a limit at any point of time to the services which are known to be effective in curing or preventing ill-health, and because doctors are expected only to authorize the use of services which are effective (including placebos which need not be expensive) that a free service does not lead to an infinite use of preventive or

47

curative services. It is only in standards of care that there is no evident limit on what could be provided.

Even after the decisions have been taken and the services provided, the patient is still not in a position to know whether they were technically good services or technically bad services. If he recovers it may be despite the services he has received which have prolonged the illness, though he does not know it. If he is left disabled, he may be grateful to his doctor for saving his life when the disability was in fact due to faulty treatment rather than the original problem which brought him to the doctor. Not only is the patient in no position to assess the quality of his treatment, he is in no position to assess whether it has been provided at a reasonable cost.

Ignorance of what is being bought is to be found in other markets. For example, few consumers are equipped to assess the technical efficiency of a machine, whether it is a car or a refrigerator. But the performance of a machine can be described. Because there are different models to choose from, each made in quantity by one or several manufacturers, information on the suitability of particular models for a particular purpose can be obtained from independent experts: indeed advice of this kind can be made regularly available to consumers in published form. When choosing a particular machine, an expert can examine it to see whether it is operating according to specification. And if it fails to perform as specified after purchase, at least the consumer comes to know that either the model he purchased was deficient or the whole series was deficient. It is possible to learn from experience and a manufacturer who intends to stay in business is wise to build up a good reputation among customers who have purchased his goods. A doctor may build up a good reputation but this is no certain indication of his technical proficiency.

There are few fields of consumer expenditure where the consumer is as ill-equipped to exercise his theoretical sovereignty as in health services. This is partly because no two medical services are precisely the same – if only because they are performed on different patients. The failure of an established medical procedure to produce the desired results may be due to peculiarities in the patient which the best-trained practitioner could not have foreseen. Nor can a patient learn by his own experiences which is technically a good doctor or a good hospital. Recommendation by other patients is also of no assistance. Reputation as assessed by the medical profession is a better guide, though even that is fallible and few patients are able to find this out. No books are published by the profession grading its members because only to a limited extent is it possible to measure the competence as distinct from the training of doctors. And even a well-trained doctor can rapidly fall behind in knowledge after qualification.[1]

Where consumers have sufficient knowledge, they can collectively regulate by their purchases what it pays producers to supply. If consumers are able to assess quality, they will decide collectively how much extra they will be prepared to pay for better quality and what minimum of quality they expect in goods to make them worth buying at lower prices. Different consumers will purchase goods and services of different quality at different prices. If, however, the consumer cannot assess quality, this regulation of supply cannot take place. Moreover if he wants medical help urgently he lacks the time to try to seek out the quality supplier or the cheap supplier of a service of a given quality or the doctor who is cost-conscious in what he commissions for his patients.

The Regulation of the Health Profession

Before the profession of medicine was regulated, some 'quacks' were able to charge high fees while competent and qualified doctors were under-employed and forced to charge low fees in the same neighbourhood. It was mainly to protect the qualified from the competition of quacks that the health professions first became regulated. The pressure for regulation came from the better-qualified doctors rather than from their patients, though much was made of the damage done to patients by unscrupulous practitioners who were unqualified.

The basic regulation of the health professions consists in registering or licensing personnel. While existing practitioners with limited training may at first be given licences or registered under a 'grandfather' clause, in the longer run a minimum of education and training is laid down for new entrants to the profession. In practice this means that a central body is established which determines which degrees or qualifications from which schools or colleges will be recognized. Such a body may come to specify what minimum periods of education and training will be required in the future and may also approve the curriculum and supervise the examinations. Where such bodies are controlled by the leaders of the profession concerned, the attainment demanded of new entrants tends to be continuously increased. This has the effect of restricting the supply of personnel and thus conferring considerable monopoly powers on the members of the profession.

In the United States when the regulation of medical education was undertaken in 1909 following the Flexner report, the number of medical schools fell from 135 to 66 within a decade. By 1971, the number of schools had risen only to 103 – less than in 1909. The number of practising doctors in the United States was 14·6 per 10,000 in 1910. It only increased to 17·0 per 10,000 in 1971,[2] despite the enormous economic growth, the vast development of medical knowledge and the various measures which reduced the severity of the money barrier. The supply of doctors increased much more slowly than demand and this conferred vast eonomic benefits on the profession.

In some other countries regulation has not had the effect of restricting supply. Over the last fifty years the U.S.S.R. has planned a vast increase in the number of doctors and secured it. The same has happened in other Eastern European countries since the war and also in such countries as Egypt. There has been a vast expansion in doctors in Argentina without any planning.

Any qualified student who wishes to enter Medical School has the right to do so. There has been no limitation of places. The population per doctor is now 600 but it rises to 200 in Buenos Aires and 170 in Cordoba. In countries with relatively easy entry to the profession the earnings of doctors are low when account is taken of the period of education and comparisons are made with other occupations. In Argentina a doctor can expect to earn about $80 a month in his first year – the equivalent of a skilled worker's salary.[3]

The earnings of doctors depend not only on supply in relation to demand, but also on the extent to which they have been granted a legislative monopoly. A state register of personnel may do no more than record those who have obtained an approved qualification in a particular field. For example, the register of nurses in Britain does no more than this. A register or licence may go further and give exclusive rights to persons on the register by making it illegal for other persons to perform these functions. Only a doctor may be entitled to issue a death certificate, prescribe certain listed drugs or undertake certain medical procedures. Similarly exclusive rights may be conferred on persons registered as dentists or certain rights parallel to those conferred on doctors may be conferred on midwives.

Registration or licensing are not the only ways by which monopoly powers may be conferred on persons. For example, the monopoly powers of doctors in Britain arise much more from the fact that only a registered doctor can normally be employed in a hospital or make a contract to act as a general practitioner within the National Health Service than from any restrictions in the Medical Act. Similarly, in the United States insurance companies and social security agencies may only reimburse expenditures authorized by a licensed doctor and a hospital may only confer privileges to act as a doctor on those who are licensed. Thus patients may be able to buy medical advice and certain treatments from nature-cure practitioners, pharmacists, herbalists, osteopaths and indigenous practitioners. But when services from doctors are made free at time of use the patients have an incentive to consult the registered doctor rather than practitioners who are not registered because the latter charge for their services.

The monopoly powers of professions therefore depend for their extent on the number of registered personnel compared to the demand for their services, on the scope of work which unregistered personnel can perform and on what incentives there are for patients to consult those who are registered. In rural areas, geography may confer monopoly power. The inconvenience and cost of travel may restrict patients to one or two doctors. When there are only a few practitioners in a neighbourhood, it is easier for them to agree to charge the same fees and not to undercut fees to attract patients.

The Doctor as Purchasing Agent

As mentioned earlier, a doctor is expected not only to decide what each patient requires but to provide or order the goods and services which are needed on the patient's behalf. In view of the patient's ignorance the doctor is expected to operate as a knowledgeable purchaser in the patient's interest. The patient expects him to provide or order only those services which are needed. If the patient is paying, he expects his doctor to secure value for money when he decides what should be purchased. He or his relatives may expect to be consulted on what standards of amenity are to be purchased if admission to a hospital or nursing home is advised. They may also hope to be consulted if the choice is between going to a specialist of high renown who can command high fees or a less renowned specialist who charges lower fees. But many decisions are in practice taken by doctors without any real consultation with the customer or his representative and little regard for cost.

In deciding what to provide or order for his patients, the doctor is expected under his ethical code to ignore considerations of his own financial gain. But the doctor in private practice, charging on the traditional fee-for-service basis, is constantly faced with conflicts of interest. The doctor is in a position to advise the patient who consults him whether further visits are required. If the patient is sick at home, it is for the doctor to decide how frequently he should call to see the patient. The patient who feels ill but has no symptoms or abnormalities which the doctor can identify may develop relevant symptoms or abnormalities later on. Should the initiative be left to the patient to call or call on the doctor or should the doctor himself take the initiative by making a call or advising a further visit? Should the doctor advise patients who feel healthy to call for regular health checks?

There is in fact no limit to the number of times patients could be examined. On any occasion the doctor might detect an illness at an early stage though the statistical odds of this occurring are extremely small. Thus some royal families have had doctors in constant attendance and the health of the President of the United States is closely monitored by his personal physician. While there is a limit to the curative and preventive actions which are known to be effective on random populations, it is not possible to say conclusively that there is no action which a doctor could take which would not be beneficial to an individual patient. A placebo may make a patient feel better and this is a service which patients are glad to receive and for which they are willing to pay.

In the case of minor mental 'illness' there is no limit to the time a doctor can spend with a patient which that patient may regard as useful. Reassurance and emotional support are what many of us seek. A sympathetic listener with the status which the profession of medicine confers can provide a service which some people want and are prepared to pay to have. How far has the doctor made the patient emotionally dependent on him? The borderline between what is necessary and what the patient appreciates, between effective cure and sympathetic care is not easily demarcated. The doctor who responds to the emotional demands of his patients is providing a service and earning his fees. It is hard for anyone, even the doctor himself, to say conclusively that a service is being provided unnecessarily for financial gains.

Conflicts of interest can also arise in the ordering of services from others. For example, the doctor may be in a position to make a profit when authorizing an X-ray or pathological examination. He may do it himself, employ staff to do it or send it out to a laboratory or centre but still charge the patient considerably more than the laboratory or centre charges him. Some laboratories in the United States give doctors a kickback for tests sent to them.[4] Similarly the doctor may have the choice between referring the patient to a surgeon for an operation or doing it himself and charging accordingly. Even if he decides to refer the patient for surgery he may derive financial benefit by 'assisting' the surgeon and continuing the care of the patient in hospital. The surgeon may also have a financial interest in 'splitting his fee' with the referring doctor to encourage further referrals. Though many professional associations rule that such practices are unethical they do occur when surgeons are paid on a fee-for-service basis. Thus the decisions on whether to recommend surgery and who should do it may be taken in circumstances where one decision is clearly more profitable for the original doctor who was consulted.

A further conflict of interest can arise when a doctor owns a pharmacy or a hospital. The decisions on whether to prescribe and what to prescribe are taken when the doctor profits from each prescription and knows that some preparations are more profitable to dispense than others. Similarly the decisions on whether to admit to hospital and when to recommend discharge may be taken with the knowledge that there are vacant staffed beds in his hospital and he will have to pay the cost if they are unoccupied. A doctor who owns a hospital, like any other owner has to decide what standards to maintain in areas where the patient is not in a position to know what is going on. For example, what proportion of his nursing and other staff are qualified? Who acts as anaesthetist while he operates? Private hospitals which doctors do not own may be willing to pay doctors for securing that patients are admitted to them.[5]

Regulations may be designed to prevent conflicts of interest and secure minimum standards. While in Japan it is not unethical for a doctor to own a hospital and sell pharmaceuticals, and many do, in

Britain ownership of a pharmacy is deemed unethical by the British Medical Association. In the United States a doctor can own a hospital, but under various state laws not a pharmacy or optician's shop.[6]

The motive of financial gain is not the only reason why unnecessary services may be requested by doctors for their patients. The fear of prosecution for negligence may lead doctors to play safe and order tests, though they do not think that they are really needed. If the ordering of unnecessary tests can lead to no financial or other penalty for the doctor, why not order them? Admission to hospital for observation and diagnosis may be motivated by similar considerations. If the patient should die at home, there is a risk of a negligence suit. If the patient dies in hospital, this fact goes some way towards preventing the suit or defending it if it is brought. It costs the doctor nothing to spend someone else's money in lavish quantities to be sure that he can defend himself in a legal case.

Few negligence suits are brought in Britain as is shown by the fact that all doctors could obtain insurance to cover legal costs and damages for £25 a year ($60) in 1973. In the United States about 10,000 malpractice claims are filed each year[7] and in California there were 18 claims for malpractice per 100 doctors. General surgeons have to pay $4000 for insurance against malpractice claims of up to $1 million. In some fields of surgery malpractice insurance cost $20,000 a year,[8] and some anaesthetists pay $34,000.[9] The United States is a litigious country and suits are encouraged by the acceptance of 'speculative actions' as ethical by the legal profession: the patient only has to pay his lawyer if he wins the case, when he hands over an agreed proportion of the money gained in the action.

A further reason for unnecessary expenditure is that the doctor lacks any clear interest in economy and is not taught how to secure it. Medical schools generally teach the doctor to seek the best he can find for his patient irrespective of cost. Indeed doctors seldom know what costs they are generating by the decisions they take. They may never see the bills for the hospital care and drugs which they have ordered. Doctors are seldom taught economical prescribing in hospital and come to learn little about the cost of new medicines introduced while they are in practice. The whole question of prescribing and the role of the pharmaceutical industry in influencing prescribing are discussd in Chapter 6.

54

The system by which health services are provided and how doctors are trained and remunerated can all affect the extent to which unnecessary or uneconomical services are provided. Unnecessary services involve economic waste. They may also be the cause of denying health services to others who need them. If the limited supply of hospital beds is used for those who no longer need or never needed hospital care, those in urgent need may have to wait for admission or be refused admission. If the accumulation of doctors in the more popular urban areas leads to no reduction of their average earnings because unnecessary services are provided, there will be no economic pressure to discourage newly qualified doctors from entering these areas and force them to seek out areas where their services are needed. As qualified personnel are always in limited supply at any point of time, unnecessary services in urban areas may prevent necessary services being provided in rural areas.

What may be fundamentally wrong is for doctors to act as businessmen rather than as independent professional advisers. But, in so far as they do act in this way, it becomes necessary to examine the financial incentives operating on doctors, hospitals, pharmaceutical companies and other suppliers of health services. It is to alter these financial incentives that governments have, in some countries, taken extensive powers to control the supply and distribution of health services and to alter the financial incentives of those working in them. It is partly for this reason that in some countries hospitals are owned by the government. Thus the government can decide what hospitals will be built, of what size and where they will be built and attempt to find methods of economical construction. Other countries use planning powers to control the construction of hospitals but do not own them. Similarly countries may regulate where doctors may practice with the aim of securing a more even distribution of personnel.

Thus the regulation of the supply of health services may have a variety of aims. One aim may be to secure a minimum of quality. A second aim may be to secure a more even geographical distribution of limited resources. A third aim may be to prevent unnecessary services. A fourth aim may simply be to limit expenditure. A fifth aim may be to secure value for money by the most economical use of each pound, ruble or rupee spent on health services.

Conclusion

The dominating feature of the health market is the consumers' lack of knowledge. They do not know their risks of ill-health. They do not normally know what precise services they want to buy, the prospects of benefiting from them or whether they have had good or bad health services after they have bought them. Few are equipped to express a preference beyond the choice of a doctor or dentist. To protect the consumer from his ignorance, standards are laid down which have to be attained by those who wish to enter the key health professions. To protect the consumer from exploitation the doctor is not ethically expected to be a profit maximizer. Similarly the vast majority of hospitals throughout the world are not expected to be profit maximizers either. The basic conditions for the rational exercise of consumer choice are absent in wide areas of the health market. Even when services are not provided free, governments which have conferred monopoly rights on doctors which allow them in practice to spend their patients' money have a duty to ensure that these rights are used responsibly in economic as well as medical terms.

It is the fear of losing business which makes firms cost-conscious. Consumers are constantly searching for the best buy. Goods or services will not sell if consumers think they can get better value elsewhere. In many other fields consumers look to specialist intermediaries to find them the best buy. In theory at least it is the job of insurance brokers to find the consumer the cover he wants from a safe insurer at the lowest cost. Their skills in doing this determine the success of their business. Consumers do not, however, select doctors for their shrewdness as negotiators or abilities as purchasing agents but for their knowledge of medicine and skill in practising it. Doctors are not taught to be cost-conscious during their medical education nor do they normally become so after they are qualified. They exercise little or no pressure on suppliers of health services to be cost-conscious.

Individual money-backed demand in the market for health services with or without insurance is a gross understatement of what many people would pay for health services taking their lives as a whole. Thus expressed preferences of voters for free or nearly free health services in most developed countries does have real significance though it means imposing majority decisions on minorities. It places on governments the responsibility for ensuring that services are available where they are needed and securing that value for money is obtained from services which are collectively purchased.

In the next three chapters we discuss three specific problems in the regulation of supply – the remuneration system for doctors, the supply of pharmaceuticals and the economics of hospitals.

NOTES

1. 'If any doctor allowed himself to lapse for several years, he was no longer a competent doctor.' Sir John Peel, former gynaecologist to the Queen, as reported in *The Times*, 7 July 1973. 'Unless the profession did something about it, the public or others would. The question was not just one of academic knowledge. A few doctors might be totally irresponsible in prescribing potentially dangerous drugs and colleagues knew this was going on but were reluctant to try to influence them' (ibid.).

2. C. M. Lindsay and J. M. Buchanan, 'The Organisation and Financing of Medical Care in the United States', B.M.A., *Health Service Financing*, 1969, p. 538, and D.H.E.W., *Health Manpower and Health Facilities*, 1973, p. 155. The two figures quoted have slightly different coverage (e.g. the inclusion of osteopaths in the later figure).

3. J. Kandell, 'Bar to Medical Students is debated in Argentina', *New York Times*, 3 February 1973, p. 122.

4. *Medical Care Review*, Vol. 30, No. 2, February 1973, p. 142.

5. Sums of $50 to $100 per patient are alleged to be paid in California. *The Times*, 21 January 1974.

6. S. E. Berki, op. cit., p. 7.

7. *Medical Care Review*, Vol. 30, No. 2, February 1973, p. 181.

8. ibid., Vol. 31, No. 2, February 1974, p. 192.

9. ibid., Vol. 31, No. 7, July 1974, p. 861.

CHAPTER 5

Tradesman or Priest: the Payment of the Doctor

In theory, the doctor should not allow financial considerations to influence the way he practises his profession. By his professional ethics he is expected to behave as a priest. But not all doctors live up to their ethical principles. Hence the need to study the financial incentives of different systems of remuneration for doctors. What systems of payment promote good medical practice, induce doctors to enter those specialties and those geographical areas where they are most needed, and encourage continuity of the doctor/patient relationship, a proper emphasis on preventive medicine and participation in continuing education?

As pointed out in Chapter 1, traditionally doctors charged on a fee-for-service basis and adjusted the fee according to the patient's ability to pay. The maximum charges of a particular doctor depended on the demand for his services among those in a position to pay high fees. Price discrimination still continues in many countries. In the United States, however, it is now more common for a doctor to have a customary schedule of fees which are charged to all his patients. Moreover fee levels have tended to become standard in each area – higher in more prosperous areas than in poorer areas.

Before the advent of government services and health insurance and where doctors were unwilling to provide extensive free services, the extent to which patients used doctors as well as the choice of the doctor they consulted depended on their ability to pay. While the wealthy consulted doctors whenever they wished, the poor went only in extreme illness. In treating a poorer patient the doctor was wise to take account of the patient's capacity to pay because if the treatments he recommended consumed all the financial resources the patient could raise, the bill which ultimately went unpaid or was only paid after extensive delay was likely to be the doctor's bill.

In a private medical market, the doctor who is in great demand does not need to provide unnecessary services. He can maximize his income simply by raising the level of his fees. His practice will then be increasingly confined to those who can afford to pay what he asks. But as doctors can, within limits, induce patients to accept and pay for more services than are really needed, they can enter areas where doctors are already plentiful and still make a living. Where patients have to pay their own doctors' bills, the amount of unnecessary services is limited – at least for some patients and some illnesses – by willingness to pay. But when doctors' bills are wholly paid by health insurance, this limit no longer applies. While demands by patients for a service will not become unlimited, what becomes critical is the number of services doctors persuade patients that they 'need'. This in turn depends on the number of doctors, hospital beds and other facilities in each area. But also important is the method by which doctors are paid.

The main methods of payment used by government services and health insurance agencies are salary, capitation and fee-for-service. The choices which have been made in different countries between these methods of payment have been strongly influenced by the system of payment already in force in the country.[1]

Fee-for-services under Health Insurance

In a unified health insurance system which aims to give all patients equal rights to services, it is hard to justify any difference in the remuneration of different doctors for the same services – unless the doctors clearly differ in their qualifications (e.g. specialists) or by some other clear indication of rank (e.g. professors, staff of teaching hospitals, etc.). Unless the level of remuneration is to be the highest received by any doctor, the introduction of standard remuneration under health insurance is likely to make some doctors worse off. Those most likely to be worse off are the leading members of the profession – the most vocal and the most influential.

One solution to this problem is to exclude the higher income groups from membership of compulsory health insurance, so that best-paid doctors can continue to practise privately among the better off. This is still the arrangement in West Germany and

Holland. This solution was rejected in Great Britain in 1948 despite a strong demand for it from the profession. The whole population was given rights to use the National Health Service, though they were free to pay for private care if they wished to do so. Earnings from private practice helped to retain existing differentials in the earnings of different doctors. In Britain, however, there was a fairly clear, but by no means complete, distinction between general practitioners and specialists. The best-paid doctors were the specialists and they could be paid on a separate basis which included extra payments for specialists judged to be of outstanding merit.

When Canada developed health insurance for doctors' services, the bulk of doctors were specialists and general practice was rapidly declining. The strong wish of the profession for fee-for-service payments limited the extent to which the most prestigious doctors could get higher rewards except in so far as they undertook the better-paid services.

The solution originally adopted under Medicare in the United States was to allow the doctor to charge the insurance fund his customary fee. It was, moreover, adopted in a situation in which the administration had only limited knowledge of the customary fees of the roughly 300,000 doctors practising in the United States, which varied widely.[2] The system was clearly open to abuse and led to complex mechanisms to examine and control claims for payment.[3]

A third solution adopted in Sweden, Australia and Switzerland and originally in France is to reimburse a standard fee to the patient for defined services and leave the doctor free to make his usual charge. The danger of this system is that it could result in some doctors increasing their usual fees - at the extreme by adding the payment from the insurance fund on to the fee they charge the patient - thus leaving the patient no better off than before, indeed worse off by the cost of the insurance contribution. This tended to happen in European reimbursement systems of health insurance and when Blue Shield was introduced to pay surgeons' fees in the United States. In Sweden, however, doctors responded with considerable restraint.

In France, successive governments attempted for twenty years to secure that doctors did not charge more than the fees paid for services by the health insurance system. Not until de Gaulle came to power in the very special political situation of 1958 were virtually all provinces of France brought into line. But concessions were made to particular groups of doctors, professors and chiefs of staff, those who had taken post-graduate courses and certain other specialists. These were allowed to charge more.[4]

Negotiating the fees to be paid for particular medical services is an extremely complex operation and the examination and payment of doctors' bills according to an agreed fee schedule involves a heavy administrative cost. Some schemes have lists of thousands of different services and the fees payable for them. This becomes essential when provision has to be made for the remuneration of every type of medical procedure, and specialist services are paid for in this way. Sweden has a narrow range of fees because the more complex procedures were always undertaken by salaried doctors working in hospital.

The general pattern under health insurance using fee-for-service payment is for standard fees to be paid for each service – in other words for doctors to be paid on a piece-work basis. This, however, creates an incentive for doctors to magnify the number of services for which payment can be claimed. Where doctors are in short supply it encourages them to see as many patients as possible. Where there is a shortage of patients, it is likely to lead to excessive services to patients and to short and frequent consultations rather than fewer and more thorough examinations.[5] This may, in turn, lead patients to consult more than one doctor on the same illness.

Thus fee-for-service payment provides little pressure for an even geographical distribution of doctors. A doctor can enter an over-doctored area and obtain work. He will find it easier if he has a specialist qualification. The more doctors there are in an area the more services are provided to patients. The young doctor may establish himself quicker in an under-doctored area but the amount he can eventually earn anywhere is limited by the number of services he can provide. In Sweden, doctors are induced by part-time salaries to practise in the more remote areas – they can supplement their salaries by fee-for-service payments. There are no mechanisms of this kind in France, Germany or Switzerland. In France there are regional differences in fees based upon differences in wages and living costs. This strengthens the forces which lead doctors to practise in the more prosperous areas. Similarly in Germany and Switzerland the urban sick funds can charge higher premiums and thus can and do pay their doctors higher fees.

Where under the fee schedule extra payment is made for undertaking procedures, the emphasis on the consultation can be distorted to doing rather than observing and listening. The quicker the doctor decides to act, the higher his remuneration and the more he acts, the more he can claim. To undertake certain procedures, the doctor needs to purchase special equipment. Once purchased the more he uses it, the more quickly he can write off the cost. If a fee is paid for an injection but no fee for issuing a prescription, there is an incentive in favour of injections. There is also a financial incentive not to refer patients to specialists. Thus doctors may attempt to interpret diagnostic tests which they have little skill in interpreting and undertake procedures beyond their competence to do well. Fee-for-service may lead to less specialization within specialties and thus less opportunity to acquire high skills in particular procedures – particularly surgical procedures. Conversely, it may lead to excessive specialization so that medical care is fragmented into an enormous variety of services provided by a large number of different specialists.

A doctor in private practice can charge on a time basis; he has the option of seeing fewer patients for longer and charging more. This option is not available under national health insurance with fee-for-service payment with standard charges, as administrators seek a schedule with clear definitions based on facts which can be checked relatively easily. Charging on a time basis could, in the long run, magnify costs and result in a shortage of doctors. Where standard fees are paid, the doctor who spends time to try and understand a patient's emotional problem is at a financial disadvantage. Systematic health inspections are also time-consuming and so is the taking of histories. Both these are discouraged by fee-for-service, payment systems when fees are standard. On the other hand, follow-up visits to check that treatment has been successful are quick and thus remunerative. So is the ante-natal or post-natal examination where much of the care can be provided by trained para-professionals.[6] The patient who is not ill but simply wants a sickness certificate to obtain sick pay or benefit is the most remunerative of all.

Thus in many respects the payment system carries the risk of distorting the practice of medicine, generating wasteful use of diagnostic tests and the excessive use of X-rays, and unnecessary intervention (including unnecessary surgery). Is the payment system partly responsible for the fact that West Germany has as many appendectomies as the United States although the population is three times greater in the latter? Already 33·7 per cent of men have had their appendices removed and 46·2 per cent of women.[7] Moreover the rate on Saturdays was 40 per cent of the weekday rate and for Sundays 25 per cent of the weekday rate, which is surprising for an operation normally regarded as an emergency.[8] Is the payment system partly responsible for the fact that the incidence of surgery was found to be twice as high in the United States as in the United Kingdom and two or three times as great for some surgical procedures?[9] Is the payment system partly responsible for the incidence of tonsillectomies being twice as high in California as in Sweden?

Good medical practice is not standard for each patient and itemized payment schedules cannot allow for this. The highest financial rewards go not to the best doctor but to the quickest and to the doctor with the least professional scruples about responding to the financial incentives of the payment system. Some doctors may even claim for services which were not performed.[10]

Special problems arise when a modified fee-for-service system is used to pay doctors for services to in-patients. Such a system is used in Holland. The normal system is to make a daily payment per case. This is said to create an incentive for the doctor to admit to hospital because a few days in hospital will bring more money to a specialist than several months of care outside hospital.[11] The rate of payment is reduced after the fifth day but the payment remains higher than if the specialist cared for the patient outside hospital. Surgeons are, however, paid lump sums for a single expensive procedure. This is said to create an incentive for early discharge in order to make room for a new patient.[12] In France, daily payments are paid for hospital care to specialists when that care is provided in the clinics they run. Until the 1960s the rate paid for care in private clinics was higher than in public hospitals and the specialists collected higher fees for procedures performed in those clinics.[13]

To protect the standards of practice and perhaps more consciously to protect the finance of the scheme, a variety of controls and regulations have been introduced in countries paying doctors under health insurance on a fee-for-service basis. Glaser describes these procedures as they operated in the early nineteen-sixties. He found that payments for certain procedures were only claimable by specialists with the requisite qualifications (Netherlands)[14] or by doctors in hospitals (Sweden).[15] Or higher payments were made to qualified specialists for certain procedures than were paid to general practitioners (Belgium).[16] Or a doctor was paid a higher fee if he consulted another doctor (France).[17] Many schemes would not pay for both a consultation and a procedure taken during it (e.g. France).[18] When two procedures were undertaken at the same consultation the payment was lower than when they were undertaken at separate consultations (Sweden).[19] A surgeon was allowed to claim only for the most expensive operation if more than one was performed through the same wound (Netherlands).[20] To prevent excessive visits, doctors were paid on a declining scale for the visits they made to a particular patient or to all patients (Sweden, Switzerland and Netherlands).[21] Less was paid if a second family member was seen during the same visit (Germany).[22] In some cases a collective fee was paid for a procedure and the necessary aftercare (France).[23]

While fee schedules are frequently adjusted to achieve particular medical objectives such as referral[24] and to create disincentives for unnecessary procedures, visits and consultations – particularly those which the doctor is most likely to be able to generate himself – fee-for-service payment is usually accompanied by administrative controls. These controls may be exercised by clerks or control doctors employed by the health insurance agencies or by the local medical profession as in the case of Germany. Thus in Switzerland, many sick funds refuse to pay for an expensive medical procedure unless approval has been obtained from the sick fund in advance.[25] Some sick funds withhold payment or reduce payments if claims exceed a statistical norm. This is the practice in the Netherlands and may be applied in Switzerland after a decision by a joint conciliation commission.[26] In France, some sick funds arrange for the control doctor to examine the patient to detect medically unnecessary over-performance or fraud.[27] An extreme method of preventing excessive services is the Austrian method of payment per case. Though fees are paid for certain procedures such as injections, punctures, pathology, obstetrics, etc., the main payment is per patient treated during a quarter year. This leads the general practitioner to hand over to specialists or to the hospital patients who require intensive treatment and to seek patients who require only superficial treatment or sickness certificates. 'Sickness certificates are not infrequently handed over without actual illness' and 'not a few elderly people are shoved into hospitals' who could be looked after at home.[28]

Paradoxically, pure fee-for-service payment which would appear at first sight to maximize the independence of the doctor from control, leads to more pervasive controls than are found under other systems of payment. The doctor's decision to undertake a procedure or provide service for a patient may be questioned afterwards by the health insurance administration through their control doctors. Did the patient need to be admitted to hospital and was the stay unduly long? Was each X-ray, pathology test and prescription necessary and was it economically provided? Did the doctor ask the patient to return for a repeat visit which was unnecessary? Such review procedures are expensive to operate and consume the time of professional personnel in making the review. Nor is it always possible to collect reliable evidence about the need for services after the event. Countries which have used this approach have developed statistical techniques to identify prima facie cases of abuse. The effect of procedures of this kind is primarily deterrent. Only the most glaring cases are likely to be brought to light. The information collected by these health insurance systems is of little use for any other purpose – particularly any epidemiological purpose as it is seldom related to a defined population in a given area. As the information is provided for the payment control system, the provision of it generates hostility among doctors and the scope of it cannot readily be extended to make it useful for wider purposes.

The extent of the waste of medical resources generated by fee-for-service payment systems is not known but the various mechanisms developed to try and prevent it are expensive to administer for the doctors and for the insurance scheme. This consumes resources which might alternatively be used for other purposes including the provision of better or more comfortable care for patients. The cost of the administration of compulsory sickness insurance in Belgium is more than 10 per cent of total expenditure compared with 4 per cent in the Netherlands.[29] In Australia operating expenses for medical funds are 18 per cent of contributions.[30] It is, however, extremely difficult to make precise comparisons of administrative costs as the administrative tasks vary in different systems of health insurance.[31]

Little significance can be attached to the number of proven cases of abuse which come to light in different countries as so much depends on the rigour of the methods used to detect it. Moreover, there are major difficulties in defining what is and is not necessary for particular patients. As research workers would find considerable difficulty in defining abuse, it is no less difficult for the individual doctor to know how much of what he does is really necessary for his patient. In Germany and Switzerland allegations of abuse are particularly made with regard to X-ray and electrotherapy and in the case of Germany also to the excessive use of health inspections which attract a separate payment.[32] Under health insurance in the United States, attention has concentrated on unnecessary surgery because this can be clearly defined by pathological test. In Japan where the doctor makes a profit on issuing pharmaceuticals attention is concentrated on excessive prescribing and injecting. Nor is this surprising as for every 100 consultations, 220 prescriptions are issued and 49 injections are made.[33]

Inevitably the extent of abuse depends on the general standards of ethics in the medical profession in different countries. The ethos of a profession is strongly influenced by its leadership. Where medical teachers and leading clinicians strongly condemn abuse, the norms are likely to be communicated to each generation of students and maintained when they go into practice. The norms of professions are moreover not uninfluenced by those of the wider society in which the profession operates. Thus suspicion of abuse appears to be small in Sweden and much larger in Germany, Switzerland, France and particularly large in the United States under Medicare and Medicaid and voluntary insurance programmes.

It is in those countries where any doctor can claim a fee for any service, procedure, or test that allegations of abuse are greatest. Moreover the use of medical resources in a wasteful way may become such an accepted part of medical practice in some countries that this becomes the norm. The professors of medicine in Switzerland, France and Germany have high standards of living built upon private practice among the wealthy. The norms they teach are those established in their own practices. It may not be a coincidence that the heavy emphasis on diagnostic tests developed in Germany under fee-for-service payment for health insurance. This emphasis spread to Switzerland. It also spread to the United States when Germany replaced Britain as the main centre for Americans to obtain post-graduate education. Payment systems may have had a major influence in shaping the way medicine is practised in different countries in the world. What now appear as traditional forms of practice may be the accumulated response to financial incentives.

From the point of view of the quality of medical care, one of the

66

most damaging effects of fee-for-service payment systems, which allow any doctor to claim any fee in the book, is the lack of specialization in a realistic sense. Surgery is dangerous and thus should only be undertaken by a doctor with specialist training in surgery and continuous experience in using this skill. Indeed there are clear advantages in surgeons specializing in particular types of operation. The more they perform a particular kind of operation the more they are likely to meet the unusual and difficult problems which occur with that type of operation and the more skill they will acquire in handling these problems. Speed is still important in surgery and the surgeon who regularly repeats the same operation will on average work faster. Similarly the administration of anaesthetics requires high skill, and poor performance in this respect is more likely to be a cause of death than poor performance by the surgeon.

The part-time surgeon is likely to be a poor surgeon but the fee-for-service payment for health insurance encourages the doctor to do his own surgery provided he can obtain facilities to do it. In Germany the insurance system allows surgeons to claim fees for anaesthetics administered under their direction. Thus most surgeons employ salaried assistants or nurses to give all anaesthetics and pocket the profits earned from the fees. Though German surgeons are very knowledgeable about anaesthetics, they cannot devote their whole attention to this aspect during an operation. In early 1965, there were only 260 specialist anaesthetists in Germany and nearly all of these were salaried members of hospital staffs.[34] Few hospitals have enough work for full-time anaesthetists. Similarly most German doctors take and interpret their own X-rays. There are therefore relatively fewer radiologists in Germany than in other developed countries.[35]

Capitation Payment

Payment by capitation requires and indeed secures a clearer division between general practice and specialist practice or the provision of comprehensive services by a multi-specialist group. The general practitioner is the primary doctor in the sense that the patient normally enters the medical care system by seeing his general practitioner. Direct access to specialists is not normally permitted under the National Health Service in Britain. The general practitioner refers the patient to a specialist when he believes that specialist care is needed. Moreover, the general practitioner chooses the particular specialist. While capitation payment encourages continuity of care by one doctor over life and creates a disincentive to consult more than one doctor for the same illness unless referred by the primary care doctor, the process of referral can lead to discontinuity of care during an episode of illness and to a sharp distinction between hospital practice and office practice.

Under a pure capitation system the general practitioner has a financial incentive to acquire as many patients as possible, particularly undemanding patients, and to discourage calls upon his time. He also has an incentive to refer time-consuming or difficult cases to specialists. One way of discouraging calls upon his time is to keep his patients well and to try and prevent frequent visits from a particular patient by getting to the root of his problem when the patient first presents himself. Another way is to discourage the patient from troubling him but this may involve losing the patient to another doctor.

The terms of service of general practitioners are therefore generally designed to ensure that no general practitioner neglects his patients and that the number of patients any practitioner is responsible for is not greater than he can properly look after. Thus in Holland, Britain, Italy and Spain there are limits on the number of patients a practitioner can have on his list. Limiting list size may also be used as part of the mechanics for securing a more even geographical spread of practitioners. In addition, the capitation system may be adjusted so that beyond a limit the capitation payment for extra patients is lower. In Britain the practitioner's terms of service specify office hours and require the doctor to make a home visit when requested by a patient. There is no attempt to limit or check on the extent to which patients are referred to specialists working at the hospitals. Specialists do however complain that a certain proportion of patients are referred to them unnecessarily and with incomplete information. In Britain specialists are paid by salary for their work for the national health service. In the Netherlands where specialists are paid according to the number of patients for which they are responsible, statistics are kept of the referral rates of general practitioners and circulated to them. Doctors who over-refer may be reported to the local medical committee and may be reprimanded, fined or even suspended from insurance practice. The profession as a whole has a clear financial interest in checking excessive referrals as any unnecessary costs falling on the sick fund limit the fund's ability to increase the capitation fee. While under fee-for-service payment administrators of health insurance complain of over-provision of services, under capitation payment doctors complain of over-demanding patients.

In Britain, Holland and Italy statistics are kept of the prescriptions issued by each doctor, and doctors employed by the sick fund (or in the case of Britain by the Ministry) visit doctors who appear to be over-prescribing, and sanctions are used in extreme cases. Under INAM, the largest sick fund in Italy, doctors who are paid by capitation write fewer prescriptions per insured person than doctors paid by fee-for-service, and this difference holds for all provinces.[36]

In a pure form capitation encourages general practitioners to be evenly spread in relation to the population served, if there is no private practice pulling in a particular direction. The amount payable to general practitioners in an urban area is limited by the number of patients. The more doctors there are in that area, the lower the average list size. Moreover as the expenses of practice, particularly rent, are higher in urban areas, less is likely to be earned per patient. On the other hand, more miles will have to be driven to make home visits in a rural area than in an urban area. The time involved may not necessarily be much greater in view of the congestion of traffic and parking problems of towns and cities.

In both Holland and Britain the natural economic incentive towards practice outside the cities is strengthened by modifying the pure capitation system to favour rural practice. In both countries mileage allowances are paid to help rural practitioners and to encourage home visits. In both countries extra payments are made to doctors working in under-doctored areas. On the other hand, in Britain, general practitioners are wholly reimbursed for rents for approved practice premises. This tends to favour urban areas. Moreover limits on list size, as mentioned earlier, also help to secure a more even geographical spread of practitioners.

In Britain the capitation system has been modified to such an extent that less than half of the money received by an average practitioner is related to the precise number of patients on his list. A basic flat rate allowance is paid, seniority payments are made, and the general practitioner is covered by a superannuation scheme to which the government contributes.

Extra payments are made to doctors who practise in defined group practice arrangements. Fees are paid for night visits, immunizations, the taking of cervical smears, maternity care and other defined services. In addition to payment for rents, the greater part of the cost of two supporting staff members (nurses, secretaries or others) are reimbursed to each practitioner.

A fee-for-service system of payment involves more competition between doctors and one way of attracting patients is to maintain a modern, well-equipped office. Moreover the delegation of work to supporting staff may enable the doctor to provide more services more profitably. A capitation system of payment involves registration with a practitioner or a group of practitioners. This results in less competition for patients and thus less pressure to maintain a well-equipped office. Any expenditure to improve the service provided to patients either by ancillary staff or equipment or by taking a course of further education will reduce the net remuneration of the doctor, unless these costs are separately reimbursed as some are in Britain. In Holland, the proportion of patients covered by health insurance is lower and private patients pay on a fee-for-service basis. It may be for this reason that the capitation system has been less modified in Holland than in Britain where many of the elements normally associated with salaried payment have been gradually grafted on to the capitation system of payment.

A problem of both capitation and fee-for-service systems of payment is that there are no clear financial rewards for providing a high quality of service. This is most clearly the case in general practice where the patient is ill equipped to judge quality of service as distinct from the attitude of the doctor. In specialist practice governed by referral, quality is more likely to be rewarded in so far as the doctors who make the referrals are in a better position to assess the skill of specialists than patients. But, nevertheless, the same service attracts the same payment whether it is well or poorly performed. A further disadvantage of both fee-for-service payment and capitation is that the older doctor tends to earn less than the middle-aged doctor because he becomes less able to manage a long list or he finds that he must lessen his pace or work shorter hours. Thus the average earnings of doctors decline in their later years of practice while average earnings in many other professional occupations tend to increase in the later years of work. This creates dissatisfaction and pressure for the whole remuneration system to be higher. This is the justification for the supplementary seniority payments which have been introduced in Britain.

Salaries

Under a salaried system of payment, merit can be rewarded by promotion to a higher grade and income can be fully maintained up to retirement. Moreover merit can, in theory at least, encompass not only good clinical curative treatment but full attention to prevention where preventive action is warranted. A further aspect of merit which could also be included is skill in the deployment of resources – the use of resources where they can be effective and the avoidance of the use of resources on ineffective therapy, and the choice of cheaper methods of therapy where two forms of therapy are equally effective. A further advantage of salaried payment is that higher rewards by promotion, or prospects of promotion or otherwise, can be used to try and secure a more even distribution of doctors. Not only can direct and indirect (e.g. subsidized housing) financial inducements be provided for those who practise in less favoured areas but the number of posts in all areas of the country can be restricted to the number of doctors available to take those posts. Thus those who fail to be selected for a post in a popular area must apply in less popular areas, or leave the profession, emigrate or enter private practice where opportunities exist. As in many other types of organization, promotion to a higher grade may be more easily secured by a move to a less popular area.

This last system has been operated in hospitals of the British National Health Service with considerable success. Moreover the merit awards paid to specialists are allocated on a regional basis. Thus a doctor who is not adjudged of wholly exceptional merit is more likely to secure an award if he practises in a less popular region than if he practises in one of the London regions.

The disadvantage of a salaried system is that doctors may become less concerned to please their patients and more concerned to please those who take decisions on promotion where these two criteria diverge. In particular the doctor may be put under undue pressure to limit the number of certificates of sickness issued to the working population. The doctor who cannot expect further promotion may become less conscientious in performing his responsibilities. No country has managed to abolish private practice completely and the

71

salaried doctor is tempted to treat private patients whether this is officially allowed under his terms of service or not. Where it is allowed, the salaried doctor may give less time than he should to his salaried practice. In Britain and Sweden where senior specialists are in general conscientious in performing their salaried work, there are nevertheless constant allegations that some are giving undue attention to their private patients. In Israel, salaried doctors provide few home visits: these tend to be provided by doctors privately after they have finished their salaried work.[37] There are some allegations of a similar kind in the Soviet Union. Some of the worst problems of this kind are found in South Europe, the Middle East,[38] and Latin America. Doctors are said to come late and leave early. In these countries the salaries are low compared with potential earnings from private practice.

In Latin America it is the common practice for doctors to be paid a part-time salary for the three or four hours' daily service leaving the doctor free to augment the inadequate salary by earnings from private practice. The temptations of this system are obvious:

> In a village post conditions are often crowded in a morning session, and the doctor may advise an anxious patient that later in his private office there would be more time for a careful examination. This happens in the large city polyclinics as well, and it occurs under social security programs as well as governmental or charity systems. The patients who can afford private fees thereby obtain a larger share of the doctor's limited time, even though they may be theoretically entitled to proper service under the public program.[39]

In countries where there is a shortage of beds and where ethical standards as well as medical salaries are low, doctors may accept bribes to give priority in hospital admission to particular patients. A less direct distortion of medical priorities for admission can occur when patients see and pay specialists privately and these patients are given priority in admission to free places in hospital. There are allegations of this type of 'queue-jumping' in the British National Health Service.

As in any other salaried organization, one would expect to find much more pressure for additional doctors to be trained under salaried payment than capitation or fee-for-service payment. There is a natural desire to lighten work loads and provide ideal standards of care. Norms of work loads become established in the profession and pressed on those responsible without much critical examination of how much if any extra benefit patients derive if more doctors are employed. Many in the West would consider the work loads officially established in the Soviet Union to be low and observers have remarked on the relatively slow pace of medical work in that country. In Britain where hospital doctors are also salaried there has been little pressure from the profession to increase complements of specialists. This may be because the appointment of an additional specialist would mean the introduction of a further competitor to share the private practice available in the neighbourhood. Thus while private practice can create many problems for a salaried service, one favourable effect may be to restrain unjustified pressure for additional medical staff.

A salaried service removes financial competition for patients and makes it more likely for doctors to be willing to work together as a team of colleagues co-operating to improve the service provided to patients. Doctors who work closely together will learn from each other and this has special importance in a profession where knowledge is rapidly extending. Many forces are influencing the spread of salaried employment of doctors all over the world – not least the expansion of formal medical teaching. One of the major drawbacks of individual competitive practice is the lack of opportunities for the practitioner to learn from his colleagues. Formal courses of postgraduate education are not all that is needed to keep a doctor's practice up-to-date.

Conclusion

There is no perfect way of remunerating doctors. Every system of payment can have undesirable effects on the use of resources and on the quality and character of care. Moreover a system of remuneration which works well in one country may work badly in another. Everything depends on the standard of medical ethics and on how far or how many doctors respond to particular financial incentives and on the profession's definition of 'good medical care'. Nor can the quantum of remuneration be ignored. If doctors are paid less than they think they deserve in relation to others with whose remuneration they compare their own they are more likely to respond to financial incentives to get more. If the incentive is towards providing unnecessary medicines, pathology and other tests and hospital admission, low remuneration can be more expensive for the total medical care system than higher remuneration. On the other hand very high remuneration may lead doctors to give less time to their medical practice because they can achieve the standard of living they want in only three or four working days. This is already a problem in some parts of the United States – particularly in the case of surgeons.

The ideal remuneration system which will encourage both quality and economy, which will secure an even distribution of services, promote effective preventive action as well as effective curative action, stimulate concern for patients' feelings as well as for their bodies, and establish medical priorities on the basis of need alone does not exist. A decision has to be taken on which are the most damaging effects to be avoided and how any drawbacks of a system ultimately chosen can be reduced to a minimum.

Under any system of payment it is the ethics and social commitment of the doctor which matter most of all. Where standards are low in these respects no financial structure can induce doctors to be what they are not. But where standards are high, salaried payment best indicates to the public the ethical stance of the doctor as a servant of the public, as a priest of medicine.

NOTES

1. See Chapter 2.

2. See, for example, *Medical Care Review*, Vol. 31, No. 2, February 1974, p. 188.

3. See Health Insurance Benefits Advisory Council, *A Report on the Results of the Study of Methods of Reimbursement for Physicians under Medicare*, D.H.E.W., 1973.

4. W. A. Glaser, *Paying the Doctor*, Johns Hopkins U.P., Baltimore, 1970, p. 185.

5. See, for example, J. P. S. Jamieson, 'The Social Security Medical Service in New Zealand', *British Medical Journal*, 5 July 1958, Supplement, p. 17.

6. Large sums of money are made under Medicaid by obstetricians in the United States for this reason. See *Medical Care Review*, Vol. 31, No. 2, February 1974, pp. 168–71.

7. M. Pflanz, 'German Health Insurance', *International Journal of Health Services*, Vol. 1, No. 4, November 1971, p. 326.

8. S. Lichtner and M. Pflanz, 'Appendectomy in the Federal Republic of Germany', *Medical Care*, Vol. 9, 1971, pp. 301–30.

9. *New Society*, 3 May 1973, p. 231. Studies quoted in G. Horobin, 'The Politics of American Health Care', *The Atlantic*, October 1973, p. 56. See also J. P. Bunker, 'Surgical Manpower', *New England Journal of Medicine*, 15 Jan, 1970.

10. In Peru, for example, the fee-for-service system of payment has resulted in the following forms of abuse:
a. payment may be claimed by the doctor for more consultations than were actually given;
b. the doctor's signature may be falsified by patients to claim cash re-imbursement for services that were not obtained;
c. fees may be claimed for surgical operations that were not done;
d. services may be rendered to family dependents who are not insured and the name of the insured employee is inscribed on the payment claim.
   M. I. Roemer, *Medical Care in Latin America*, p. 32.

11. W. A. Glaser, op. cit., p. 145.

12. loc. cit.

13. ibid., p. 191.

14. ibid., p. 161.

15. ibid., p. 169.

16. In Belgium specialists are paid more and the refund to the patient is 100 per cent compared with 75 per cent in the case of general medicine. This system 'makes patients with minor diseases choose a specialist'. It also makes it easy for the specialist 'to use expensive means of diagnosis and treatment where cheaper ones are at hand'. J. Van Langendonck, 'Organisation and Financing Medical Care in the Netherlands and Belgium', B.M.A., *Health Services Financing*, 1969, p. 466.

17. W. A. Glaser, p. 147.

18. ibid., p. 146.

19. ibid., p. 146.

20. ibid., p. 146.

21. ibid., pp. 146–8.

22. ibid., p. 148.

23. ibid., p. 161.

24. For example, subscribers to the Medical Benefit Scheme in Australia receive a higher rate of refund for specialists' fees if they have been referred to a specialist. J. M. Last, 'How Australia Pays Doctors', *New Society*, 14 April 1966, p. 144.

25. W. A. Glaser, op. cit., p. 141.

26. ibid., p. 151.

27. ibid., p. 188.

28. H. Kohlmaier, 'The Organisation and Financing of Health Insurance in Austria', B.M.A., *Health Services Financing*, 1969, pp. 338–9.

29. Van Langendonck, op. cit., p. 469.

30. A. Seldon, 'Organisation and Financing of Medical Care in Australia', B.M.A., *Health Services Financing*, 1969, p. 320.

31. See, for example, R. J. Vogel and R. A. Blair, 'An Analysis of Medicare Administrative Costs', *Social Security Bulletin*, August 1974.

32. See for example, Pflanz, op. cit., p. 324.
33. From the Health Insurance Medical Benefit Survey 1963. The author wishes to thank Mr Tei Seki for supplying this information.
34. W. A. Glaser, op. cit., p. 168.
35. loc. cit.
36. ibid., p. 262.
37. ibid., p. 213.
38. ibid., p. 209.
39. M. I. Roemer, *Medical Care in Latin America*, p. 260.

CHAPTER 6

The Pharmaceutical Industry

The most common treatment ordered by a doctor is a pharmaceutical. In Britain about two-thirds of consultations with general practitioners result in a prescription for one or more drugs. The number of drugs prescribed is about five per year per head of population in both Britain and the United States. In France over six drugs are prescribed per head per year and in the Netherlands nearly ten. In most countries the use of drugs has been steadily increasing. One reason for this increase has been the expansion in the range of effective drugs and a second is the fact that prescribing a drug is the most comfortable way for a busy doctor to end a consultation. Prescribed drugs are used more by women than men, by the elderly than the younger age group and by the higher than lower social classes.[1]

Throughout the world patients also buy a wide range of medicine without a medical prescription. In the United States, the average citizen spent $21.52 for prescribed drugs and $14.14 for other drugs and sundries in 1971.[2] In more developed countries, aspirin and its derivatives, vitamin preparations, tonics and laxatives represent substantial shares of the non-prescription drug market. In many developing countries, people incur heavy expenditure on traditional herbal remedies.

In most, but not all countries,[3] the public is prevented by law from buying 'ethical' pharmaceuticals without a prescription from a doctor. It is with these 'ethical' preparations which we are concerned in this chapter. The scope of the restriction varies between countries. For example, Sweden requires a prescription for many preparations which can be bought over the counter in the United States.[4] The object of these restrictions is to limit the consumption of the more dangerous substances to circumstances which are approved by a medical practitioner. The ban normally extends far beyond drugs

77

which are or can be dependence-producing. Only registered or licensed doctors are authorized to prescribe these preparations as they alone are regarded as qualified to determine in what circumstances they should and should not be used. In making such decisions, doctors are expected to be governed solely by their professional knowledge. Society has thus made doctors trustees of the health of patients who consult them. But paradoxically there is little emphasis in Western medical education on therapeutics compared, for example, with diagnostic medicine.[5] Medical education has yet to come to terms with the vast growth of effective drugs over the last twenty years.

Originally, the pharmacist mixed and prepared medicines according to the instructions contained in the prescription and some doctors prepared their own medicines. Increasingly medicines have been manufactured in factories as greater reliability and purity can be achieved in an industrial setting. In the United States pharmacists now only compound about 5 per cent of prescriptions. The majority of products are now prescribed by brand name in most countries. The growth of proprietary preparations has undoubtedly improved the quality and reliability of medicines and more complex products can be produced at lower cost when made in bulk. But these economies of mass production have to some extent been countered by elegant presentation and attractive packaging.

The number of products on the market in developed countries runs into tens of thousands, though much depends on the definition of the product. Many products are very similar, many consist of mixtures of chemical substances and the same substance can be presented in a variety of different forms. Most of the preparations prescribed today did not exist when the average doctor in practice finished his medical course. It is estimated that in the developed countries 'upwards of 90 per cent of the total volume of drugs prescribed is now represented by drugs which are less than twenty years old.'[6] Throughout their career, doctors need to learn about new drugs and their uses. About forty wholly new products are registered each year in the United States though the number of new preparations, including new mixtures and new presentations of existing products, marketed each year is several hundred.

Research and Development

Most of the important new drugs have been developed from research undertaken by the pharmaceutical industry rather than from research by universities or other academic institutions. While the original discovery of antibiotics was made by Fleming in 1929 and penicillin was isolated by Florey and Chain some ten years later, all the subsequent antibiotics originated in industrial laboratories. None has depended on chemical scientific departments or on the kind of chemical science which they teach. While insulin was first extracted by a physiology laboratory, academic medicine or departments of therapeutics played no part in the origins of tranquillizers, anti-malarials, anti-histamines, hypotensives, oral contraceptives and most of the vitamins and anaesthetics.[7] 'Modern medicine treatment seems to have depended almost wholly on non-clinical, often non-medical scientists frequently working in, or in close collaboration with, the pharmaceutical industry.'[8] Whatever may be said in criticism of the world pharmaceutical industry, there is no doubt that it has been responsible for introducing the major part of the modern doctor's drugs.

New medicines are sought by isolating natural products, by imitating existing products, by applying the theory of biological processes and by random screening of chemical substances. Each of these methods has produced important new products in the past and there is no way of knowing which of these methods will be the more cost-effective in the future. Large pharmaceutical companies may therefore use all four methods of research. It is probable that the pharmaceutical industry finds more new products than academic and research institutions because this is the sole purpose of the research: academic institutions tend to be more concerned with 'elucidating basic principles'.[9]

For a drug to be of value in medical practice, it must be not only effective but safe for use on humans and produced with consistent quality. The safety of a new drug is established by tests on animals and then ultimately on man. Many promising preparations have to be rejected because they fail to achieve acceptable levels of safety and in some cases preparations have to be withdrawn from the market when unforeseen and damaging effects come to light (for example, thalidomide). The nature, extent and severity of unwanted effects have therefore to be established in so far as possible before a product is marketed and estimates have to be made of the doses which will be effective and safe in human beings. This work is of immense importance in view of the severe risks of adverse drug reactions. It is estimated that about 30,000 persons die annually in the United States from adverse drug reactions – possibly 80 per cent of them preventable.[10]

In most cases the effectiveness of a preparation can only ultimately be estimated by controlled clinical trials. In view of the placebo effect, these trials need to be conducted in a situation where neither the doctor nor the patient knows which of two preparations is being used. By statistical method it can be established whether a new preparation is more effective than a placebo or more effective than another preparation.

Pricing and the World Market

Some groups of countries attempt to produce most of their pharmaceutical requirements and heavily restrict imports of products from other countries. This is on the whole true of the Eastern European countries. Countries which do not restrict imports are served to a large extent by international companies which manufacture in several countries and sell to particular sectors of the market from their different companies. The world market for pharmaceutical products was over £7,000 million in 1970 and is expected to increase to between £15,000 and £20,000 million by 1980.[11] The United States is by far the largest producer in the world and its main companies have subsidiary companies in a large number of different countries.

Companies protect the market for each of their new products by patents. In addition products are protected by brand names which are normally different from and simpler than the official names given to products by W.H.O. Brand names provide market protection for a product simply because doctors are induced by advertising to use the brand name rather than the official name when writing a prescription. By specifying a brand name they are not only selecting a particular product but also specifying one particular manufacturer of it. While the laws of each country specify how long protection by patent is to last, the right to use a brand name is the permanent industrial property of the company who 'owns' it.

Patents and the widespread use of brand names greatly limit the role of price competition in the industry. Some valuable pharmaceuticals for which the patent lapsed many years ago are produced by several manufacturers who compete by price. Some hospital pharmacists, with the support of their medical staff, buy in bulk on a generic basis and can thus take quotes for products from several manufacturers. But most of the sales of pharmaceuticals in the more developed countries are of patented products and the vast majority of prescribing is done by doctors outside hospital. Thus competition in the industry is mainly between products rather than by price. This is because most doctors prescribe what they consider to be the best preparation to meet the needs of each patient irrespective of price. Manufacturers do not generally quote prices in advertisements to doctors and few doctors are well-informed about this aspect of the products they prescribe. A new product will be prescribed if doctors are led to believe that it is the preferred medication for patients with particular conditions. It will continue to be prescribed until doctors come to believe that a new or different product is preferable for those conditions. Thus it is the custom of the industry not to price new drugs 'on the basis of cost, but on the basis of what the market will bear. A new drug's price is set by considering the prices of existing drugs, and then adding to that price whatever the product improvement is thought to be able to command.'[12]

This pricing policy has induced Italian firms to undertake raw material production as Italy is the one Western advanced country which does not recognize pharmaceutical patents. Some Eastern European countries which do not recognize pharmaceutical patents have also entered this field. Thus countries which are prepared to ignore patent infringement have been able to obtain raw materials for local manufacture far below the prices charged by the patent holders. There are thus two world markets for the main pharmaceuticals – the patent market with prices set by the multi-national companies and the non-patent market where prices are much more competitive. In the latter section of the world market there is a greater risk of purchasing products of unreliable quality.

Sales Promotion

At any point of time, each of the large multi-national firms sells a number of branded products for which it holds the patent and perhaps also a number of other products which are still branded but no longer patented. At any stage a new product from another firm may take over the market for any of their products. As the commercial life of most, if not all, of its products is limited each firm must produce new products if it is to maintain its level of profits. Firms are competing for the preferences of doctors. Thus when a firm produces a new and useful product, it advertises it to doctors to secure that it comes to be used as rapidly as possible. If all doctors diligently read their medical journals and participated regularly in continuing education on the subject, they would learn of all useful new developments from professional sources. But they do not. Thus genuine informative advertising has in the past performed a useful function not by the most cost-effective methods which society could devise, but by the most cost-effective methods available to the separate firms which constitute the industry.

A doctor needs to learn how to use a wholly new type of product correctly. But by no means all advertising is of this type. By far the major part of sales promotion activity today is not needed 'to support pharmaceutical education, but to induce brand preference. This means that new drug introductions have had to be acompanied by increasing amounts of promotion.'[13]

Profits can be made by persuading doctors that a new product is better than it is, that the range of conditions for which it is the best choice is wider than it is,[14] that the quantity necessary for successful treatment is larger than is actually required, that the product is produced at a higher and more consistent quality level than can be truthfully claimed. In so far as sales promotion leads to an over-use of drugs or more powerful drugs than are justified for the treatment of a particular condition, this is by far the most serious consequence of it. An American study showed that 5 per cent of patients admitted to hospitals have drug-induced illness and 10 per cent to 31 per cent of hospital patients experience untoward reactions to prescribed drugs at some time during their hospital stay.[15]

The number of preparations which are real improvements on existing products are about five or six out of the roughly forty new products registered each year in the United States. Two-thirds of the new products put on the market contain two or more older drugs in a new combination and nearly a fifth are duplicates or minor modifications of products already in use. While fixed combinations of drugs offer some convenience and some are necessary and useful, the 'locked-in' proportions of the drugs 'may or may not fill the needs of individual patients'.[16]

The pharmaceutical industry spent about £33 million on sales promotion of prescription drugs in the United Kingdom – nearly 14 per cent of home sales revenue. This proportion of sales revenue spent on promotion is lower than in many other countries and by no means the highest for industries in the U.K. But while other sales efforts are directed to the whole consumer population, the efforts of the pharmaceutical industry in promoting ethical preparations are devoted almost exclusively to doctors and mainly to the 35,000 specialists and principals in general practice. At current rates, more is spent on drug advertising to each doctor over his working life than was spent to train him in the first place. In 1971, the pharmaceutical industry in the United States spent more than 1 billion dollars on all forms of promotion of prescription medicines – about $5,000 per doctor.[17]

Expenditure on pharmaceutical advertising in both the U.K. and the U.S. vastly exceeds the cost of continuing education for doctors in every aspect of practice. Indeed it is the failure to develop continuing education which makes genuine informative advertising necessary. For the cost of sales promotion activity in the United Kingdom, it would be possible for each general practitioner to have a teacher of medicine or therapeutics spend about a month a year working with him in his practice and giving him advice. A month would, however, be much more than would be required to inform a doctor about the five or six really valuable new preparations produced by the world pharmaceutical industry in a year.

The industry would not incur this vast expenditure on sales promotion unless each firm believed that the extra sales it obtained more than covered the cost. Detailed evidence on the impact of advertising is available from a special study of a random sample of general practitioners in the United Kingdom undertaken for the Sainsbury Committee. About half the practitioners thought that the sales efforts of the companies were the best way of finding out about the existence of new drugs and 16 per cent thought that it was the best way of finding out about the efficiency of new products. Over a third thought that there was usually enough information in drug firm literature to decide whether to use the drug and nearly half thought that they had enough information after seeing the firm's representative. A half thought that they would lose an important source of information if they did not receive drug firm literature and 70 per cent if they did not see the drug firm representatives. Yet over a half had, in the past year, felt that a drug firm representative had had insufficient information to tell the practitioners what he wanted to know, had made less of the side-effects than justified, and had claimed more uses for a product than were justified.

Some firms employ pharmacists as representatives. Others prefer to recruit representatives without a professional background and train them in psychological techniques of presentation. Still others select salesmen from other fields of experience and brief them as if they were selling soap powder: bonuses and prizes may be offered to the most successful salesman.[18] If firms with low ethical standards increase their share of the market, those who have previously behaved more ethically may be tempted to lower their ethical standards. Within limits the bad drives out the good.

To support the claims of effectiveness made in advertising matter, references are normally given to articles in medical journals. These articles often consist simply of testimonies by doctors who have been induced to try out the drug in their own practice. They seldom represent scientific evidence because the study was not properly controlled or because the sample was too small to be statistically significant. Some companies in the United States are said to maintain lists of doctors willing to write testimonies of this kind and some doctors write to companies offering to provide testimonies and expecting to be paid for them.

A firm which is known to have told doctors in its advertisements what was later found to be untrue or a distortion of the truth, may damage its reputation with doctors so that later claims made by that firm are less likely to be believed. But the scope for misleading advertising is still large simply because a doctor can seldom establish the safety or effectiveness and particularly the relative effectiveness of a product by using it in his own practice. Some companies guarantee that every item of sales promotion material is prepared under the supervision of, or has been approved by, a doctor. But this does not ensure that all their advertisements tell the whole truth.[19] And even the most objective briefing will not control what a representative actually says to the doctors he visits. Representatives are the most powerful influence on prescribing behaviour.

Sales promotion activities include efforts to influence every channel by which information about the effects of pharmaceuticals may be acquired or disseminated. Medical teachers, research workers and leading specialists become important targets for this activity. Thus gifts of equipment and other facilities may be given to departments of medical schools to win goodwill among medical teachers. Generous consultancies may be offered to those who conduct clinical trials and those conducting trials may be offered generous expense allowances or direct payments. Postgraduate education meetings may be financed, sponsored or conducted by firms at which lavish entertainment is provided and time or space allocated to promote the firms' products: one U.S. firm recently arranged a seminar in Bermuda. Medical students may be given gifts of equipment or expense-free trips, providing in the latter case a visit is made to the firm's factory. Politicians and other opinion leaders may be invited to visit factories and provided with generous entertainment when they do. Gifts may be distributed to doctors – gramophone records, golf-balls, blotters, diaries and inkstands to win goodwill and encourage doctors to open packets of advertisements and study their contents. Larger gifts in the United States include colour TV sets and deep-freezers.[20]

Advertising in medical journals is on such a large scale that many of them are heavily dependent on this source of revenue. One leading medical journal in Britain derives 60 per cent of its revenue from pharmaceutical advertisements and some others 40 per cent. Firms promote newspapers and journals which are given free to all doctors and contain among other matter articles which appear to be independent and authoritative to promote the merits of the firm's products: the financing of the publication may not be revealed to the doctors receiving it. One doctor in the United States reported that he had received 40 medical publications for which he had not subscribed.[21]

The effectiveness of particular efforts of sales promotion depends not only on the skill of those who run them but on the critical judgment of doctors and the integrity of research workers, medical teachers and journal editors. How far do editors of journals and newspapers maintain their independence when pressed by advertisers whose continued support may be essential to the commercial success of their publication? Do university teachers and research workers stand clear of association with particular firms or maintain complete academic independence when they are associated? Do they avoid situations involving conflicts of interest? Are they prepared to criticize products of firms from which they are deriving direct or indirect advantages as readily and forcefully as they would if they were not receiving these advantages? The answers to these questions will vary according to the ethical standards current in particular societies and the personal integrity of individuals in the face of strong commercial pressures.

In connection with the Sainsbury Committee's enquiry into the pharmaceutical industry in the United Kingdom, two independent teams of experts assessed the therapeutic value of the 2,657 proprietary preparations available on National Health Service prescriptions in December 1965. The two panels were completely agreed on the classification of 84 per cent of these preparations. The proportion of these preparations considered to be undesirable for one or several reasons was 35 per cent.[22] In the United States, 75 out of 263 biological products were 'not recognized as being effective' by most of the medical profession and 32 vaccines were 'generally regarded as ineffective by the medical profession'.[23] A study by the National Academy of Sciences of about 4,300 products marketed in the United States before 1962 found substantial evidence supporting only 30 per cent of the 16,500 claims of effectiveness for these drugs. Only 434 products met all the claims made for them.[24]

The use of ineffective drugs is of course justified if the doctor is consciously using them as a placebo. If, however, the doctor accepts false or, more often, misleading claims made by the manufacturer, he may be denying his patient a drug which would be effective. Or he may use an effective drug for a wider range of conditions than is warranted. For example, 'according to the Food and Drug Administration [in the U.S.] as well as the American Medical Association Council on Drugs, chloramphenicol is the drug of choice only for typhoid fever. Due to its toxicity, in the form of serious blood dyscrasia and deaths, its use is rarely indicated. In the light of repeated warnings about its toxicity and the fact that annually there are only a few hundred typhoid fever cases in the whole nation, how can we justify the mass prescribing of this drug?'[25] In Belgium, the Netherlands, Sweden and the United Kingdom it constitutes 1 per cent of the sales of antibiotics. In France it is 5 per cent of the sales of antibiotics and in Western Germany 25 per cent.[26]

Profits

The sheer number of new preparations which the industry attempts to persuade doctors to prescribe creates confusion and distracts attention from the few important advances. It also makes it much more difficult for a doctor to be an economic prescriber. The more products there are on the market the less can he be expected to know or try to find out the price of each. The more literature he studies, the more difficult it is to select the best product for each purpose and the less time he has to give to independent publications which attempt to advise him on good and economical prescribing. The less price conscious doctors are, the less the industry has to worry about the prices charged for its products and the higher the margin between cost and price which can either be ploughed back into further research or sales promotion or taken as profit.

Data comparing the cost of production of particular products with the prices charged for them do not necessarily prove that excessive profits are being made. Profit margins on successful products have to cover the costs of research and of developing products which prove to be ineffective or too toxic to be marketed. Nevertheless the difference between the price charged by the multi-national companies for raw materials and that charged by other, primarily Italian, firms is remarkably big. In Table 1 data are shown for some popular drugs taken from a study conducted for the Colombian government. In interpreting this table it should be appreciated that the multi-nationals' prices are what they charge local manufacturers and it is not clear whether the prices for the 'other' firms are one-time offers or prices which will be maintained for a continuous supply. Prices for the same drug vary markedly between countries. Some products cost three or four times more in the United States than in Britain or Ireland.[27]

Data on the profits of a pharmaceutical company as a whole can be misleading where, as is often the case, a company is producing other products as well as pharmaceuticals. Moreover the profitability of multi-national companies cannot be established without looking at their activities in every country. Transactions between the country units of multi-national companies are not arm's-length transactions. What a company will charge its subsidiary in another country for raw materials, technical and managerial services and

87

manufacturing know-how will depend on the tax laws of the two countries and on wider political and economic considerations.

TABLE I

Selected Drug Price Comparisons –
Multi-national and 'Other' Firms

Chemical Name	Trade Name	Price Per Kilo in U.S. $ 'Other' $	Multi-national $
Chlordiazepóxido	Librium	18.90– 20.00	1,250.00
Diazepan	Valium	30.00– 45.55	2,500.00
Sulfafurazol	Gantricín	7.20– 8.75	35.00 ⎱ 15.00 ⎰
Nitrazepan	Nogadón	108.70	2,088.00
Ampicilina	Pentrexil	162.50–200.00	420.00
Tetracilina Base	Bristaciclina	23.50– 26.00	110.00
Erytromycina	Ilosone	100.00–145.50	275.56
Prometacina	Deinal	17.75– 21.00	140.00
Indometacina	Indocid	72.50–110.00	320.00
Metrenidiázol	Flagil	11.15– 14.80	38.00
Acetazolamida	Diamox	13.50– 16.85	53.00
Tolbutamida	Rastinón	2.40– 3.20	28.00
Furosemida	Lasix	77.00–100.00	1,177.00
Cloranfenicol	Chloromycetin	13.00– 15.95	80.00

Source: Data gathered for Colombian Government quoted in L. H. Wortzel, *Technology Transfer in the Pharmaceutical Industry*, UNITAR Research Report, No. 14, 1971, p. 52.

Nevertheless it is significant that while the U.S. price of bulk penicillin which was not patented dropped from $2·50 to 21 cents per milligram in the period 1951 to 1960, the price of tetracycline sold under different names by five companies remained at $5·10 per bottle of sixteen capsules during the same period. Since then the price has fallen well below a dollar. As the U.S. Task Force chaired by Dr Philip Lee remarked, 'The rigidity of prices of patented antibiotics is clear evidence of the lack of competition benefit to consumers.'[28] The Task Force also pointed out that 'since 1952 drugs and medicines have consistently ranked about the three most profitable of 41 industrial groups whose sales profitability is charted annually by the First National City Bank of New York. Based on net income after taxes as a percentage of net worth, the drug industry ranked first in six years, second or third in five years and never lower than ninth. Among 31 major industries, drug-makers have averaged an 18·1 return on capital as compared with 9·7 per cent for the whole

88

group.'[29] In Canada, whether measured as profit on capital employed or on total equity, the pharmaceutical industry did twice as well as manufacturing industry as a whole.[30]

The Sainsbury Committee in the United Kingdom ascertained, subject to qualifications some of which are set out above, the rates of profit on employed capital of 27 companies with home sales of N.H.S. products in excess of £2 million for years between 1963 and 1967. There were 17 of these 27 companies with returns in excess of 20 per cent; three of them coming within the range of 50 or 55 per cent and five within the range of 30 to 40 per cent.[4] The committee concluded that the profits of some of these companies were 'much higher than is reasonable'. 'The figures suggest that the cost of the National Health Service has been inflated by excessive prices to the extent of several million of pounds over this period of three years.'[31]

In its propaganda, the industry emphasizes that it is 'science-based' as if this gave it the right to some special dispensation in the matter of profits. While the industry in common with all other major industries employs scientific methods, much of its research owes more to chance than to the application of scientific theory. In defending its level of profits the industry claims that it is subject to special risks. But the Sainsbury Committee pointed out that firms with 'a research programme involving a substantial number of research personnel have emerged with encouraging regularity with products which have remained dominant in their field of therapy for a considerable time'.[32] The Task Force in the United States concluded that they had been 'unable to find sufficient evidence to suggest the concept of the drug industry as a particularly risky enterprise'.[33] Risk does not justify such a high level of profit nor does the need to ensure the quality of products. Indeed despite the high level of profits over many years, there have been substantial lapses in the quality of products even in the case of large firms. The prospect of profit is undoubtedly needed in any private industry to secure the continuation of research. What is not clear is that profits at their current levels are necessary or that this is the only way by which this research could be financed.

The Regulation of the Marketing and Advertising

In view of all these problems, many countries have been imposing tight regulations on the operations of the pharmaceutical industry to achieve one or more of the following purposes:

- to ensure that no new medicines are marketed unless there is evidence of their effectiveness;
- to ensure that all medicines which are marketed are of acceptable safety;
- to ensure that all effective medicines which are produced are of reliable quality;
- to ensure that doctors become rapidly aware of valuable new medicines and the correct uses of them;
- to ensure that misleading claims are not made by manufacturers, so that doctors' decisions on prescribing are 'rational';[34]
- to ensure that prices paid for pharmaceuticals are reasonable.

To secure the first two of these aims more and more national governments have established central government agencies to decide what products may be marketed. No new medicine may be put on the market unless the manufacturer satisfies such agencies that it is (a) effective and (b) of acceptable safety. These agencies may also seek similar evidence about products already on the market and have powers to require unsatisfactory products to be withdrawn. While these agencies have had some success in preventing new ineffective products from being marketed, they have been less successful in removing from the market ineffective or undesirable preparations which have long been available. For example, in the United States in November 1970, the Food and Drug Administration had only actually removed from the market 157 drugs out of 369 it had declared to be ineffective,[35] though it had limited considerably a number of unjustified claims in sales promotion. As doctors need on occasions to prescribe placebos, the enormous effort needed to try and take old ineffective products off the market seems unjustified. What is, however, important is that claims should not be made about them in sales promotion which cannot be substantiated.

The extreme solution to the problem of pharmaceutical advertising would be to forbid it altogether and substitute an independent information service. Moreover doctors could be required to take further education at regular intervals or lose their registration or licence. The task of keeping doctors abreast of new developments would seem to be most appropriately performed by professional associations, medical schools and research institutes rather than by commercial firms. Thus government subsidies could be channelled towards such bodies to provide continuing education which would not, of course, be concerned only with pharmaceuticals. It would, of course, be difficult to define sales promotion and some form of evasion would always persist. Moreover firms would still attempt to influence indirectly opinion leaders in the profession.

But the banning of visits by representatives would be a great step forward. This was envisaged by the Sainsbury Committee in Britain in the long run.[36] If, however, written advertising were banned, the professional journals would be faced with a major financial crisis and the provision of government subsidies to replace the advertising revenue would present grave practical problems. How should such subsidies be distributed – on the basis of past revenue, circulation or what other criteria? How would it be possible for a new journal to enter the field and thus preserve the vitality of medical publishing? How should the total level of subsidy to all journals be determined in the long run? In 1974, the Trustees of the American Medical Association recommended a ban on advertising in its professional journals because the Association was accused of being biased towards pharmaceutical manufacturers because of its dependence on drug advertising.[37] This recommendation was rejected by the delegates.[38]

An alternative to a ban on written advertising is the regulation of the wording used in advertising. The examination of advertisements after they have appeared requires a large and highly qualified staff, leads to endless disputes and the control operates after the major part of any damage has been done. In the United States, the Food and Drug Administration has, since 1962, attempted to monitor written advertising matter but it has never been properly staffed to perform this task very effectively. In the United Kingdom, the industry has established a Code of Marketing Practice and a special committee to adjudicate on alleged infringements under an independent, legally qualified chairman. This does not, however, ensure that all infringements are brought before the committee and the only ultimate sanction available in the industry is to require the offending company to leave the Association of the British Pharmaceutical Industry.

As part of the control of marketing, many countries require an approved 'label' or statement about effectiveness, safety and use to be drafted for each product. This system could be extended to cover older products as they are brought under control. Legislation could be introduced to require the precise text of this label to be reproduced in any advertisement without any addition or omission. This was the type of solution favoured by the Sainsbury Committee in

Britain.[39] Alternatively all advertisements can be required to be submitted for approval before issue. This is required in Australia and in France for new products.

The Regulation of Prices and Profits

Unreasonable profits are made because of the limitation of price competition by patents and brand names. If doctors were more aware of the prices and merits of similar and identical products there would be more price competition after the end of the patent period. Thus legislation could require the price of each product to be included in advertising matter and literature could be sent to doctors indicating the relative prices of identical or similar products. The latter is done both in Britain and Canada but with limited effect.

In the case of patented products, the statutory period of patent protection could be reduced, licences could be granted to competitors to use patents where the prices charged by patent holders are excessive or patent protection of pharmaceuticals could be abolished altogether. In Canada where most of the large pharmaceutical companies are subsidiaries of United States firms, the Restrictive Trade Practices Commission recommended that 'patents with regard to drugs be abolished. In the opinion of the Commission this is the only effective remedy to reduce the prices of drugs in Canada'.[40] In Britain, which has a substantial industry of its own, the Sainsbury Committee favoured a shorter patent life for pharmaceuticals. A similar recommendation was made for the United States which has the largest pharmaceutical industry in the world, by the U.S. Task Force chaired by Dr Philip Lee in 1968. None of these proposals has been implemented.

In 1969, the Canadian Government introduced legislation to enable Canadian firms to manufacture drugs imported under patent. Though many licences were granted by the Commission of Patents, their decisions have been challenged in the Courts. Thus firms seeking compulsory licences could expect 'delays of up to two years and count on legal expenses of up to $100,000'.[41] Later on they may face deliberate underpricing by the original patentee. There is, moreover, no certainty that compulsory licences will be used.[42] Established producers may agree not to invade each other's patents and less established firms may fear that doctors will still prescribe well-known brands.

Brand names confer considerable market protection when patents have expired. In the United Kingdom the Sainsbury Committee proposed that the name first given to a new product by its manufacturer should have to be approved by the Medicines Commission and any manufacturer should be entitled to use this name after the expiry of the patent period. A similar proposal was made by the United States Task Force in 1968. Any doctor who wished to specify a particular manufacturer would still be free to do so but he would have to make the conscious effort of adding it after the name of the preparation on the prescription. Where no manufacturer was specified the chemist would be free to prescribe the cheapest source of supply. Indeed he could be induced to do so if he were paid under health insurance or a national health service for the cheapest product whether he had filled the prescription with it or not. Thus the purchasing by chemists would introduce the price competition which the medical profession fails to generate at present.

A variant of this proposal is simply to allow chemists the right to substitute a similar drug or different brand when it is cheaper than that specified by the doctor on the prescription. Thus it was proposed by the American Pharmaceutical Association in 1970 that the laws of the States which forbid substitution by the chemist should be amended to make it legal.[43] In 1974, it advocated the abolition of the use of brand names altogether.[44]

In 1962 the Province of Alberta (Canada) legislated to allow substitution by the chemist unless the doctor specifically indicated that no substitution should be made. This had limited effects as doctors tended to write 'no substitution' on all their prescriptions. Under the Pharmaceutical Act passed by the Legislature of Manitoba (Canada) in 1972, chemists are required to sell the cheapest genuine equivalent of a range of drugs to a patient when the doctor has not specified a brand name. In Ontario, such substitution is permitted but not required. A comparative drug index is circulated and there is evidence that generic prescribing and substitution by chemists is increasing. In any scheme of this kind, it is particularly important to ensure, by continuous monitoring and inspection, that drugs of inferior quality are not marketed.

A further way of securing that the cheapest drug is used where there are equivalents or close equivalents is for the range of products which a country allows to be marketed to be restricted. This procedure is most likely to be adopted by countries which are heavily dependent on imports. Thus, for example, Norway tightly controls imports of drugs and takes tenders from international suppliers for each category of drug. Such a system has been proposed by an official committee in the Province of Manitoba (Canada) for a range of 42 drugs no longer patented with sales in Manitoba of over $3 million.[45] Such arrangements have also been introduced in many developing countries – particularly those with very limited resources and balance of payment problems. Where drugs are only close equivalents, two or three alternatives may be selected as some patients may benefit more from one close equivalent than another. Few of the more developed countries are willing to impose such severe restrictions on what a doctor may prescribe – particularly in private practice. It would, however, seem more practicable and acceptable to apply such a restriction to drugs provided free or at nominal charges in a health insurance or health service programme.

The principle of restricting the scope of free drugs under such programmes is well established, though the criteria for inclusion in such free lists vary in different countries. The extreme case is Norway where 'life-saving' drugs are available free but the patient has to pay the full cost of any other drugs. In Australia, important drugs for treating acute cases are provided free and without restriction, while other drugs are restricted for use only for the treatment of specific diseases. Inclusion in the formulary is used as an indirect means of price control. 'If the price is considered too high, in relation to its therapeutic advantages by a committee of medical advisors, a drug may not be included in the list.'[46] In New Zealand prices are laid down for each medicine admitted to the Drug Tariff which are paid to the pharmacist: if certain expensive proprietary brands are prescribed, the patient has to pay the extra cost above that laid down in pricing rules. Prices are negotiated. The criteria for admission of drugs to the tariff are therapeutic value, safety and side effects, and cost, in that order. Where there is already a therapeutically equivalent drug on the list, a new item may only be accepted as a part charge on the scheme: the patient has to pay the pharmacist the extra cost.[47] In Saskatchewan (Canada) the Provincial Government is introducing a drug formulary and an agency to purchase drugs centrally. In the United States it is government policy not to pay under the Medicare scheme for medicines designated as 'ineffective' or 'only possibly effective' by the Food and Drug Administration. And under both Medicaid and Medicare a plan has been announced to limit reimbursement to the lowest-priced of chemically identical non-patent drugs generally available to pharmacists.[48]

Under the British National Health Service, the general practitioner can only order appliances which are on a limited list. If the practitioner thinks that the patient needs a particular appliance not on the list he has to refer him to a hospital. But in the cases of drugs there is no limitation. Thus the doctor orders, the patient receives and the government pays the bill except for the notional charges falling on the patient. There is a voluntary agreement with the pharmaceutical industry (V.P.R.S.) under which prices are negotiated, but this agreement is backed by statutory sanctions. The scheme has, over the past decade, succeeded in reducing considerably the extent of unreasonable profits identified by the Sainsbury Committee. The main problems occur with foreign-owned firms where it is difficult to establish the profits arising out of sales in Britain.[49]

A limited list of drugs prescribable under a national service or insurance programme gives governments greater bargaining power in negotiating prices. Thus the authorities can threaten to exclude a product from the list if the price quoted for it is held to be unreasonable. Doctors can be left free to prescribe products not on the list but in this case the patient has to pay the full cost or the extra cost. But this does create a burden for chemists in sorting out who should be charged for what and there is a risk of free-list drugs becoming regarded as inferior. For such a system to be potentially acceptable to the profession, the choice of products for the list has to be made by a committee which enjoys the confidence of the profession. This is the procedure used in such countries as Denmark and New Zealand, where it works well.

Conclusion – an International Responsibility

Each country has an interest in regulating what pharmaceuticals are sold, how they are promoted and either the prices at which they are sold or the profits emanating from the prices. These matters cannot be left to the free operation of the market. But the key drug firms are multi-national and control should be similarly multi-national as it is difficult for a country to act alone in these matters. Medical journals have an international circulation. Doctors emigrate and world tourism is on a vast scale. It is undesirable for the same drug to be known by different names in different countries. It is also of limited value for some countries to exercise a tight control on advertising matter in journals while the journals of other countries in the same language are not controlled. Moreover countries with patents of international importance hesitate to reduce the patent rights of foreign pharmaceutical firms lest this should lead to reprisals against their own patents in other countries. Patents are to reward innovators but they also benefit those countries which make the innovations.

Developing countries with few patents of their own benefit little from the patent system, but pay their share of the rewards to innovators abroad if they purchase from multi-national companies. Thus some of these countries have encouraged local manufacture. The fabrication of dosage form is where a start can most easily be made. Thus high tariffs have been put on finished goods and low tariffs on raw materials or alternatively imports of finished goods have been severely restricted. This has induced the multi-national companies to license or contract with local firms to manufacture. But these local firms have found themselves blocked from using the technology they have learnt under contract or licensing arrangements by the control of the multi-national companies 'over raw materials, patents and trade-marks for the most desirable drugs'.[50] It is not surprising that many developing countries faced with these restrictions or the prospect of them have chosen to ignore patent agreements and either purchase from non-patented sources or nationalize companies owned or controlled by the multi-national companies.

But the main problem facing the developing countries is that of securing that the products they purchase from non-patented sources are of the requisite quality. A cheap product is of no value if it is ineffective. Moreover, there have been cases of multi-national companies dumping inferior products on countries which lack the facilities to assess quality. In countries which allow free importation and allow drugs to be bought without prescription (such as Vietnam) drugs which are forbidden to be sold in the United States because they are harmful or worthless are readily available. According to an American doctor, the drugs in Vietnam are killing people and causing unnecessary sickness.[51]

The developing countries need assistance with the testing of drug samples whether they are purchasing from the patent or non-patent market or attempting to formulate dosage or manufacture themselves. Only if these countries can be really sure of what they are buying can they decide the best way of securing value for the limited money they can afford to spend on pharmaceuticals.

More and more countries are duplicating efforts to ascertain the facts about both new and old pharmaceutical products, to assist them in controlling marketing and advertising. Which products are effective and of acceptable safety and which are not and which are more effective than others? Every country has an interest in the quality of its health services as well as in the profitability of its exports. These interests are to some extent in conflict though in some areas this conflict can be avoided – if by dubious international ethics.

The task of ascertaining the full facts about all medicines has proved a formidable task for the richest country in the world and is well beyond the resources of developing countries. This is a task which the World Health Organisation might undertake on behalf of member countries. It is an international responsibility to secure not only that there is a common drug nomenclature but that this nomenclature is the one which is actually used by all doctors throughout the world. The introduction therefore of generic prescribing is of international importance. W.H.O. should be invited and financed by member countries to play a much larger role in the regulation of the world pharmaceutical industry. The smaller and poorer countries of the world particularly need protection from the unethical marketing of dangerous or ineffective pharmaceuticals just as the whole world needs to police the trade in addictive drugs.[52]

Given technical guidance from W.H.O., each country needs effective legislation which is properly enforced to ensure that as far as possible medicines are used only when they ought to be used, and to secure that the prices paid for them are reasonable. First, there needs to be restriction on what preparations are marketed. Second, regular inspection of manufacturers' premises and testing of products is required to ensure both safety and quality. Thirdly, written advertising matter needs to be strictly controlled. Fourthly, the use of company representatives should be forbidden and instead each country needs to develop extensive continuing education for doctors to keep them up-to-date with new pharmaceutical developments. Finally, the role of patenting and branding needs to be curtailed to stimulate greater price competition. Ideally the control of marketing and advertising should be international rather than national. What is paradoxical is for countries to license doctors and encourage professional standards and yet allow the doctors they have licensed to be exposed to such enormous commercial pressure.

NOTES

1. D. L. Rabin, 'Use of Medicines', *Medical Care Review*, Vol. 29, No. 6, 1972, p. 669.

2. D.H.E.W., *Prescription Drug Data Summary*, 1972.

3. In most countries in Latin America and in some in the Far East (e.g. Thailand) the public can buy any pharmaceutical without a prescription either because laws are not enforced or because there are no legal restrictions.

4. D. L. Rabin, op. cit., p. 672.

5. L. Christopher and J. Crooks, 'Are we Overconsuming?' *World Health*, April 1974, p. 19.

6. L. H. Wortzel, *Technology Transfer in the Pharmaceutical Industry*, U.N.I.T.A.R. Research Report, No. 14, 1971, p. 15.

7. Lord Platt, 'Medical Science: Master or Servant', *B.M.J.*, 25 Nov. 1967, pp. 439–44.

8. ibid.

9. *Report of the Committee of Enquiry into the Relationship of the Pharmaceutical Industry with the National Health Service, 1965–7* (Sainsbury Committee), Cmnd. 3410, H.M.S.O., 1967, para 211.

10. Quoted in *Medical Care Review*, Vol. 31, No. 4, April 1974.

11. N.E.D.O., *Focus on Pharmaceuticals*, H.M.S.O., 1972, p. xii.

12. L. H. Wortzel, op. cit., p. 33.

13. ibid.

14. For example in a testimony to the U.S. Senate on 17 September 1968 an official of the Food and Drug Administration quoted from a bulletin evidently prepared by a regional sales manager of Merck & Co. to help his detail men sell Indocin. 'It is obvious that Indocin will work in that whole host of rheumatic crocks and cruds which every general practitioner, internist, and orthopaedic surgeon sees every day in his practice.' Dr McLeery stated that Indocin had been authorized for use only against four specific conditions: rheumatoid arthritis, rheumatoid spondylitis, osteo-arthritis of the hip and gout. 'It has many side effects, contra precautions and warnings that must be heeded for its safe and effective use'. *Medical Care Review*, 1968, p. 830.

15. P. Gardner and L. E. Cluff, 'The Epidemiology of Adverse Drug Reactions', *Hopkins Medical Journal*, Vol. 126, February 1970, p. 78.

16. Task Force on Prescriptive Drugs, *Final Report*, U.S. Department of Health, Education and Welfare, Washington, D.C., 1969, p. 8.

17. *Medical Care Review*, Vol. 29. No. 5, 1972, p. 521.

18. According to the former medical director of a major drug company 'innumerable prizes ranging from cutting boards to sets of monogrammed glasses are given to those detail men who reach or exceed a present quota

of sales. Many of them had convinced, or confused, a doctor to prescribe one of our products by telling the doctor that they were only one step away from winning a prize'. *Medical Care Review*, 1969, p. 675.

19. A medical director who resigned from a major drug company in the U.S. described the pressures on him as follows: 'he must learn the many ways to deceive the F.D.A. (Food and Drug Administration) and, failing in this, how to seduce, manipulate, or threaten the physician assigned to the New Drug Application (for marketing) into approving it even if it is incomplete. He must learn that anything that helps to sell a drug is valid, even if it is supported by the crudest testimonials, while anything that decreases sales must be suppressed, distorted or rejected because it is not absolutely conclusive proof. He must learn to word a warning statement so it will appear to be an inducement to use the drug rather than a warning of the dangers inherent in its use. He will find himself squeezed between businessmen who will sell anything and justify it on the basis that doctors ask for it and doctors who demand products they have been taught to want through the advertising and promotion schemes contrived by businessmen.' *Medical Care Review*, 1969, p. 673.

20. See *Medical Care Review*, Vol. 31, No. 4, April 1974.

21. Province of Manitoba, *Report of the Advisory Committee on Central Drug Purchasing and Distribution*, 1972, p. 75.

22. Sainsbury Committee, p. 209.

23. *Congressional Record*, Vol. 118: S 5287, 30 March 1972.

24. *Medical Care Review*, Vol. 30, No. 7, 1973, p. 715.

25. *American Pharmaceutical Association Newsletter*, 17 June 1972, quoted in *Medical Care Review*, Vol. 29, No. 7, 1972, p. 775.

26. O. Wade, *The Lost Discipline and ἁμαρτια*, Birmingham University, 1972, p. 17.

27. E. N. Jacoby and D. L. Hefner, 'Domestic and Foreign Drug Prices', *Social Security Bulletin*, May 1971.

28. *Medical Care Review*, 1968, p. 65.

29. Task Force on Prescriptive Drugs, op. cit., p. 14.

30. A. P. Ruderman, 'The Drug Business in the Context of Canadian Health Care Programs', *International Journal of Health Services*, Vol. 4, No. 4.

31. Sainsbury Committee, para 122.

32. ibid., para 132.

33. Task Force on Prescriptive Drugs, op cit., p. 14.

34. Rational prescribing has been defined as 'prescribing the right drug for the right patient, at the right time, in the right amounts, and with due consideration of relative costs', ibid., p. x.

35. *Medical Care Review*, Vol. 29, No. 9, 1972, p. 994.

36. Sainsbury Committee, para 351.

37. *Medical Care Review*, Vol. 31, No. 10, November 1974.

38. op. cit., Vol. 32, January 1975, p. 36.

39. The Committee was, however, divided on whether advertisements should be made to contain nothing other than the approved statement. Sainsbury Committee, para 347.

40. *Report of the Restrictive Trade Practices Commission*, Ottawa, 1963, p. 522.

41. Province of Manitoba, op. cit., p. 30.

42. See R. W. Lang, *The Politics of Drugs*, Lexington, 1974.

43. *Medical Care Review*, Vol. 29, No. 7, 1972, pp. 773–4.

44. op. cit., Vol. 31, No. 9, 1974, p. 1052.

45. Task Force on Prescriptive Drugs, op. cit., p. 29.

46. W. M. Wardell, 'Control of Drug Utilisation in the context of a National Health Service: the New Zealand system', *Clinical Pharmacology and Therapeutics*, Vol. 16, No. 3, Part 2, pp. 588–9.

47. *Medical Care Review*, Vol. 29, No. 6, 1972, p. 661.

48. See 'The Battle over Equivalence', *Medical World News*, 8 November 1974.

49. For example, in the case of one Swiss manufacturer (Hoffman-La Roche), anti-monopoly legislation was used to fix a price for a particular range of products. The French government is tackling the same problem under compulsory licensing provisions. Legal proceedings are also being taken against the same company in Germany. *The Times*, 13 January 1975.

50. L. H. Wortzel, op. cit., p. 26.

51. *Medical Care Review*, Vol. 30, No. 4, April 1973.

52. Warnings which American producers are required to put on their products when sold inside the United States are not necessarily put on their products when sold abroad. A leading company which manufactures Chloromycetin refused to provide doctors abroad with the same warnings as provided to doctors in the United States. *Medical Care Review*, Vol. 29, No. 6, June 1972, pp. 661–2.

CHAPTER 7

The Efficient Use of Hospitals

In most countries the majority of hospitals are non-profit organizations owned by trustees or by governments. In some countries profit-making hospitals are socially disapproved. This may be partly based on a vague belief that it is wrong to make profits out of sickness and partly on a fear that the search for profits could lead some owners to provide low standards of care. On the other hand, as pointed out in Chapter 2,[1] in France, Japan and some other countries doctor-owned hospitals, sanatoria or 'cliniques' are on a considerable scale. They tend to be small as they are used only for the patients of their doctor-owner. His personal reputation is intimately bound up with his hospital or 'clinique'. Large profit-making hospitals are few, and only in the last decade have commercial corporations in the United States begun to develop chains of hospitals like chains of hotels.[2]

A 'system' of private non-profit hospitals also tends to result in the bulk of hospitals being small[3] even where the population is sufficiently concentrated to justify one or more large hospital. This is true of Germany[4] and other European countries as well as of North America. This may be because the funds originally raised by the sponsors were insufficient to build a larger hospital and the site became surrounded by other buildings which it would be uneconomic to try and purchase and demolish. It is not remarkable that those who are willing to endow hospitals generally prefer to endow a separate one of their own rather than an extension for existing hospitals. A second reason may be the reflection of religious or class divisions in the population in sickness as well as health or in rivalries between factions of doctors. Thirdly, donors may have wished at the time of construction to make provision or better provision for a particular social group, or professional group (for example, women doctors) an unmet medical need or a new method of treatment. The separate hospital may survive long after the special need for it has ceased to operate.

Hospitals which are built according to the initiatives of community groups, religious groups and the caprices of donors are unlikely to conform to any rational plan. Many countries in Africa and Asia have small mission hospitals sited often according to the work of the religious group sponsoring them. In much of the mainland of Western Europe and in North America there are small denominational hospitals and in some countries small proprietary hospitals competing for patients. In Latin America many cities have separate hospitals for different occupational groups. While some communities may end up with too few hospital facilities, others may end up with an excess of beds. Although voluntary initiative has played a major role in hospital construction in many countries, it has played a much smaller role in providing services to care for the sick at home. It is not remarkable that donors have wanted to provide for the most serious type of illness for which hospital care is needed.

If hospitals were owned by profit-making companies and the doctors who used them for their patients were cost-conscious there would be profit incentives for mergers and take-over bids. The assets of under-used hospitals would be stripped and they would be sold for their site value. There would be profit incentives for the competing hospital companies to find the optimum size of hospital units and the hospital structure serving each area would gradually be rationalized. But where control is in the hands of non-profit organizations there is by definition no profit to be made by merging and thus mergers seldom occur unless tough outside pressure is exerted. Thus, in the United States, old and new, large and small hospitals, non-profit hospitals and profit hospitals struggle on side by side even though there may be in total an excess of hospital beds for the area – even for any stand-by need or 'option-demand'. They are enabled to survive partly by the affiliation of doctors with particular hospitals but also by the lack of a competitive urge by doctors to try and secure the most favourable terms for their patients.

It is not only in the more developed countries that under-used hospital facilities are to be found. In developing countries wards and whole hospitals may stand empty not because there are no patients who need hospital care but because the staff are not available to run the hospital or the running cost of the hospital cannot be afforded out of the health budget or for other reasons. In not a few developing countries, priorities have been distorted by the receipt of not wholly disinterested gifts of hospitals which are either used at intolerable cost or under-used with unacceptable waste.

An excess of hospital beds involves waste whether the extra beds are used or not. If they are empty, one (or more) hospital is running at below capacity and thus wasting its capital plant. If they are used, further unnecessary costs are incurred. Hospital managements which are free to set their charges usually base them on average costs at an estimated level of occupancy. If occupancy is lower than estimated there is a deficit in the accounts. If occupancy is higher there is a surplus. Though there may be advantages for appeal purposes in presenting accounts in a form which makes it look as if the hospital had a deficit, non-profit hospitals have, in the long run, to balance their books. Indeed, a surplus is needed out of which new equipment can be bought and expansion can be financed.

Some have suggested that managers of non-profit hospitals try to maximize cash flow or net return. Others have argued that the non-profit hospital is controlled by the doctors working in it so as to maximize their incomes.[5] Some have suggested that the non-profit hospital is engaged in conspicuous production analogous to Veblen's conspicuous consumption. Whether this is so or not, administrators, medical staffs and trustees seem to be motivated by the quest for prestige. They want their organization to grow and prosper. Non-profit hospitals, like profit hospitals, appear to be engaged in competition to attract patients, unless they are already overloaded with demand. They are also in competition for gifts and endowments to finance expansion, rebuilding programmes and new units or equipment. This is likely to be true whether it is the policy of the hospital to accommodate paying patients or not. The prestige of a hospital determines the extent to which doctors seek affiliation with it and competition for prestige and the search for gifts can lead to attempts to acquire new and particularly news-worthy units and equipment, the 'need' for which can be used when making appeals for funds. In the U.S. medical staff who 'meet none of the payrolls, own no shares in the hospital and pay none of the high fees'[6] can demand what they want and usually get it. Thus, hospitals may acquire whole units which they do not often use – intensive care units, cardiac surgery units and transplant units – and lack the specialized staff to use well. For example, '. . . 30 per cent of the 777 hospitals equipped to do closed-heart surgery had no such cases in the year under study. Of the 548 hospitals that had cases, 87 per cent did fewer than one operation per week. Of all hospitals equipped to do open-heart surgery, 77 per cent did not average even one operation per week, and 41 per cent averaged under one per month. Little of this work was of an emergency nature, and the mortality rate for both procedures is 'far higher . . . than in institutions with a full work load'.[7] Similarly, there were in 1965, 72 hospitals in the State of New York with cobalt bombs.[8]

This theory of competitive prestige is at least one possible explanation for the duplication of under-used facilities which is to be found in non-profit hospitals of some poor countries as well as rich ones. These facilities confer reflected glory on the doctors that staff the hospitals and the trustees responsible for their management. But instead of patients being concentrated in a limited number of units planned so that each will work near to capacity and fully use its plant, patients become scattered among competing units. Specialists may, as a result, be denied the quantity of experience which would be needed to acquire the highest skills. The same applies to nursing staff. The system may, therefore, not only be wasteful of resources but deny high quality service to patients who do not find their way to a hospital which is one of the winners of the prestige battle and thus has a unit which is in frequent use by experienced staff.

The theory of competitive prestige also explains the preference for short-stay patients. They help to promote the hospital's image as a curing institution. In the United States it is said that administrators want to achieve high occupancy and medical staffs want to secure rapid turnover of patients which inevitably requires a lower level of occupancy. Rapid turnover is also sought by medical staffs in the more prestigious British hospitals. Where medical staffs with these policies control admission, it is the patient with the least prospect of cure and the greatest need for care who will end up in the least prestigious hospital.

In Britain, before the National Health Service, the patients which the voluntary hospitals did not want ended up in the local authority hospitals, many of which, though by no means all, provided low standards of care. The same occurs today in the United States where 20 per cent of the short-term beds are in non-federal government hospitals – in the case of New York City 40 per cent of the short-term beds – established to provide care for indigent patients. These hospitals are crowded, short-staffed and housed in dirty, crumbling and dreary buildings,[9] and patients get fewer drugs and cheaper drugs than in the voluntary hospitals.[10]

The provision of hospitals whether by private interests, charitable bodies, social security agencies or governments in response to apparent demand leads to the waste of the community's resources. It can also lead to pockets of bad medical care. These problems are likely to be greater when different social security funds build separate hospitals to meet the needs of different occupational groups. This is also likely to be true in a country which has not introduced national health insurance, provided that a large section of the population is rich enough to purchase hospital insurance, and provision by government and/or charitable bodies is made for those who have no insurance. In an unplanned system there is by definition no one responsible for seeing how far demands for hospital care are real needs and for developing alternative forms of care which are no less effective and at lower cost.

Decisions on admission to and discharge from hospitals are taken by doctors, and patients seek wherever possible to follow the advice they are given. It is because doctors do not take responsibility for the costs which they are generating that inducements for doctors to take a positive interest in economy in the use of the nation's resources are lacking in most systems of medical care organization. But they are particularly lacking in the voluntary hospitals of the United States because until recently costs could so easily be passed on by the insurers in higher premiums. As Professor Somers has pointed out, 'in no realm of economic life are payments guaranteed for costs that are neither controlled by competition nor regulated by public authority, and in which no incentives for economy can be detected'.[11]

To be efficient a hospital system has to be planned to provide units of the right size, in the right places, to admit only those patients who need to be admitted and to discharge them as soon as they no longer need care in hospital. Hospitals are an expensive way of providing medical care. Nevertheless the special services they provide are cheaper to provide there than at home. While some highly technical services could not be provided in the home at all, at least without virtually rebuilding it, many could, but at fantastic cost. It is a misuse of the hospital for it to care for patients who do not need any of the special services it provides.

Economies of Scale

This *relative* cheapness of hospitals may arise from a number of different reasons, of which the first is the sharing of nursing services. If a patient needs 24-hour nursing, this could be provided at home, but three nurses would be required to man three 8-hour shifts and still more nurses to cover meal breaks, holidays and sickness. By bringing patients into a hospital, a 24-hour nursing team can look after a group of patients, and the number of staff on duty at particular times of the day and night, on particular days of the week, can be adjusted to the work load. Thus economies of nursing staff deployment come from bringing patients together in a hospital. A hospital which provides little more than nursing care needs to be of a certain size to achieve these economies.

A hospital which provides acute treatment services as well as nursing care needs specialized equipment, specialized staff and rooms which are specially designed to limit cross-infection and house equipment. No longer is it safe to operate on the kitchen table. Since the operation on George VI in 1951, even the British Royal Family has gone to hospitals for surgery rather than adapt at short notice a palace room for the purpose. In theory it would be possible for a pantechnicon containing an operating suite and a recovery room to be parked outside each patient's home in turn, but this would be absurdly expensive. An acute hospital should be a place where specialized equipment and staff with a variety of different specialized skills are brought together so that they can be used by different patients in succession, in such a way that skilled teams and expensive equipment are used as fully as possible. The concentration of patients in one complex cuts travel time for staff and secures a continuous flow of work for expensive apparatus.

The principle of division of labour applies in a hospital just as in a factory or hotel. Tasks which require extensive knowledge and high skills should be performed by those who have acquired them and tasks which require less knowledge and skill should be delegated to persons with lesser training who also specialize in their allocated functions. While some medical specialties have evolved from the history of medical practice (e.g. the distinction between medicine and surgery) or of hospitals (e.g. psychiatry, infectious diseases), others have arisen as a response to the extensive widening of knowledge and techniques. The practice of surgery has become increasingly confined to doctors who specialize not only in it but in particular types of operation. Pathology became a speciality and has since broken up into separate divisions of pathology. Internal medicine has similarly fragmented. The greater the expansion of both knowledge and techniques, the narrower has become the field in which a doctor can be expected to know all that can be known or practise with the highest skill.

Specialization in medicine has been accompanied by delegation. As treatment and diagnostic procedures have become routine, they have been delegated to trainee doctors, nurses and other personnel. Many specialties have developed their own para-medical workers – physiotherapists, radiotherapists, occupational therapists, pathology technicians, and many others. The development of medical technology has made it possible for more effective treatments to be provided and thus more manpower and equipment are needed to service a population with a given incidence of disease. But the greater the extent of specialization and the greater the delegation of tasks, the larger the catchment population from which the more esoteric specialists need to draw their patients.

A third stage of development has also occurred – mechanization. The concentration of work has made it possible to develop machines to handle some of the routine work. Not only is this more economic when the annual cost of the machine in interest and depreciation is compared with the cost of staff saved, it may also result in a higher quality of work. A well-designed machine can reduce human error. For example, a large sterilizer is cheaper and more efficient than a small one. Autoanalysers have been developed to undertake certain common pathology tests. These machines can now work at a very rapid pace and require a heavy load of work if they are to be used to maximum economic advantage. For all these reasons some specialties with their supporting staff and equipment require a large catchment population if they are to provide high quality services at the lowest cost per service provided. A larger hospital facilitates the division of labour and delegation of tasks and can make full use, or fuller use, of specialized equipment.

The daily patient cost of a hospital is lower the higher its average occupancy. This is because the bulk of hospital costs cannot be varied at short notice. The building has to be heated and maintained and equipment is installed for full-capacity working. Only within narrow limits can the staff be adjusted according to short-term fluctuations in occupancy. While some hospitals engage temporary nurses or private duty nurses when they are pressed, manpower costs per patient/day are lower where staff are regularly employed and the bulk of the costs of a hospital are usually manpower costs. The short-term marginal costs of hospitals, those costs which can be varied with occupancy – catering, drugs and other supplies – are a small proportion of the total.

Small hospitals are likely to have a lower average occupancy than large hospitals as emergency admissions become more predictable for a large unit. A small unit is likely to be faced with a larger daily fluctuation in the proportion of emergencies referred to it. The full advantages of scale in this respect can only be attained if the beds of a large hospital are used flexibly – if patients are admitted to those wards or nursing units where beds are vacant.

For all these reasons it would seem likely that the larger the hospital the lower the cost at which it can provide services of a given quality. But there are considerations which pull in the reverse direction. First the larger a hospital becomes, the further it has to be from some of those who need to travel to it. Thus patients, visitors and staff are forced to incur higher travel costs.[12] The larger a hospital becomes the more difficult it is likely to find the problem of staff recruitment: some staff, particularly married women, will not work far from home unless they are paid considerably more or have special transport provided. While all these costs may not fall on the hospital, they are part of the social costs of larger hospitals. Secondly, the cost and inconvenience of travel may deter visitors and reduce the extent to which the hospital is used. The further people live from a hospital the less use they tend to make of it.

Thirdly, problems of management may increase with the size of the operating units: the larger the units, the more difficult administrators may find it to run them efficiently. Fourthly, delegation of tasks can lead to communication problems for staff. How far the problems of management and communication which increase with the size of the hospital can be overcome by better organizational technique is not yet clear. Some large hospitals operate in practice like a series of small hospitals on one campus. Space is allocated permanently to particular specialties. Thus some wards may be full to capacity and accumulating a waiting list while other wards are used far below capacity.

In Britain, where there are doctors who are full-time or nearly full-time engaged in hospital work, it is believed that acute hospitals need to have at least 500 beds to provide a full-time job for the doctors in the main specialties and senior staff in the main diagnostic departments. It is argued that there are advantages for patients if doctors in one specialty can readily consult doctors in other specialties who are also on the spot. This is an argument based on quality considerations, though empirical evidence is lacking to support it because of the difficulty of measuring quality. Moreover, if rationally planned and operated according to the plan, one would expect a hospital of this size to be able to provide on average cheaper courses of treatment of a given quality than a much smaller hospital. This is because the main skills are available throughout the work week and the equipment needed can be more fully used than in a small hospital which attempts to provide the same range and quality of services.

Using regression analysis, Feldstein has shown that there are economies of scale in British hospitals with the turning point at 300 or 900 beds depending on how the statistical results are interpreted.[13] While he made adjustments for variations in the proportion of patients in different specialties by size of hospital, it was not possible to control for age, severity or diagnosis or to assess quality of service.

Data for the United States using similar techniques has been summarized and criticized by Berki. Different studies have come to different conclusions. 'Depending on the methodologies and definitions used, economies of scale exist, may exist, may not exist.'[14] But again none of the studies was properly controlled for diagnosis, age or severity or the quality of service provided. American non-profit hospitals do not operate on limited budgets, and their administrators are not, therefore, under the same pressure as administrators in Britain to try and secure that the best services are provided out of the money allotted to them. If there are economies of scale in British hospitals and fewer economies of scale or no economies of scale in American hospitals it may be because American hospitals, large or small, were until recently under much less pressure to operate efficiently: insurance carriers paid the charges determined by the hospitals and surpluses were used to extend facilities.

While one would expect there to be potential for considerable economies of scale in acute hospitals, the maximum economies are likely to be achieved with small-scale hospitals which provide little more than nursing care – hospitals for convalescent patients, for mentally or physically handicapped persons who can use local facilities for training and occupation, or for patients admitted to hospital for social reasons (because their home is unsuitable or there is no one at home to provide simple care). There may be positive advantages in certain types of psychiatric hospitals being small and intimate to avoid the rush and authoritarianism which tend to be the characteristics of general hospitals throughout the world.

In many countries specialized hospitals have been developed for particular categories of patients – for example, children's hospitals, maternity hospitals and tuberculosis hospitals. While such hospitals may be preferred by patients it is argued that specialists in one field of medicine should not be isolated from specialists in other fields as medical progress is fostered by cross-fertilization of ideas. Such hospitals may also be uneconomic if supporting services are occasionally required, such as X-rays, pathology and physiotherapy, which are more economically provided on a large scale. The small user who has his own supporting service on the spot is likely either to have a service of poor quality or an unduly expensive service because specialized staff and equipment are not fully used.

The Siting of Hospitals

At first sight, the most economical location for a hospital to serve a district would seem to be where the travel costs including the cost of travelling time of all who need to use it (patients, staff, trainees and visitors) will be lowest. But this ignores the cost of land. The annual rental value of land used for hospital purposes is established by what others are prepared to pay for the site for alternative uses. A non-central position may be cheaper when *both* land costs and travel costs are taken into account. Also relevant is the cost of recruiting and retaining all the different types of staff needed to run it. Can staff be recruited at prevailing rates of remuneration? Will the hospital need to provide or subsidize transport for staff to get to work? Will subsidized accommodation need to be provided? If the hospital is to be used for teaching, siting in relation to the basic science facilities of the university may also be important. Moreover, the construction of a large hospital in any position can generate so much travel that the capacity of local roads proves inadequate. Either the travel costs of others using the same roads are increased or road improvements are made to ease the congestion when hospital traffic is added to the existing traffic. All these costs need to be considered even though they will not all fall on the hospital budget.

Up to this point we have discussed hospitals as if they were indivisible units. In practice a hospital may perform a variety of different functions. While many hospitals provide education and training and serve as bases for research, their main function is to provide treatment and care. To do so, a hospital may need a catering department, laundry facilities, sterilizing facilities, a pathology department, a storage and supply system and many other facilities with which the patient may make no direct contact. The economies of scale for one or more of these activities may be greater than for the hospital itself. Thus it may be economic to have one vast laundry serving a dozen or more hospitals. Part of the catering requirements may be met more cheaply on a factory basis even allowing for the cost of regular deliveries to the hospital. The same may be the case with part of the sterilizing requirement. Certain pathology tests can be more cheaply done on a scale much greater than that of one hospital. It may be economic to keep certain stores at a depot serving many hospitals. Economies of this kind may only be achieved if a hospital system is planned on a regional basis.

The Length of Stay

The length of hospital stay for patients with particular conditions tends to become a matter of local custom and tradition. In Eastern Europe these customs have tended to become frozen into administrative 'norms'. Traditional practices may survive because alternative, less costly, services are not provided or not provided on a sufficient scale. In many countries separate convalescent units are not available and even minimal home care services, such as visiting nurse and home help services, are not developed. Other practices survive despite the availability of alternative forms of care which are inadequately or inappropriately used. If the doctor in charge of the case in hospital expects to continue to be responsible for the care of the patient after discharge, retaining the patient in hospital may be more convenient for him or more economic for him but not for whoever has to pay the cost of the patient's care. Alternatively, the hospital doctor who hands over his patient to another doctor on discharge may lack confidence in this second doctor – particularly if he does not know him personally. Traditions may persist in one country or area of a country even though quite different traditions operate elsewhere without any evident difference in the patients for whom care is provided.

There are less likely to be important differences in the needs of appendicitis and maternity cases than in many other types of patients. 'But the average length of stay of patients with appendicitis in Britain is 10·3 days which compared with 6·4 days for all hospitals in the United States.[15] In the early nineteen-sixties, the average maternity case stayed 3 days on the West Coast of the United States, 7 days on the East Coast and 10 days in Britain. Yet, paradoxically, Britain had much better developed home care services than the United States. It is only in recent years that more and more obstetricians in Britain have been introducing 48-hour discharge policies, and the average length of stay has fallen to 6 days. The length of stay for maternity cases fell not because it was found that this was better or cheaper but because of a desire to ensure that as many deliveries as possible took place in hospital.

The length of stay for particular conditions is found to vary not only between countries and regions but between consultants in the same region.[16] For example, the median duration of stay for the surgical treatment of peptic ulcers under the care of surgeons in Scotland who treated at least 20 patients during the year varied from 6 to 26 days. The median duration of stay for the medical treatment of myocardial infarction under the care of specialists in medicine varied from 10 to 36 days.[17] Lengths of stay for many conditions have been found in general to be lower in the United States than in Britain.[18] Lengths of stay in Sweden are, however, as high or higher than in Britain.[19]

There has been little research to establish the optimum length of stay and the best deployment of hospital and out-of-hospital services. Random control trials could establish the effectiveness and costs of care and consequences for patients and their families of lengths of hospital stay with appropriate home care services. Too readily doctors assume that they are conferring a benefit on patients by allowing them to stay in 'their hospital' for a further day or two. But many patients may not want a longer stay, however 'good' the hospital. They wish to go home as soon as they are advised that it is safe for them to do so.

There is for any patient a minimum necessary length of stay in hospital. How long a patient needs to be in hospital depends on (i) the rapidity with which the diagnosis, curative and other procedures are applied, (ii) the availability, suitability and costs of alternative plans for the continuation of care if the patient is discharged. Each day of hotel or nursing care costs money. Thus the quicker any diagnostic tests are initiated, completed and interpreted the fewer days of care are needed. The addition to the cost of X-ray and pathological departments in providing a rapid service which may involve under-utilized facilities at certain periods needs to be compared with the cost of a longer stay. Moreover, the doctor responsible for the case has to find a balance between requesting initially tests which *might* later be needed and waiting for the first test results before deciding whether a further batch of tests is required. The second alternative may involve the cost of extra days of care and the first may involve the cost of ordering tests which are found later to have been unnecessary.

Once a treatment procedure has been selected it should be swiftly administered, unless there are medical reasons for delay. For example, orders for pharmaceuticals need to be rapidly met unless the additional costs of providing a speedier service are greater than the cost of a longer stay. If an operation is required, it should be performed as soon as the patient's condition permits, unless again the additional cost of more rapid service exceeds the cost of a longer stay. Thus the economic efficiency of a hospital depends upon the correct 'gearing' of its facilities – for example, on whether the provision of pathology or X-ray facilities is sufficient to process reasonable in-patient and out-patient demands without undue delay and on the number of theatres and theatre teams and the number of hours for which they are used.

The efficient running of a hospital depends to a considerable extent upon the decision-takers being available when decisions have to be taken. And the main decision-taker is the doctor in charge of the case. The doctor who visits only on certain days or is only available at certain hours, increases the length of hospital stay unless he has delegated the responsibility for taking decisions to other doctors who are on the spot. In each case a balance has to be struck between the provision of facilities to meet all demands immediately both by day and by night which would involve considerable under-utilization of staff and facilities, and the extra costs generated not only for the hospital but for the patient (e.g. loss of working time) by waiting for the next procedure or the next decision to be taken. An efficient hospital is one which can provide the required standard of service at lowest cost including as part of cost the amortization and interest charges on buildings and equipment and the rent of land.

On each day of care the practicability of discharge needs to be considered for each patient. Is further bed-rest needed for this patient?[20] If this patient were discharged on this day where could he or she go to? What services does the patient need and where else could these services be provided? Would this be at lower cost and could the treatment be continued at the necessary standard? Can the patient continue treatment at home? If so, what would be burdens for the patient and his family and what would be the costs of this alternative?

In calculating the cost of extra hospital days of stay it is wrong to look at the average daily cost of the hospital, or of the ward, or even of patients with the particular diagnosis. A day of care for a convalescent patient costs much less than average costs, and it is this 'marginal' day cost which needs to be compared with the cost of alternative forms of care. There are essentially three elements in the running costs of a hospital – hotel cost, care cost and diagnostic/treatment cost. The hotel cost is roughly the same for each day in the hospital. The care cost depends on whether the patient is confined to bed and has to be fed and washed and whether the patient can get up to perform bodily functions. Patients who are seriously ill normally progress from total dependency to self-care. They need a decreasing amount of care as they advance towards recovery. Diagnostic and treatment cost varies greatly between patients depending on what diagnostic tests are requested, whether surgery is required and the cost of other treatments. Normally treatment costs are highest in the first few days of the hospital stay. Thus the average cost per day of a hospital will vary according to the precise functions it is performing. What proportions of patients, for example, are surgical patients? What type of surgery is practised.

Payments made to hospitals at a standard rate per day cannot reflect real costs. If the rate is right for the average hospital, it will be too high for some and too low for others. A hospital management which knew its costs could make a surplus by discriminating in the type of patient it was prepared to admit. Secondly, whether or not costs are covered by standard daily payment will depend on how long the patient stays in hospital. Days at the end of the stay, when the patient normally costs the hospital less, are needed to compensate the hospital for the early costly days of stay. This point is important as it is common practice in continental Western Europe for hospitals to be paid at a daily rate by health insurance agencies. If the payment is inadequate for a particular hospital, a deficit can nevertheless be avoided by lengthening the length of stay. Thus in both France and Western Germany hospitals tend to keep patients as long as possible in order to increase their income.[21]

Unnecessary Admissions

However hard it may be to establish it in practice, there is in theory a maximum number of hospital beds needed to serve a given population with given demographic structure at any given time. This maximum depends not only on the length of time which patients need to stay but on the avoidance of 'unnecessary' admissions. While a more developed country may be able to afford to provide hospital services on the required scale, a developing country may be unable to do so. To secure an efficient use of resources, patients should only be admitted to hospital when a given standard of care can only be provided in hospital or can be provided more cheaply in hospital.

At one extreme there are some medical procedures which it would be more expensive to provide at home and some which could not be provided as safely at home. But it is still important to be sure that these procedures do actually improve the prospects for the patient. For example the treatment at home for acute ischaemic heart disease was recently compared in a random controlled trial with hospital treatment, including a variable term in a coronary care unit.[22] The results for those patients accepting the trial did not 'suggest that there is any medical gain in admission to hospital with coronary care units compared with treatment at home'.[23]

While some procedures may need to be undertaken at a hospital it does not follow that the patient has to stay in the hospital overnight. Patients are often admitted to hospital for diagnosis tests: more of this testing might be undertaken on an out-patient basis. A procedure may be performed at the hospital on an out-patient basis and the patient may be discharged to his home where follow-up visits may be made by doctors, nurses and others and whatever else is needed for good care may be provided. For example, several experiments are in progress in Britain to examine the total effects of performing operations for varicose veins, hernia and abortion on an out-patient basis. It has been found that day care was considerably cheaper than in-patient care for the treatment of varicose veins and hernia.[24] Treatment at or from home may not necessarily be cheaper than treatment in hospital. It has, for example, been found that normal confinements cost less in hospital consultant units than in home care programmes.[25]

The admission rate may vary according to whether (as, for example, in Canada and the United States) doctors who practise in the community have access to hospital beds where they can treat their own patients, or (as, for example, in Britain and Sweden) doctors practising in the community do not normally have beds under their control. In the latter system of organization decisions about admissions are made by the separate medical staff of the hospitals. It appears that where beds are in short supply there are pressures on these doctors to adopt stricter criteria on admission and these criteria become known to doctors practising outside hospital. When hospital beds are readily available, more patients are admitted for short spells for diagnostic and other reasons including those who could be looked after at home.[26]

In both systems of medical care organization there are advantages in admission to hospital for the doctor whom the patient first consults. British general practitioners are paid on a broad capitation system. If they pass on to the hospital those patients who need more time and care and are most likely to need home visits, this will lighten their work load without any loss of remuneration. In North America, quite apart from economic incentives to patients and doctors, the admission of a relatively ill patient to hospital involves less time and trouble for the doctor than care at home. In hospital there is a trained staff: this relieves the doctor of the task of instructing relatives of the patient on how to care for and nurse the patient. While the ultimate responsibility for the patient remains with the doctor responsible for his admission, unless he transfers it to a colleague, he can delegate much of this responsibility to the nursing and other hospital staff.

Whether a patient needs to be admitted to hospital depends on the quality of service that could be provided at home and on the social situation of the patient and on what services can be effectively provided in the patient's home and at what cost. What is the cost of suitable transport to take the patient to and from hospital? Frequent, even daily visits may be required for some patients to receive proper treatment. Some patients may need to stay in hospital because daily travel would be an excessive strain or involve risks. In others, hospital care may be required because of the social costs of care at home and the attitudes of the patient and the relatives. In other cases a balance should be found between the cost of moving staff and equipment to the patient's home and the cost of taking the patient to the hospital. First, there are the costs which fall on the health services. Second, there are the costs which fall upon the patient and the household, including indirect costs. For example, having a patient at home may mean that a family member has to give up work to care for the patient or work less. Admitting a mother or father of dependent children to hospital may mean that someone has to stay at home from work to look after the children or that a relative or paid help has to come and stay or other extra costs are incurred by the family. All these wider costs need to be considered when the decision on admission is taken.

Supply Creates Demand

It has been shown both in Britain and in the United States that hospital beds which are provided tend to be used. The more beds, the more patients are admitted to hospital and possibly also the longer the length of stay. Within limits, supply creates demands by doctors for the extra beds. The first statement of this proposition in the United States is attributed to Roemer in 1959[27] who studied bed use in different counties and states. In a county of upstate New York, he found that an increase in bed supply of 42 per cent led to an increase in patient days of 28 per cent within three years. Later evidence is available from a careful study by Rafferty.[28] In England this conclusion was reached by Feldstein who analysed bed use and bed availability in different hospital regions,[29] and by others.[30]

While extra beds tend to be used, this does not indicate whether either the original or the final number of beds was more or less than was 'needed'. While some patients may be admitted to hospital unnecessarily and some stays may be unnecessarily long, there may be other patients who need hospital care and do not receive it. Some who need medical care do not seek it and some may be sick at home who should be in hospital, particularly those who live far from a hospital. Where there are financial barriers to the use of hospitals or where poorer patients are stigmatized or admitted to inferior accommodation, it is these patients who are likely to be over represented among under-users.

Conclusion

The principles governing the efficient planning and operation of hospitals apply in both developing and more developed countries. While a more developed country can provide hospitals for all who might benefit from care in hospital, the resources of a developing country, particularly in trained manpower, in the ability to purchase equipment and supplies and in taxable capacity may make it impossible to provide hospital services on this scale. Thus priorities need to be established for the use of hospital services, and the design, equipment and organization of hospitals have to be adjusted to the local situation. Hospitals may be constructed in local materials using traditional methods. More labour-intensive methods of operating may be used and simple equipment installed which can be used and repaired by staff without elaborate training. In view of the shortage of hospital beds, it is particularly important that the length of stay should be kept to a minimum. As much treatment as possible should be provided outside the hospital and the hospital should only be used for patients with a high prospect of deriving benefit from the special services which can only be provided in a hospital. We develop these themes at greater length in Chapter 11.

Not only in more developed countries but in developing countries the major part of national health resources are usually devoted to hospitals. For this reason it is of special importance to avoid waste and make sure that the highest quality of service is secured for those who really need hospital services out of such national resources as can be spent on them. This can only be secured by planning the hospital system to ensure that the size of units is such as to provide quality service at economical cost, that hospitals are rationally located, and that the number of beds provided is adjusted to the need, which, in turn, depends on appropriate lengths of stay and the avoidance of unnecessary admission. It is by no means easy to plan a hospital system: much of the information needed to do the job is difficult to collect and interpret. But the price of not attempting to do so is high – not only in wasted resources but in pockets of poor quality service.

NOTES

1. See p. 23, above.

2. D. Neuhauser and F. Turcotte, 'Cost and Quality Plan in Different Types of Hospitals', *Annals of the American Academy of Political and Social Sciences*, January 1972, p. 53.

3. For example, the average size of non-federal short-term hospitals in the United States was 123 beds in 1963, 11 per cent had less than 25 beds. Quoted in C. M. Lindsay and J. M. Buchanan, 'The Organisation and Financing of Medical Care in the United States', B.M.A., *Health Service Financing*, p. 545.

4. The average size of German hospitals is 188 beds. S. Eichhorn, 'German Federal Republic', *Health Service Prospects*, Lancet and N.P.H.T., 1973, p. 84.

5. M. Pauly and M. Redisch, 'The Not-for-Profit Hospital as a Physician's Cooperative', *American Economic Review*, March 1973.

6. C. M. Lindsay and I. M. Buchanan, op. cit., p. 549.

7. H. and Anne Somers, *Medicare and the Hospitals*, Brookings, 1967, p. 198.

8. S. E. Berki, op. cit., pp. 13–14.

9. Piel report quoted by S. E. Berki, op. cit., p. 196.

10. ibid., p. 204.

11. H. M. Somers, 'Delivery of Health Care: Do we know where we are going?' in *Social Economies for the 1970s*, ed. G. F. Rohrlich, Dunellen, 1970, p. 102.

12. In the United States travel costs for all concerned have been estimated as 19 per cent of a hospital's operating costs. Quoted in H. E. Klarman, *The Economics of Health*, Columbia University Press, 1965, p. 143.

13. M. S. Feldstein, *Economic Analysis for Health Service Efficiency*, Markham, Chicago, 1968.

14. S. E. Berki, op. cit., p. 115.

15. J. Simpson, A. Mair, R. G. Thomas, H. N. Willard, H. J. Bakst, *Custom and Practice in Medical Care*, O.U.P., 1968, p. 41.

16. See M. A. Heasman and Vera Carstairs, 'Inpatient Management: Variations in some Aspects of Practice in Scotland', *British Medical Journal*, 1971, vol. 1, p. 495–8.

17. loc. cit.

18. Simpson et al., op. cit., p. 43.

19. For short-term general hospitals in 1968 the length of stay was 11·9 days in Sweden, 11·6 days in Britain and 8·4 days in the United States. Odin W. Anderson, *Health Care: Can there be Equity?* Wiley, 1972, p. 131.

20. It has been shown, for example, contrary to earlier views, that bed rest is not important for patients with pulmonary tuberculosis. For evidence, see A. L. Cochrane, *Effectiveness and Efficiency*, N.P.H.T., 1973, p. 45.

21. M. Pflanz, 'German Health Insurance', *International Journal of Health Services*, Vol. 1, No. 4, November 1971, p. 325. The point is also made more generally in R. F. Bridgman and M. I. Roemer, *Hospital Legislation and Hospital Systems*, Public Health Papers, No. 50, W.H.O., Geneva, 1973, p. 168; and P. Cornillot and P. Bonamour, 'France', in *Health Service Prospects*, Lancet and N.P.H.T., 1973, p. 74.

22. H. G. Mather *et al.*, 'Acute myocardial infarction: home and hospital treatment', *British Medical Journal*, 1971, Vol. 3, p. 334.

23. A. L. Cochrane, op. cit., p. 29.

24. D. Piachaud and J. M. Weddell, 'The Economics of Treating Varicose Veins', *International Journal of Epidemiology*, Vol. 1, No. 3, p. 287 and J. H. Babson, *Disease Costing*, Manchester University Press, 1973.

25. Babson, op. cit., the same finding was made by Ferster and Pethyridge, *Hospital and Health Service Review*, July 1973.

26. S. E. Berki, op. cit., pp. 147, 158.

27. Max Shain and Milton Roemer, 'Hospital Costs Relate to the Supply of Beds', *Modern Hospital*, 92, No. 4, April 1959, pp. 71–3, 168.

28. J. A. Rafferty, 'Patterns of Hospital use', *Journal of Political Economy*, Vol. 79, No. 1, 1971, pp. 154–65. Discussed in S. E. Berki, op. cit., p. 147.

29. M. S. Feldstein, op. cit., pp. 193–222.

30. For example, G. Forsyth and R. L. Logan, *The Demand for Medical Care*, N.P.H.T., 1960.

CHAPTER 8

The Search for Priorities

In virtually every country, health services are taking a large and growing share of health resources. As an increasing proportion of the cost is falling on government and social security, more and more countries are searching for ways of containing the cost and securing better value for money. How much are costs increasing and why are they increasing? How is it possible to contain cost and secure better value for all the money which is spent?

Trends in Health Expenditure

Recent comparative data on health expenditure in different countries is not available.[1] It is not possible to identify all the separate services and activities which contribute to health, it is only possible to measure those activities which different countries group together under health services and the coverage of these services is not standardized between countries. There is, for example, no clear and uniform international definition of a drug, a hospital or of nursing staff. In some countries health services are responsible for services which in other countries are provided by the social services. Moreover virtually all developing countries lack reliable data on private expenditure on health.

While comparisons between the expenditure of different countries cannot be made with great accuracy, trend data conforming to definitions established by each country is more reliable. For this purpose we are concerned with expenditure on real resources whether paid for by government, social security, voluntary insurance, charity, industry or patients and their families. In view of the difficulty of applying meaningful price indices to health services, the trends are shown in relation to measures of total resources.

In the United States health expenditure has risen from 3·6 per cent of gross national product in 1928–9 to 5·2 per cent in 1959–60 and 7·7 per cent in 1973–4.[2] In the Netherlands the total cost of health care has risen from 3·3 per cent of gross national income at market prices in 1953 to 5·4 per cent in 1968.[3] In France the consumption of medical services has risen from 3·2 per cent of gross national product in 1950 to 5·5 per cent in 1971.[4] In New Zealand, health expenditure increased from 5·8 per cent to 6·7 per cent of national income between 1960–61 and 1968–69.[5] Estimates for the U.S. Department of Health, Education and Welfare of the growth of expenditure in a number of countries during the sixties are shown in Table 2.[6]

TABLE 2

Health Expenditure in Seven Countries

Country	Year	Per cent of G.N.P.	Year	Per cent of G.N.P.
Canada	1961	6·0	1969	7·3
United States	1961/2	5·8	1969	6·8
Sweden	1962	5·4	1969	6·7
Netherlands	1963	4·8	1969	5·9
Federal Republic of Germany	1961	4·5	1969	5·7
France	1963	4·4	1969	5·7
United Kingdom	1961/2	4·2	1969	4·8

In 1969, Canada, United States and Sweden were all spending about 7 per cent of their resources on health services. What perhaps is more significnt is the rate of increase. All the countries except the United Kingdom were expanding their health services at such a rate that between 0·1 per cent and 0·2 per cent of national product more was being devoted to them per year. If this trend continues there will be several countries who will be devoting a tenth of all their resources to health services before the year 2000. Indeed in France forecasts show that medical expenditure could represent 11–13 per cent of gross national product by 1985.[7] At present rates of growth health services in Australia which consumed 5·3 per cent of gross national product in 1973 could rise to 12 per cent of gross national product in 25 years.[8]

In all these countries national product was growing, so the rate of increase in real terms was faster than these figures suggest. If the consumer price index is used to give a rough indication of price rises, Canada, Sweden and the Netherlands were all spending around 10 per cent more each year on health services; the rate of increase drops to 5–8 per cent if a wage index is used to correct for changing prices.[9]

One might expect countries with low rates of growth (e.g. United States and the United Kingdom) or extensive free services to have higher increases in the proportion of G.N.P. devoted to health services than countries with a faster rate of growth (e.g. France or the Netherlands). This is not borne out by the Table. The United Kingdom with its financing of largely free health services primarily out of central government funds has restricted the growth of health services expenditure more than all the other countries. Sweden, on the other hand, which relies heavily on government financing (particularly local government) has had one of the fastest rates of growth.

Six main reasons can be given for the growth of health services expenditure in real terms (i.e. excluding the impact of rising prices and levels of remuneration). First, in some countries the role of government health services and insurance, particularly social insurance, has been increasing. A higher proportion of the population has been covered by such schemes. This is noticeably the case in the United States. Moreover in the United States, up to 1969, little had been done to limit the costs which providers could pass on to consumers.

Secondly, people are expecting more from health services. They seek help with minor conditions and disabilities which they would have treated themselves or just tolerated years earlier. They expect to be cured and cured rapidly of each and every ailment.

Thirdly, health services consist to a large extent of personal services rendered by doctors, nurses and others. The introduction of mechanization can reduce the labour requirements in some areas of the health services and provide a service of similar or better quality at lower cost. For example, this is the case with laundries, certain laboratory services, and methods of transporting supplies and equipment. But the scope for mechanization is considerably less than in manufacturing industry or agriculture. Moreover productivity advances in hospitals have tended to increase the sophistication of care rather than save labour. The health services sector is also under pressure to improve standards of personal care and reduce hours of work of care staff as the economy gets richer. Thus the health sector employs more staff per patient and for this as well as other reasons has to pay a higher proportion of its resources for each staff member of a given skill whom it employs.

Fourthly, not only has the population been growing in these

countries, but the proportion of the aged in the population has been increasing faster still: the aged consume much more of health services than younger persons. In the United States it is estimated that in 1973 28 per cent of personal health care spending was devoted to those aged 65 or over.[10] People who would have died 25 or 50 years ago relatively young from some infectious disease are living longer to become victims of the degenerative diseases of old age, many of which are costly to treat. There are more infirm and elderly needing care.

Fifthly, and most important of all, the expansion of medical knowledge, new pharmaceuticals and new treatment procedures, from transplants to kidney machines, have greatly extended the range of care which physicians can provide for the individual patient. These new techniques, both of diagnosis and treatment, have greatly increased both the staff and equipment needed to treat certain categories of patients. The process can be most readily identified by comparing what younger doctors request for a patient with a given diagnosis with what older doctors request. What is less clear is precisely how much of this increase contributes to the treatment of the patient. But what is certain is that 'medical advances leave a progressively more difficult set of problems to be faced. With the conquest of infectious diseases less tractable forms of illness such as cancer – whose causes are more complex, and whose treatment tends to be more expensive – claim proportionately more lives.'[11]

A sixth reason for rising cost in some countries is an increase in unnecessary or inappropriate services. There are quite wide variations in what countries are spending on health services and in what they have been spending over the past ten or twenty years. This is true whether one makes comparisons by translating expenditure per head into dollars at prevailing rates of exchange, or whether one looks at the proportion of gross national product spent on health services. It is true also if one tries to escape the difficulties of varying prices and remuneration levels by comparing such input statistics as are available – for example, doctors or nurses per head or hospital beds per head.

What however is important is that it is hard to find any correlation between resources spent and level of health at least as indicated by mortality rates. Robert Maxwell recently put together some of the key data.[12] According to his estimates in 1969 the United States spent 298 dollars per head, Sweden 234 dollars, France and Germany about 150 dollars, the Netherlands 116 dollars (in 1968) and U.K. 93 dollars. The U.S.A. and Sweden at that time spent about 6½ per cent of G.N.P. on health services, France, West Germany and the Netherlands 5·7–5·9 per cent and the U.K. 4.6 per cent.

The U.S. spent most by both criteria, yet its mortality indicators were the worst at the perinatal stage, for men aged 35–44 or 45–54, for women aged 35–44 or 45–54. It was also nearly the worst for infant and maternal mortality. On the other hand, Sweden and the Netherlands had, on the whole, much better results than the other countries. Britain, the lowest spender by both criteria, had better mortality results on six of these indicators than either Germany or France.[12] Measured simply by mortality indicators, spending more on health does not necessarily buy you better health.

There are many possible explanations of this lack of correspondence between spending and these crude health indicators. The first is that postponed mortality is only part of what health services are trying to achieve. The second is that some of the important causes of premature death lie in the environment in which people live, and how they live. Thus some countries may need more health services in the widest sense to achieve the same level of health as other countries, or alternatively, these societies want the best health they can attain without giving up their unhealthy habits. For whatever reason, health services are failing to come to grips or have no power to influence the major causes of ill-health. If these societies wanted good health, they were over-investing in health services compared to other methods of social intervention. But there is also a third explanation. Much of what is currently spent on health services in many countries is not spent efficiently even for the achievement of the somewhat limited objectives of current services.

The Search for Priorities

The simplest way to control health spending is to make each individual pay part of the cost when services are used. Thus most of the Bills for comprehensive health insurance in the United States envisage what is called in that country co-payment, deductibles and co-insurance – or what in other countries would be called charges on consumers. But the consequence of such policies is to restrain the consumption of the poorer and place virtually no restriction on the expenditure of the better off. Charges of any kind frustrate the objective of securing that health services are readily available to all.

An alternative approach is to try to assert priorities and in particular to secure that unnecessary services are not provided and, if further choices have to be made, to ensure that the more important services are retained and less important services are not provided. But this raises fundamental questions. What criteria can be used for judging what are necessary and unnecessary services and who should decide? What is the objective of health services? Is the provision of services the most cost-effective way of securing this objective? How can one measure progress towards the objective?

The objective of health services is to improve standards of health. People want good health for its own sake not because it may enable them to work more or earn more. Members of all societies would rather be well than sick and wish to live longer or at least as long as life is enjoyable or has a prospect of being so. Indeed, in many cultures, to want to die or be ill is in itself regarded as evidence of sickness. Ill-health restricts the way in which people spend their lives and it may also involve pain. Thus the objectives of health services and other services which contribute to health standards are to prevent and cure ill-health and restore health wherever this is possible. In so far as cure cannot be effected, then the objectives are to relieve pain, or the distressing symptoms of mental illness, compensate for disability, to provide care, either directly or to give support and assistance to family members providing care.

Improved health is the goal, and prevention, cure and care are the three strategies for reaching this goal. But how much can actually be done for a co-operative population other than to provide care, either in the preventive field or in the curative field, depends on medical knowledge. Hence the need to advance medical knowledge by research. It also depends on the number of people who have absorbed the relevant knowledge and acquired the relevant skills. Hence the need to educate and train health personnel.

The Role of Preventive Medicine

The causes of ill-health and disability lie deep in the fabric of the societies in which we live and many of them are not precisely known. In addition to diseases transferred directly from human to human through the air or physical contact, or through contact with insects and animals, there are diseases caused by the inhalation of polluted air, the consumption of polluted food or drink, or by the consumption of too little, too much, or improperly balanced food or drink. For example, a lack of Vitamin D can cause rickets and an excess can cause renal disease. Too much physical and mental exertion may cause strain and too little physical and mental activity can create other health problems. What diseases an individual contracts depends not only on the environment to which he is exposed but on whether he is in a receptive state – on his immunity status, on the standard of his nutrition, on his previous illnesses and on many other physical and psychological factors.

The body may be damaged by accidents in the natural environment, by accidents involving man-made machines, by the violence of men or animals or by inappropriate or inadequate medical care – particularly ill-chosen pharmaceuticals. Disability may be caused by the malformation of mind or body or by the natural deterioration or wearing out of mind and body. The climate, customs, technology and living standards of each country affect its pattern of disease. Hence the need to provide adequate housing and food, to limit the risks of accidents and violence, to promote habits of work, diet and exercise which are healthy and discourage those which are not and to monitor all the effects on health of a changing environment. For example, in France 'over 40 per cent of the total expenditure for health services is attributable to the treatment of alcohol-related diseases and about 50 per cent of all hospital beds are occupied by patients suffering from such diseases.'[13]

One cause of ill-health is pregnancy which occurs when the mother is still debilitated by an earlier birth or still weaning an earlier child or is in poor health. This can endanger both the mother's health and the health of the child. Moreover excessive reproduction is a major cause of low levels of living – perhaps the largest underlying cause of ill-health in the world today. In countries faced with this problem, the control of births can be the key to development and higher standards of health. Methods of birth control have been known and practised in most, perhaps, all societies for centuries, but it is only in the past few decades that really effective and cheap methods of family planning have been developed, other than obstacles to or interruption of sexual activity. Hence the need to make these methods available to all, to inform people about them and encourage them to use them for the benefit of their own health, that of their family and national well-being and development.

Scientific knowledge limits the amount which can be spent with any certainty that it will be useful in preventing ill-health. It is known, for example, that vaccination against smallpox can be highly effective, that examining the blood of pregnant women can prevent serious morbidity and fatality in newborn infants, and that it is useful to screen newborn infants for phenylketonuria and congenital dislocation of the hip and to examine the hearing and vision of young. children.[14] But there is at present insufficient evidence to justify screening for carcinoma of the bronchus, breast or cervix.

Many more causes of ill-health are known than can be prevented. While cigarette smoking is known to be correlated with lung cancer, little is known about how to persuade people not to smoke. While obesity is known to be correlated with earlier death, little is known about how to persuade people to diet. While certain observable abnormalities are known to be associated with certain diseases, nevertheless the vast majority of people with these abnormalities will not contract these diseases. This is the case with arterial blood pressure, blood-sugar levels, iron deficiency anaemia in non-pregnant women and intra-occular pressure. The number of screening procedures which are at present of practical value in the early detection of disease is very small. Moreover, some procedures produce clear results but only for a tiny proportion of the population (e.g. for porphyria variegata). It would be extremely costly if these procedures were applied to the whole population as a routine basis. In the more developed countries, this position is being reached in the case of screening for tuberculosis.

There are other fields where preventive actions could be taken but are not for other reasons. More and better roads would reduce the incidence of accidents but at substantial social and economic cost. Cars could be made much safer but also at greater cost. More effective safety devices could be fitted on machines in factories but often at the cost of reduced production. Industrial pollution could also be reduced but at considerable cost to industry.

The growth of travel – particularly rapid travel – within countries and between countries is responsible for considerable spread of disease. Not only may bilharzia be spread throughout continents by migrant workers but air travellers are constantly transferring such diseases as typhus, smallpox and cholera from countries where they are endemic to countries normally free of them. No longer is a 'cordon sanitaire' policy practicable for any country. Rarely is it acceptable to restrict travel to improve health.

Legal restrictions could be imposed to improve health. For example, driving in a motor vehicle without wearing a seat-belt could be made a legal offence. The importation or sale of cigarettes could be banned but this would involve a vast loss of tax revenue which would have to be found from another source. The importation and manufacture of asbestos could be prohibited but at the cost of a much higher incidence of fires or of the use of much more expensive methods of construction. There are limits to the extent to which societies are prepared to spend money, raise costs and restrict individual liberty to promote higher standards of health and secure a safer environment.

Action to prevent ill-health extends far beyond the health field. Some preventive activities are undertaken by specialized health workers and others by those with a variety of other skills. It is therefore not possible to measure precisely what a society is spending on preventive health. For example, health education is undertaken by parents, teachers, safety committees and many others besides those employed by the health services to prevent ill-health. Action to improve the environment, nutritional standards and to secure a more equitable distribution of income involves many different sectors of government activity.

The Role of Curative Medicine

The term 'cure' is used here to mean intervention to interrupt or mitigate the natural history of disease, or improve the functioning of mind or body which is impaired for any reason. It includes social and occupational rehabilitation in so far as this improves the functioning of the patient.

The body will fight off many illnesses without intervention. It is therefore difficult to be sure that intervention has expedited the process, reduced the severity of symptoms or secured an improvement which would not have occurred without the intervention. Neither the patient nor the doctor can always be sure that intervention has been more effective than non-intervention. Cures are not only effected by health personnel. In all societies many conditions are treated effectively within the household.

The most reliable proof that a particular intervention is effective is by random controlled trial. This method of testing remedies has only existed for some fifty years and only been used on a considerable scale for twenty years. Much of what is taught in medical schools was never validated by evidence of this rigour. There are probably many forms of intervention which are in frequent use, including some which involve the use of large resources, but may not actually improve the prospects of recovery: some may even be harmful. There are however ethical problems in testing established medical procedures and in many cases such tests could not be justified as the theoretical evidence and animal evidence in support of a treatment are so strong. But no random control trials have been undertaken, for example, to test the usefulness of dietetic therapy for phenylketo-nuria or of surgery for carcinoma of the lung.[15] Thus while there is a definite limit to what can be usefully spent on cure, it is not at present possible to establish the amount.

The Role of 'Care'

The phrase 'medical care' is often used loosely to include both cure and care. By *care* is meant here the provision of standards of bodily comfort and emotional or psychological support. It includes helping patients and those close to them to accept and adapt to the limitations imposed by illness or disability. It includes support for the patient if relapse or recurrence occurs and assessment of changing social, psychological and medical needs. In the case of fatal illness, it includes the management of the physical problems and emotional distress of the dying person and the support of the family.

The ultimate assessment of the effectiveness of the care of a patient can only be made by that patient, though others may have to try and form a judgment on the patient's behalf. For, while the patient can assess standards of amenity and bodily comfort, he cannot know what standards of comfort could have been achieved with his condition nor can he know the long-term effects of different methods of relieving pain. Care in all its aspects can only be indirectly and imperfectly measured.

There is no clear limit to what can be spent on care. More can be spent to improve, if not standards of physical comfort, at least the amenities and support available to the sick, disabled and dying just as it can be spent to provide greater amenities and support for those who are well. Somehow decisions have to be taken on what standards of amenity to provide, bearing in mind that it will normally cost more to provide a given standard of amenity to a sick or disabled person than to a person in normal health. There is, however, no evident limit on what can be spent to provide emotional or psychological support. This aspect of care is provided by many others than those trained in the health professions. But substantial demands are made on doctors and other health workers for help with emotional problems some of which make the 'patient' feel sick. Care is quantitatively important in the health services of the more developed countries. Some rough indication of its importance is given by the fact that 22 per cent of reimbursements under Medicare in the United States are for aged persons who died in that year.[16] In Britain it is estimated that between 25 per cent and 30 per cent of hospital beds are occupied by people who will be dead within twelve months.[17] Some of these beds were of course used in valiant attempts to save the patient's life which were unsuccessful. But there were also large numbers of further beds used by long-stay patients for whom neither cure nor discharge was a serious possibility with given medical technology. In general practice a third or more of consultations are viewed by some practitioners as having an emotional or psychological origin.

The Role of Research

Research relevant to the health field includes the study of what causes ill-health and what will cure it and what may prevent or cure it, either more effectively or more efficiently – with a smaller use of resources. There is no limit to what could be spent on research. No one can be sure that a particular line of research could not possibly be useful to society. Judgments can, however, be made on whether a particular line of research looks more promising than another.

Among the relatively neglected fields of research is assessment of standards of care. How far, for example, can bodily comfort be increased? How best can emotional support be given and by whom? How can people be enabled to live the fullest lives with a given extent of disability? Also relatively neglected is research to establish how desired results in prevention or cure can be secured with a smaller use of resources.

The Role of Education and Training

Standards of health in the future depend partly upon the transfer of knowledge and skill to later generations. Decisions about the level of investment in training and education depend upon the priority to be given to health in the future. If the coverage of the population with preventive and curative services is judged to be inadequate and extra resources are to be provided, decisions have to be taken about the period of time after which it is planned to achieve adequate coverage. Similarly in countries where cure and preventive services are well developed, investment in education and training will be needed to maintain services in the future and provide such further services as greater medical knowledge will require.

What Priority to Health?

While some societies appear to attach more importance to health than others, no society gives it absolute priority. People are left with considerable liberty to harm their health and that of others though financial and other penalties may be imposed on those who do so. If better health were made the supreme objective, vast resources would be devoted to health research and severe restrictions would be placed on individual liberty.

Changes in health status cannot simply be attributed to the relative success or failure of past or present health services. This is because of the vast range of environmental and other influences which cause changes in health status. If the environment is generating more ill-health, more services are needed to prevent, cure and care. As not all states of health can be prevented or cured, a decline in health status over time can occur despite better health services or an improvement in health status can occur despite deteriorating health services. Indeed in the more developed countries, such changes in health status as occur are only to a small extent due to changes in health services. Wars, accidents, changes in social habits, speed limits and car safety requirements and even the weather seem to have more effect on year-by-year changes in mortality and morbidity than changes in health services. Similarly despite the vast scientific capability for the cure and prevention of disease in developing countries, epidemics and changes in rainfall are still usually the major causes of short-term changes in mortality. Even in the case of longer-term changes in health status, it is only in relatively narrow fields that it is possible to differentiate the effects of health services activity from other changes affecting a particular society.

In developing countries, inadequate nutrition is a major cause of death – particularly in children. 'Taking the world as a whole, about

10,000,000 children are at great risk of death, and even if treated, one-third of them would probably still die from hunger and malnutrition. In addition, the condition of 90,000,000 children with moderate forms of malnutrition may suddenly be aggravated by an infection . . . It is estimated that several hundreds of thousands of children become blind every year for lack of Vitamin A in the diet.'[18]

Therefore while factories produce goods and farms produce food, we cannot say precisely how much improved health status has been 'produced' by health services. Nevertheless, improved health status, and care where health status cannot be improved, are still the ultimate objectives of health services. Doctor consultations, drugs consumed, hospital bed-days provided, nursing hours of care, pathological tests performed or X-rays taken and read are useful or useless depending on whether they contribute towards these objectives. They are inputs – or perhaps it is more helpful to think of them as through-puts. They are certainly not outputs.

If we could measure all the influences on health status other than those of health services, we could indirectly measure the effect of health services as a residual. But we know even less about the precise effect of these variables on health status than we do about the effects of health services. At least this is true of health status as an aggregate. Only in narrow areas do we know both the causes of ill-health and the effectiveness of measures to combat them.

In the case of the young and middle-aged it is often possible to identify one specific cause of ill-health. But in the aged, multiple causes of ill-health are more often operative: health services are engaged in a constant battle to postpone the ill effects on health status of the aging process. Thus it is difficult to establish a norm. What, for example, would be the health status of an average person aged 80 if there were no health services? Or, more difficult still, what would be the health status of *that* person of 80 if health services had not been provided at different stages of life? And how important is the care of an 80-year-old compared with a 20-year-old or a 10-year-old?

A Health Status Index

At first sight the concept of the health status of the population may seem to have a clear meaning and be capable of measurement either on a single dimension or on a number of different dimensions which could be readily aggregated together in an agreed and objective way. In practice, however, no country has regular statistics purporting to measure health status as a whole and there is no agreement on how an index of health status should be constructed. Many countries have data on death by age, sex and cause, but the prevention of 'premature' death (whatever that means) is only a part of health status. We need to be able to measure the quality of life as well as the quantity. And this is where the main difficulties lie.

Should health status be measured in clinical terms? For example, should health status be measured from levels of blood haemoglobin and cholesterol and the results of urinalysis, from measures of height and weight, from the absence of certain physical defects and from tests of mental functions? Or should measurement be subjective? Should it be based on what people say they feel about their health? Or should it be based on how some consensus of doctors or others would scale the importance of the effects of certain health conditions and disabilities? Or should the measurement be behavioural – for example the extent to which people are independent of others and can bath, shop, cook, clean, dress, go to the toilet, move about without the help of others? There are obvious practical advantages of using behavioural measures rather than clinical measures as we lack tools to measure all we would want to measure in objective clinical terms. Moreover it would be very expensive to apply regular clinical tests to large samples of the population, assuming that the cooperation of a sufficient sample could be obtained. In the case of subjective measures we cannot be sure that any method of measurement has recorded what is most relevant. Who is to decide what is relevant?

A behavioural measure, such as the restriction of usual activities,[19] will not be sensitive to minor health failings which people take in their stride. Moreover, the appropriateness of particular measures depends on the culture and on the environment and thus no one measure is necessarily suitable for comparison between countries or between different parts of a country or over long periods of time. For example, the amount of effort required for daily living depends on whether there is water piped into the house or water has to be fetched and on whether there is an indoor W.C. It depends on the tasks which people of different age, sex and social class want to undertake – on what they are culturally expected to do when they are well. All measures of what people do, fail to tell us what they *could* do. Nor do they tell us about the discomfort and time taken by those who attempt to function 'normally' or more 'normally' despite their disabilities. Indeed, they tell us nothing about pain, discomfort, emotional stress, psychological deprivation or any other aspect of being 'sick' which may be unpleasant. For example, some dependent bed-ridden persons may be in great pain, while others suffer little pain. Moreover the effects of ill-health are not only suffered by the sick or disabled person: relatives and others may suffer social, psychological and economic costs due to responsibilities for the care of the sick or disabled person.

A health status index needs first of all, to be capable of measuring the health status of a population at a point in time. To become a single indicator, weights have to be given to different states of health below 'the normal' with a particularly large weight for a person who has died prematurely. We are thus deep in the uncharted sea of inter-personal comparisons where there are methods of drawing maps but no agreement on what is sea, land and frontier. Secondly, health status needs to be measured over a period of time. How many of the population died prematurely or had how many spells of ill-health or disability, of what severity and what duration during the course of (say) a year? And if a health status index is to be used to determine priorities in the allocation of a health service budget, we need to know the probabilities of intervention improving health status over a period of time; or, alternatively, the probabilities of preventing a deterioration to lower health status or death or postponing such a deterioration or death. If choices are to be made between different programmes, these probabilities need to be known for each programme and indeed for each method of securing the programme's objective. At present, epidemiological knowledge is far too limited for health planning to be based on a health status index even if agreement were reached about how such an index should be weighted or constructed. Moreover there is no possible method by which the care output of health services can be weighted against the health improvement output of health services.

There have been no lack of attempts to construct health status indices and some have been demonstrated operationally in narrow fields.[20] Economists and other social scientists have proffered bold solutions which have attracted more interest among their professional colleagues than among those for whose guidance they are ultimately intended. If such indices are to become operational, they will need to be in accord with prevailing social values. They will also need the support of those who make policy and those who implement it. Such support is not easily won. The health professions are suspicious of any intrusion on their professional discretion and well aware of the complications of the problem. Daily contact with patients makes them conscious that a given illness can cause much more distress for one patient than for another. In view of the attitudes of the health professions, many politicians who have considered the problem see advantage in sheltering under a belief in freedom of action for individual professionals. They want to avoid being held accountable for health service priorities except in the broadest terms. In developing countries where choices are more often made and seen to be made between identifiable programmes, indices of some kind may come to be used in comparing alternative policies, but probably only over a narrow range of alternatives.

Conclusion

Value premises must underlie any choice of priorities whether or not these premises are formalized in a health status index. Is restricted activity, pain and discomfort to be regarded as of the same importance at any age, in either sex, in every geographical area, for each socio-economic strata? What is the cost of pain? What is the value of human life?[21] By what scale do we relate the different effects of disability which it is possible to measure? It is important that these value premises should not be chosen by an expert of any professional denomination acting in isolation, particularly an expert from an alien culture. Such choices should reflect the values of a particular society. Ideally each community should be enabled to participate in the choice of its own priorities.

The search for an index is the search for a tool to guide those who have the task of allocating resources *on behalf* of others. In the next chapter we discuss one of the considerations which may influence governments in taking their decisions – the relation between health and economic development.

NOTES

1. For estimates for 1961 see B. Abel-Smith, *An International Study of Health Expenditure*, Public Health Papers, No. 32, W.H.O., Geneva, 1967.

2. D.H.E.W., *National Health Expenditures, Fiscal Year 1974*, Research and Statistics Note No. 32, 1974.

3. Netherlands Central Bureau of Statistics, *Cost of Health Care in the Netherlands 1968*, The Hague, 1972, p. 9.

4. Calculation provided by Centre de Recherches et de Documentation sur la Consommation, Paris.

5. J. T. Ward and P. M. Tatchell, 'Health Expenditure in New Zealand', *The Economic Record*, December 1972, p. 512.

6. J. G. Simanis, 'Medical Care Expenditure in Seven Countries', *Social Security Bulletin*, March 1973.

7. P. Cornillot and P. Bonamour, 'France' in *Health Service Prospects*, Lancet and N.P.H.T., 1973, p. 75.

8. *The Australian Health Insurance Program*, Canberra, 1973, p. 2.

9. Simanis, op. cit.

10. D.H.E.W., 'Age Differences in Medical Care Spending', *Research and Statistics Note*, 27 March 1974, Washington, D.C.

11. R. Maxwell, *Health Care: the Growing Dilemma*, McKinsey, 1974.

12. R. Maxwell, op. cit., p. 7.

13. W.H.O., *Expert Committee on Drug Dependence*, W.H.O. Technical Report Series, No. 551, Geneva, 1974, p. 67.

14. A. L. Cockrane and W. W. Holland, 'Validation of Screening Procedures', *British Medical Bulletin*, Vol. 27, No. 1, 1971, p. 3.

15. A. L. Cockrane, *Effectiveness and Efficiency*, N.P.H.T., 1973, p. 23.

16. P. A. Biro and T. Lutens, 'Utilisation and Reimbursements under Medicare for 1967 and 1965 Accidents', *Social Security Bulletin*, May 1973.

17. Ann Cartwright, Lisbeth Hockey and J. L. Anderson, *Life before Death*, Routledge, 1973, p. 79.

18. J. M. Bengoa, 'Hunger and Malnutrition', *World Health*, Feb.-March 1974, p. 6.

19. For example, Sally Sainsbury, *Registered as Disabled*, Occasional Papers on Social Administration, No. 35, Bell, 1970.

20. For a summary of different attempts to construct an index and a discussion of the requirements see S. Fanshel and J. W. Bush, 'A Health-Status Index and its application to health services outcomes', *Operations Research*, Vol. 18, No. 6, November-December 1970, pp. 1021–67. See also C. L. Chiang, *An Index of Health: Mathematical Models*, National Center for Health Statistics, Series 5, 1965; W. L. Kissick, 'Planning, Programming and Budgeting in Health', *Medical Care*, No. 4, 1967, pp. 201–20; J. Ahumada *et al.*, *Health Planning*, P.A.H.O., Washington, D.C., 1965.

21. See, for example, Dorothy P. Rice and Barbara S. Cooper, 'The Economic Value of Human Life', *American Journal of Public Health*, Vol. 57, No. 11, 1967, pp. 1954–66; and T. C. Schelling, 'The Value of Preventing Death', in M. H. Cooper and A. J. Culyer, *Health Economics*, Penguin, 1973, pp. 293–321.

CHAPTER 9

Health and Economic Development

Every society has to choose what priority to give to social development (including improvements in health) as against economic development. But the two sectors do not operate in isolation. There are health effects of economic developments and there are economic effects of health improvements. The inter-relationships are complex. By no means all of them are known or understood, nor can they always be expressed in quantitative form.

Economic developments may reduce some causes of ill-health – particularly malnutrition. Economic progress may also make it easier to maintain high standards of personal hygiene. Economic and educational advances may assist the acceptance of family planning as may the prospect of better health and the greater chances of children surviving into adulthood. While economic development often proceeds in a way which benefits only the urban population leaving the rural population no better off than before, redistribution in favour of the rural poor may be more acceptable in a society enjoying economic growth. Much depends on how the benefits of economic progress are distributed.

Economic development either in industry or agriculture generally leads to aggregations of population in limited living space. Habits of living which cause only minor health risks when the population is dispersed can create major health problems when people are crowded together in cities or rural settlements. Water channels for agricultural irrigation can spread cholera and other water-borne diseases. If standards of health are to be maintained systematic methods of sanitary disposal and protected water supplies are essential. For example, trachoma is said to be responsible for 20 million people being blind or purblind: improved sanitation could bring trachoma under control.[1] Communicable diseases of all kinds will spread when people are herded together at work, at leisure and in residential accommodation.

Mechanical agriculture and factory production generate risks of accidents and disease. It was many years before the risks of handling asbestos, lead products or P.V.C. were appreciated and many other occupational risks are probably unidentified. Economic development increases travel for business and travel for leisure which spread diseases within countries and between countries. With economic progress come new strains and stresses from work and the separation of kin: new services may be needed to care for the sick, the aged and the disabled. A wider range of health services may be needed to stop health status from declining as economic development proceeds. New eating habits do not necessarily lead to better nutrition and they may lead to the introduction of diseases previously unknown. A striking example is the reduction of breast-feeding and the increase in bottle-feeding with preparations from cow's milk. First, this is much more expensive. In Kenya the decline in breast-feeding is estimated to have involved a loss of $11·5 million – equivalent to two-thirds of the national health budget or one-fifth of the average economic aid. If all children in Asia were fed with cow's milk, Asia would need 114 million extra cattle. Secondly, human milk has unique nutritional and anti-infective properties.[2]

Just as economic progress changes the character and geographical distribution of health needs and the services required to meet them, so the provision of health services has economic effects. Some of these effects may be indirect. For example, health programmes may demonstrate the value of Western science. To show that vaccination can eradicate smallpox, that the suppression of mosquitoes reduces fevers or that the ugly symptoms of yaws and gonorrhoea respond to a simple injection are powerful demonstrations that the application of science can cause drastic changes. They may persuade people to be more willing to accept not only further health services but advice on new methods of cultivation and production.

Other economic effects may be more direct. Some of them may be favourable to the improvement of economic standards. Poor health and malnutrition restrict the amount of work which people can do. Others may be unfavourable. They may simply consume resources to provide health benefits. The real cost to a society providing health services is 'the opportunity cost' – the manpower and materials used for health services are not available for other uses.

Some health services, however, are clearly of an investment character – they reduce costs and increase production. This is analogous to other forms of investment. For example, the man who pays for the construction of a house can receive thereafter a flow of income from renting it out to others or he can save himself rent by occupying it himself. The owner of a factory installs a machine because it will produce goods at lower cost including the amortization and interest charges on the machine. The concept of investment has been extended to education services. The cost of education, including the loss of income from studying rather than working, can prove a profitable investment if a better job is obtained as a result of the extra education. The extra pay throughout life provides a continuing reward or a 'yield' which can be compared with the original investment.

Research and the education of health personnel are wholly investment expenditures. Research is investment with the aim of adding to knowledge. Its yield may be more effective ways of preventing or curing ill-health or cheaper methods of doing so. Education of health personnel is the development of human tools to provide cure, care and preventive services in the future.

Investment in People

In crude economic terms, health services can increase the yield of human capital by keeping it in good repair, prolonging its working life and enabling more children to reach the age when they start to produce. But what does not follow is that economic considerations are the only reasons for providing health services. Thus it is unhelpful for an economist to write: 'On economic grounds, approximately the same rules that govern when to maintain and when to scrap machine capital and that determine the optimal rate of maintenance expenditures for machine capital also apply to human capital.'[3]

Abortion, infant and child mortality are every bit as much of a waste of world resources as the destruction of crops. Nor is the economic cost of a lost child only measured by its consumption and the extra consumption of the pregnant mother but also by the loss of the value of other work of the mother and others during pregnancy, delivery and the care of the young child. Added to the social effects – the emotional distress of the parents and others at the death of the child – is the loss to the community of the whole investment in bearing, delivering, suckling and nurturing the child. If the child survived long enough to attend a formal education, this investment is lost as well.

Just as a machine tool becomes more and more valuable during the process of manufacture, so the investment in a human being increases each year from conception until the time comes when the child is able to contribute more to the community's resources than that child consumes. But whether a child can eventually make a net addition to the community's resources depends on whether there are opportunities for additional workers to increase production.

If this economic analysis is extended throughout life, a point is reached when consumption starts to exceed production. This may occur when a man or woman becomes disabled – for example, by blindness. In crude economic terms diseases which cause chronic disability are more costly to society than diseases which cause early death. While a dead person, at least if cremated, does not consume and does not need care, the disabled person not only needs to consume like others but may, in addition, need care by others. In industrial countries where retirement practices have been developed, superficially it would seem that the most 'economic' point for death is around the age of retirement. If, however, a retired person takes over the care of a child, or a disabled or handicapped person and thus enables someone else to take over work, then the retired person may continue to make an indirect contribution to production. Otherwise average economic levels of living are reduced by an increase in the proportion of population over retirement age. But what may be questioned is whether an age of retirement appropriate for a lower expectation of life is still appropriate if the expectation of life increases at higher ages.

This type of economic reasoning could be used to support compulsory euthanasia for the elderly and particularly for the permanently disabled and to justify the withdrawal of health services from those who want them *most*. But such reasoning is not only unacceptable in social terms but superficial in economic terms. If we are entitled to compare the benefits of work with the pleasures of leisure in working life, why cannot we be allowed the choice of storing up leisure for old age. Moreover it cannot be assumed that production would not be different in a society that slaughtered its members the moment they ceased to be productive. Why invest in children who are planning our destruction? Why save so much if one can expect no retirement and no old age? In the more developed countries vast funds are built up in pension schemes to provide for retirement and this saving releases resources for investment. It can be advantageous for society in economic terms for people to *expect* to survive into old age.

But even if the yield from investment in human life were shown to be negative after a certain point when analysed in *investment* terms, it does not follow that it would be 'wrong' for health services to be provided. If an individual or a society makes a conscious decision to consume resources in health services, whether for the young or old, for those who may return to paid work or for those who will not, this is by definition the chosen use of resources for that individual or that society. There can be no criteria to decide how a community *should* spend its resources other than informed choices, made with popular support and understanding. Some uses of resources add to production and others do not. But these economic effects as well as the social effects need to be understood in development planning. Where a particular health expenditure can be shown to contribute to economic progress, this is an additional argument which can be used by public health administrators seeking to secure an increase in their health budgets.

The most dramatic impact of economic and social development is on the expectation of life. Rising economic standards (particularly higher standards of nutrition) and rising health standards (particularly the reduction of the dysentry diseases and of malaria) increase the proportion of children surviving the early years of life. The decline in the incidence of those communicable diseases which strike adults increases the proportion of the population who reach old age. Within a generation, the expectation of life in some societies has been doubled. The major contribution to this change has come from a switch from 'wasteful' reproduction to relatively 'efficient' reproduction but at a rate which has led to a more rapid growth of population than of work opportunities. In a sense the social progress of many societies has outstripped their economic progress. Though output has increased, output per head has declined.

Many countries throughout the world are currently in this painful transition stage of development when reproduction rates appropriate to a society with a high mortality rate are retained when mortality rates have fallen. To describe it as a transition stage may seem unduly optimistic, but all societies which are now well developed went through a similar stage to that described above. Birth rates came down and on the whole stayed down. Many economic and social changes were occurring at the time and it is not possible to establish whether one particular change was the main cause. But what is important is that the drop in the birthrate occurred long before the age of condoms, pills, sterilization or legalized abortion. It may be that it takes a generation or more for parents to revise their expectations about the survival of their children, but when parents have come to want smaller families they have found means of achieving this. The challenge for the developing countries is to find ways of expediting this process. They start with two advantages over societies which went through the process earlier. First, more techniques are available. Second, many of these countries have a network of services in contact with a large proportion of the population. The key problem is to generate the motivation where this does not exist.[4] The rapid growth of population has frustrated many valiant and successful efforts to promote economic growth. Potentially the most important preventive health measure from the point of view of economic development is a birth control programme but such a programme may be expensive for a poor country if it is to be effective.

The Cost of Ill-Health

Ill-health and the risk of ill-health involve economic as well as social costs. The economic costs are of two kinds. First, there are primary or *direct costs* – expenditure on services to prevent, cure or care. Next, there are secondary or *indirect costs* – any fall in production or school attendance due to temporary sickness or more permanent losses due to chronic disability or premature death. The loss of income due to sickness may be made good to the individual in whole or part by sick pay or sickness insurance. But this does not extinguish the loss to the community: it only spreads the cost among a larger number of people. Finally there are *tertiary costs* – any by-products of the provision of health services on economic development. It was estimated for the United States that in 1963 the direct costs were $22·5 million and the indirect costs $71 million – more than three times greater.[5]

The direct costs of providing health services are real economic costs to the extent that the resources used in providing health services could actually be used in meeting other needs. The opportunity of enjoying other goods and services may be foregone because resources are used in health services. Whether there is a secondary loss of production depends on whether there are work opportunities in countries or parts of countries or times of the year when the illness (or disability) occurred. If there is chronic unemployment and/or under-employment, the work normally done by a sick worker is likely to be done by someone else, so that sickness may not lower production but give jobs to other people. There may, however, be some people in such countries with rare skills or specialist training whose work cannot be readily replaced.

Work opportunities, capital plant and skills are not evenly spread through the world nor is land evenly distributed among those who wish to use it. One of the characteristics of a developing country is chronic unemployment and under-employment. In the wage-earning sector of such economies, the place of a man who is sick may be filled by hiring a man who was previously unemployed. Where there is subsistence agriculture and land is limited, the tasks which are traditionally done may well be done by others from the wider kinship if one or more family members becomes ill or disabled. But there may still be peak periods of labour demand (such as the time for planting or gathering a crop) when morbidity will cause a major economic loss.[6] A country with widespread unemployment or under-employment is suffering from its failure or inability to apply an appropriate balance of labour-intensive investment, training and birth control policies at an earlier stage.

Nor is this type of problem only to be found in developing countries. Many countries which are regarded as developed have regions where pockets of unemployment persist and localities where women want paid work but cannot obtain it. Nor is there a clear relationship between the health status of a country and the amount of absence from work which is attributed to sickness. Where there are arrangements for sick pay or provision for sickness insurance, people may stay away from work with conditions which though not disabling are perceived as sickness, and some with no real illness at all. Both in Britain and the United States there have been more spells of sick absence in the working population over the past decades despite evidence that health standards have improved.[7] Even where there is full employment, production loss from sickness may be made good by overtime worked by others, though this is likely to involve the employer in higher payment to get the work done.

When the attempt is made to measure a loss of production, three questions must be answered. First, how is production to be defined? People work for themselves as well as for others. They grow vegetables and flowers in the garden and do their own household repairs. Should housewives' services be included as part of production and the work of mothers and fathers in caring for children? If the housewife goes sick, a substitute housewife may expect a considerable wage. A family member who comes and helps may be given food and presents. If children are sent away to be looked after at a children's home, this can be very costly. It is difficult to put a satisfactory price on the services of housewives and mothers and for this reason the value of their work is often excluded in calculations of losses due to sickness. For similar reasons no value of these services is included in calculations of the gross national product – the conventional measure of total production in the economy.

When economic effects are calculated over a period of years, the question arises of whether losses and benefits occurring in later years should be considered to be the same value as losses and benefits occurring in the first year. Economists normally treat later gains and losses as of lower value: the longer the period the lower the value. This is because governments and individuals tend to prefer benefits this year to benefits in later years and similarly prefer costs to be incurred later rather than earlier. Moreover the yield from investments in health services needs to be compared with the yield of other potential investments. In a developing country the potential yield of investments is likely to be high and thus a high discount rate may be appropriate. Some have, however, argued that there should be no 'discounting' of this kind when making calculations for society as a whole, as society *should* be as much concerned with later generations as with the present.

When calculations are made of the loss of production due to sickness, the loss of the value of housewives' services is often but not always omitted.[8] The measure generally used is earnings before tax and other deductions, partly because this data is relatively easy to obtain. The calculation is often simplified still further by assuming that all workers are average earners. But some illnesses strike the richer more than the poorer and vice versa. Workers are not, however, necessarily paid the value of their contribution to production.

Indeed this is seldom precisely known. Moreover the unexpected absence due to sickness of a member of a work team can involve extra costs becouse of the disruption of the work team or because of overtime payments or because regular provision for the risk of sickness is made by the employer keeping extra workers standing by.

The economic effects on the family of the sickness of a family member will be different from the economic effects on society. The family will lose not the gross earnings of the worker but the net earnings after tax and other deductions and save the cost of the worker's travel to work and any costs due to working. The family may receive sick pay and sickness insurance benefits which may or may not be taxed, depending on the tax laws of the country. If the family member is sick at home this may generate extra costs quite apart from the direct cost of medical treatment. If the family member is admitted to hospital there may be savings in the family budget, but extra expenses may also be incurred – the cost of travel to visit the patient in hospital, gifts and other incidental expenses. The cost of sickness to society cannot therefore be calculated by adding together the costs falling on families.

The costs of sickness falling on government funds (including social security funds) are again different. If a worker falls sick, government loses the tax which he would have paid out of his earnings and may have to make social security payments to him and his family, and, depending on the financing of medical care, bear the direct costs of health services provided to him. Similarly if a man dies at work, government loses the tax on his earnings but may have to make provision for his dependents. Government is however saved any pension which may have been paid to him on retirement and the cost of any services which he may have used.

One preventive health programme which is almost certainly of economic benefit in terms of primary or direct savings, at least in more developed countries, is the fluoridization of water to prevent dental decay. In countries with well-developed dental services, this preventive action is likely to pay for itself at a reasonable rate of discount solely in terms of the saving in future treatment costs. It was estimated that in the United States in 1964 the saving in dental treatment which would be made unnecessary by fluoridization amounted to $700 million a year.[9]

In theory, one would expect a disease to be cured the more effectively and with the smaller use of resources, the earlier it is detected. This is true of some conditions but not of others. A policy which encourages early access to health services (for example, the removal of money barriers to the use of the health services) is medically desirable in so far as some conditions may be detected while they are still treatable, or before the patient has in ignorance made them worse. But such a policy is not necessarily cheaper in the long run. Indeed it may be more expensive if the cost of checking on false alarms exceeds the savings from early treatment.

Tertiary effects can arise in many different ways. For example, the provision of a safe water supply may be made as a disease-preventive measure. If piped water is supplied near or in the home, there is a saving in payments made for the delivery of water or in the time and effort needed to carry water to the home or go to the water to wash. This means that more time is available which may be devoted to other activities including economic production. In addition the provision of a convenient water supply is in itself an addition to the standard of living and more water is likely to be used. A water supply provides joint benefits – partly health and partly amenity.

A further example is the elimination of diseases in animals. The tsetse fly can lead to the loss or illness of farm animals and thus to lower yields of meat and milk and also of arable crops because of the loss of manure. Similarly animals may be slaughtered to eradicate bovine tuberculosis. While this involves a substantial loss in the short run, in the long run the lower incidence of tuberculosis in cattle reduces the risks for humans. In addition the food conversion ratio of the animals may be raised to give a greater yield of milk and meat, their energy may be greater when used for traction quite apart from the yield of dung whether used for fuel, fertilizer or as an alternative to cement. Nor is the fall in the food conversion ratio confined to animals. There is a waste of calory intake in humans suffering from fevers and parasitic diseases.

Other tertiary effects may occur where fertile stretches of a country have become depopulated and under-cultivated because of health risks. Areas where malaria is endemic are normally highly fertile as mosquitoes like a wet and warm climate. These areas may be under-cultivated because of the risk of fever and the discomfort of mosquito bites. Similarly river blindness (onchocerciasis) is transmitted by a fly which breeds in water. The bites of the fly irritate and cause painful itching. As a result, fertile land goes uncultivated or under-cultivated. In the African savannah, agricultural land is often abandoned over distances of 10 or 20 kilometres from the rivers. 'Only the driest and least fertile lands can be cultivated and the drier the climate the more capricious the rainfall on which the farmers depend for their meagre crops.'[10] The situation is most serious in certain West African states such as Mali and the Upper Volta where there are estimated to be over a million sufferers from the disease – 70,000 of them blind.[11] The most effective method of control is to add insecticides to the water in which the flies breed. It has been calculated that the economic benefits of this control will justify the costs quite apart from all the social costs of the disease.[12]

A further type of loss may occur because restrictions are placed on international trade and the tourist industry is interrupted because of outbreaks of infectious diseases or a general fear of health risks. When an outbreak of cholera hits a country which is normally free from the disease – exports, particularly of perishable goods – from such countries are often banned on world markets. Tourists stay at home or go elsewhere. In the past few years Hong Kong, Italy and Spain have all suffered in this way. Substantial direct costs are also incurred. Even in a country with a good medical infrastructure, a sudden outbreak of cholera, typhoid, smallpox or bubonic plague can cause heavy expenditure on tracking suspects. It is indeed possible that the expenditures caused for countries by an occasional outbreak of cholera have been greater than those incurred in countries where cholera is endemic. The elimination of cholera from the world might bring greater direct financial rewards to the richer countries than to the poorer.

The elimination of smallpox from the world which W.H.O. plans to achieve within a year or two would certainly bring greater *economic* gains to the richer countries than to the poorer. In many countries of the world people are still given regular vaccinations. Moreover travellers to continents where there is smallpox are required to have valid certificates. Vaccination is expensive when the costs of medical manpower are high. In the United States alone about 150 million dollars was estimated to have been spent on smallpox in 1968.[13] The annual cost in other high-income countries is not known, but much less was spent on smallpox in those countries where there was still a focus of infection. For many years it has been in the economic interest of the high-income countries to pay for the whole world programme to eliminate smallpox. This may be true of other diseases as well, such as measles. Spencer and Axnick have shown that the benefits have exceeded the costs of immunization against measles in both Senegal and the United States.[14]

It is commonly assumed that whatever the disease, prevention must always be cheaper than cure. This is not necessarily true. Whether it is depends on the cost and effectiveness of the preventive measure as compared with the cost and effectiveness of cure. Costs will vary according to the number of people to whom the preventive measure needs to be applied and the number of people who need to be cured. For example, when the incidence of poliomyelitis or tuberculosis is low it can be cheaper to treat those cases which arise than to undertake mass screening to find early cases of tuberculosis or to immunize the population against polio. By studying figures for the year 1961 it was found that immunization for polio in Britain did not pay in economic terms at the current level of prevalence.[15] On the other hand, Weisbrod in the United States discounted future costs and benefits and found that polio immunization showed a high rate of return.[16] In the case of tuberculosis, Pole found that in Britain early screening did not pay in economic terms as so few cases were found.[17] He also found that the cost of screening for breast cancer was high in relation to the costs of treatment.[18]

Some preventive measures are of an investment character; once applied they do not have to be applied again though some regular maintenance expenditure may be needed. For example, the provision of a water supply system or sewage disposal plant is a permanent capital investment which only needs maintenance once it has been installed. The drainage of swamps can also be a permanent improvement. On the other hand such measures as spraying homes to eliminate mosquitoes or immunization have to be repeated regularly. Once malaria has been brought under control, it is important to continue to keep it under control. If this is not done, the cost of fighting malaria can be much higher in the long run. Control measures were relaxed in Ceylon when the incidence of malaria reached a low level. The incidence rose again and expenditure over the past two decades has had to be much greater than if more had been spent earlier on control and surveillance. India now faces the formidable problem of selective strains of mosquitoes which are resistant to DDT, breed in fast flowing water and fly long distances. One sad consequence of the costly but unsuccessful efforts in the nineteen-fifties and sixties to control malaria before an effective infrastructure of health services was established has been to make the eradication of malaria even more costly in the future.

To find the most cost-effective preventive measure the average annual costs of alternative preventive measures need to be compared with the benefit obtained in terms of cases prevented. In the case of investments the annual cost consists of the interest on the investment, amortization where appropriate (e.g. in the case of water pumps) and maintenance charges. The most cost-effective preventive measure then needs to be compared with the cost of curative treatment where an effective treatment is available and the other economic effects of the disease. If a disease causes great suffering, economic calculations may be irrelevant because the social costs are reckoned to be such as to justify a preventive approach even though this may be more expensive. For example, the cure of cholera is quick, simple and efficient provided proper treatment is started early enough. Nevertheless cholera is greatly feared because of the rapidity with which it can spread and kill if untreated. Thus countries use immunization against cholera even though it is only about 50 per cent effective and the protection seldom lasts more than six months. Effective prevention can be secured by the combination of personal hygiene, a safe water supply and the effective disposal of excreta, but such a programme cannot be rapidly introduced for the whole population. It is possible that investment in water supplies and sanitation could be more economic in the long run than regular immunization, care and surveillance.

While there are immense complications in studying all the economic effects of health services, not all these complications need to be introduced when studying every health problem. For example, the economic value of fluoridization can easily be established by looking solely at savings in treatment costs. It is not necessary to go further and examine the loss of working time when people go for dental treatment or any loss of production due to pain.

Much of the work on the economic effects of health problems has been undertaken in the United States.[19] For example, there have been studies of polio, tuberculosis and cancer,[20] of ulcers,[21] mental illness,[22] alcoholism,[23] and syphilis.[24] In many countries there have been studies of the value of measures to prevent motor accidents.[25] Many attempts have been made to calculate the economic value of birth control in developing countries,[26] but it is extremely difficult to calculate at all reliably how much expenditure will prevent how many births. A complex model was used by Barlow to estimate the effects of malaria eradication in Ceylon on income per head over a 30-year period.[27] He calculated that the initial effect was favourable and became more favourable in the succeeding years but in the long run it would probably be unfavourable.

Cost-benefit analysis could be used to establish priorities between particular health programmes. For example in terms of averting deaths it was estimated that certain programmes to reduce motor vehicle deaths would be more cost-effective than other programmes studied and that next came programmes for cervical cancer, lung cancer, breast cancer, syphilis, tuberculosis, head and neck cancer, and colon rectum cancer in that order.[28] This was assuming that it did not matter who died or at what age, and that morbidity and disability could be neglected. Moreover the calculations were based on average costs: it was not clear what could actually be achieved by devoting extra money to one programme rather than another. An alternative approach is to base policy on the economic saving achieved from particular health programmes but this method of weighing morbidity and mortality involves values which are, to say the least, controversial.[29] The key problem is what value do people place on reductions of their chance of death as against disability.[30]

Conclusion

Some health measures can be justified in terms of costs saved for society quite apart from their social value and some may even compete with other possible fields for investment aimed at increasing production either by increasing output or saving treatment costs or both. Other health measures may increase the costs which have to be borne by healthy members of society. They are a form of consumption expenditure. The practical application of calculations of this kind is restricted by limited knowledge of how effective many health programmes really are.

NOTES

1. G. Edsall, 'The Control of Communicable Diseases', in C.I.B.A., *Human Rights in Health*, 1974, p. 175.

2. See D. B. Jelliffe and E. F. P. Jelliffe, 'Food supplies for physiologically vulnerable groups', in C.I.B.A., *Human Rights in Health*, 1974, p. 137.

3. S. Rothenburg, 'The Allocation of Biomedical Research', *American Economic Review*, May 1967, p. 111. Quoted in S. E. Berki, *Hospital Economics*, op. cit., p. 62.

4. See B. Abel-Smith, *People Without Choice*, I.P.P.F., 1974.

5. Indirect costs were calculated employing the concept of earnings lost in the year from illness and disability and the present value of future earnings lost from death in that one year (employing a 4 per cent discount rate). An imputed value of housewives' services was included. Dorothy P. Rice, *Estimating the Cost of Illness*, Health Economics Series, No. 6, D.H.E.W., 1966.

6. Dr Griffiths argues that an outbreak of Asian 'flu at planting time reduced the output of rice in Thailand in 1957. D. H. S. Griffiths, 'Some Reflections of Paddy Growing in South-East Asia', *Studies on Health Planning*, Series 2, U.N. Asian Institute for Economic Development and Planning, Bangkok, 1969.

7. In Western Germany on the other hand, there has been a decreased rate of sick absence since 1963. M. Pflanz, 'German Health Insurance', *International Journal of Health Services*, Vol. 1, No. 4, November 1971, p. 327.

8. They are included in Dorothy P. Rice, op. cit.

9. G. E. Mitchell, 'The False Economy of Dental Neglect', *Economic Benefits from Public Health Services*, D.H.E.W., 1964, p. 21.

10. J. Hamon and L. Kastman, 'Poverty and Blindness', *World Health*, October 1973, p. 6.

11. F. J. Tomiche, 'Man versus Blackfly', *World Health*, May 1974, p. 28.

12. J. Hamon and L. Kastman, op. cit., p. 11.

13. D. J. Spencer and N. W. Axnick, 'Cost Benefit Analysis', paper presented at the Conference on the Vaccination of Communicable Diseases, March 1973, Monaco.

14. N. W. Axnick and J. M. Lane, 'Costs associated with the protection of the United States against Smallpox'.

15. Office of Health Economics, *The Price of Poliomyelitis*, London, 1963.

16. B. A. Weisbrod, 'Costs and Benefits of Medical Research: a case study of Poliomyelitis', *Journal of Political Economy*, Vol. 79, 1971.

17. J. D. Pole, 'The Economics of Mass Radiography', in M. M. Hauser, *The Economics of Medical Care*, Allen & Unwin, 1972.

18. J. D. Pole, 'Economic Aspect of Screening for Disease' in *Screening in Medical Care*, O.U.P., 1968, p. 741.

19. For a description and discussion of the studies mentioned in this paragraph see Jennifer Roberts, 'Economic Evaluation of Health Care: a Survey', *British Journal of Preventive and Social Medicine*, Vol. 28, No. 3, August 1974, pp. 210–16.

20. B. A. Weisbrod, *Economics of Public Health*, Philadelphia, University of Pennsylvania Press, 1961.

21. I. S. Blumenthal, *Research and the Ulcer Problem*, Rand McNally, 1959.

22. R. Fein, *The Economics of Mental Illness*, New York Basic Books, 1958.

23. A. G. Holtman, 'Estimating the demand for public health services: the alcoholism case', *Public Finance*, Vol. 19, 1964.

24. H. E. Klarman, 'Syphilis Control Programmes' in R. Dorfman (ed.) *Measuring the Benefits of Government Investment*, Brookings, 1965.

25. See, for example, R. F. F. Dawson, *Cost of Road Accidents in Great Britain*, R.R.L. Report, No. 79, 1967 or J. Thédié and C. Abraham, 'Economic Aspects of Road Accidents', *Traffic and Engineering and Control*, Vol. 2, 1961.

26. See, for example, A. J. Coale and E. M. Hoover, *Population Growth and Economic Development in Low Income Countries*, Princeton University Press, 1958.

27. R. Barlow, 'The Economic Effects of Malaria Eradication', *American Economic Review*, Vol. 57, 1967. See also A. Kuhner, 'The Impact of Public Health Programs on Economic Development', *International Journal of Health Services*, Vol. 1, No. 3, August 1971.

28. R. N. Crosse, 'Cost-Benefit Analysis of Health Service', *Annals of the American Academy of Political and Social Science*, Jan. 1972, p. 93.

29. ibid., p. 94.

30. See T. Schelling, 'The Life You Save may be Your Own', in Stuart Chase (ed.), *Problems in Public Expenditure Analysis*, Brookings, 1968.

CHAPTER 10

Planning in More Developed Countries

More developed countries in this context are those which can afford to meet all the major needs for health services. All curative and personal preventive procedures known to be effective can be applied. In addition standards of care can be provided for all those in need which are reasonable in relation to the general standards of living. In such countries the object of health planning is to secure that all necessary services of the right quality are provided at the right place at the right time, that the health services are in a balanced relationship to the associated social services, and that this is achieved at the lowest cost in real resources consistent with these aims.

The broad aim of health planning can only be stated in one sentence by using words which need further definition. The word 'right' is used to denote effective, curative and preventive services and levels of care appropriate for the general living standards of the society. It is also used to conceal the difficult problem of achieving a balance between quality considerations which mean that some services cannot be made available in every locality at reasonable cost, and the convenience and social advantage that would accrue if every service were readily available to the patient and his relatives on a local basis. While some services ought to be available on a twenty-four hour basis seven days a week it would be wasteful if all services were so available. The balance between health and social services implies the need for joint planning so that people who need social care (at home or in homes) are not given health services because the social services are inadequately provided, and similarly that those needing health services are not given social care. The phrase 'lowest cost in real resources' poses the problem of whose resources – the balance between the time and travel cost of patients and their relatives and the costs falling directly on the services.

It is increasingly accepted that a health market cannot be left to plan itself by the invisible forces of self-interest and the sovereignty of informed purchasers. The unpredictable character of the need for health service is such that money-backed demand falls far short of meeting need for a wide section of the population. Hence the initiatives in virtually all more developed countries to lower if not remove the money barrier to health services. But the payment of bills presented by providers whether by health insurance or government still does not ensure that all needs are met. At one end of the market there may still be an accumulation of unmet needs, while at the other end services may be provided which are not needed at all or are of poor quality.

The health market is virtually unique in the lack of mechanisms for self-regulation. The consumer wants health but does not know what he needs to do to get it, other than to take professional advice. The doctor may know what the patient needs but has no incentive to see that it is provided at competitive costs – whether he is providing it or acting as a purchasing agent. In so far as the doctor owns hospitals, pharmacies, laboratories or radiology establishments he is faced with conflicts of interest between his entrepreneurial role and his professional role. And in so far as he does not own them, their use may still be more profitable to him than their non-use. And as the doctor is not seeking a best buy for his patient, there is no incentive on these providing agencies to be cost-conscious. The supply of hospital beds generates within limits the demand for hospital beds. Doctors can enter over-doctored areas where unnecessary services are already provided, leaving other areas devoid of medical manpower.

Competition in particular sectors of the market can lead to unnecessary surgery and all surgery is dangerous, to unnecessary prescribing of powerful drugs and all powerful drugs are dangerous, to unnecessary use of hospitals which also involves the patient in risks. Competition can also lead to poor quality service in other respects – lack of specialization in performance and lack of regular exercise of skill and the lack of the protection of teamwork. Product competition by the pharmaceutical industry can lead to the distortion of such knowledge as doctors possess and the implanting of non-knowledge.

Not only are there competitive forces which can have undesirable consequences but there are opportunities for the abuse of monopoly power. Doctors and dentists enjoy monopoly rights conferred by law and/or enforced by regulations of the health insurance or service system. As a result tasks which could be delegated may not be delegated so that there is an apparent shortage of highly trained manpower. The patent system provides high profits for the pharmaceutical industry and price competition is limited by the lack of substitution rights conferred on pharmacists. The latter also enjoy some degree of monopoly power in price fixing. The patient urgently needing to have a prescription filled does not explore the market with the same care as the customer making a more leisurely and planned purchase. The pharmacist, insecure as he has become in his professional role since the bulk of dispensing has been transferred from his shop to the factory, does not readily present himself as a cut-price tradesman.

The key problem of a private medical market is fragmentation. There are doctors, dentists, hospitals, pharmacists and diagnostic services all operated separately on a profit or, as is often the case with hospitals, on a non-profit basis. There is no single organization pledged to provide the best health service possible out of a limited budget. The professional ethos and restrictive practices obstruct this coming about in a private market without intervention by government or charitable effort.

As the problems of a private medical market have become recognized, the response of health insurance agencies and governments has been to try and regulate the system. This regulation has been of two different kinds. First there are attempts to control supply through the mechanisms of demand by specifying what will be paid for and what will not and negotiating the prices which will be paid for particular services, or by establishing new financial incentives for particular suppliers. The second has been by regulating the supply of manpower and health facilities and their siting. A more drastic solution has been the decision to take control over the whole system of supply and attempt to bind it together into one unified and planned system.

Regulation through Purchase

While profit-making insurers have an interest in satisfying themselves that they do not pay for services which were not provided and in restricting demand by deductables, co-insurance and financial limits on their liability, they have little incentive to try and regulate suppliers either to ensure that services are necessary or that they are provided at reasonable cost. Provided the costs for which they are insuring are reasonably predictable, higher costs can be passed on to the customer in higher premiums. The larger the turnover, the greater the business from which profit can be secured. Moreover an individual company in competition with many others would be in a weak position to argue that charges, which were regularly paid by its competitors without being questioned, were nevertheless unreasonable or unnecessary charges. If it attempted to do so, it might well lose clients to competitors. The patient is more likely to believe his doctor than his insurance company, if the latter started a dispute about what were and were not necessary services. The insured person may well prefer a policy at a higher price which covered him for what his doctor said he needed to a policy at a somewhat lower price which covered him for what his insurance company said he needed.

Attempts to regulate through purchase have therefore tended to come more through consumers' cooperatives and compulsory health insurance than profit-making insurance. The cooperative and compulsory insurer exists, or at least should exist, to serve the interests of the insured person rather than those of its management. In a unified scheme covering all or virtually all the population, the compulsory insurer is in a clear monopolistic position to bargain with suppliers who normally associate together in any negotiations. A unified scheme covering even one section of the population (for example, the aged under Medicare in the United States) can be in a powerful negotiating position. And separate sick funds can, as in Germany, form a powerful coalition to negotiate terms with suppliers.

Regulation through purchase can take three forms – requiring prior approval before services are undertaken, scrutiny after the service is provided to ensure that the service was necessary and of appropriate quality, and the negotiation of fee schedules which stipulate the cost of each service in the attempt to limit incentives to provide excessive services.

The urgency of so many medical services limits the scope for regulation by prior approval. While an insurer can refuse to pay for the repair of a car until the damage which needs repair has been inspected and a price for repair agreed, people do not want to wait and often should not have to wait before they obtain health services. Prior approval is used for certain dental procedures under the National Health Service in the United Kingdom and for certain 'cold' surgical procedures in the Netherlands. It involves a duplication of the examination and diagnosis by a second doctor or dentist and is thus costly in the use of professional manpower.

Post-event regulation can take many forms. The looser and older form is to allocate the costs generated to each providing or authorizing doctor and identify those whose payment claims or requisitions for services are noticeably above the average. These doctors are then approached and asked to explain why they are providing more services, prescribing more drugs, using more diagnostic facilities or hospital beds than their colleagues either locally or nationally. Divergencies may, of course, be simply explained by the demographic or other characteristics of their patients. Further analysis by diagnostic test requested, by category of drug prescribed or by the diagnosis of patients admitted to hospital may be used to pinpoint the problem. The process of drawing the attention of the doctor to an unexplained divergence, of which he may have been previously unaware, may lead him to modify his behaviour. But if the behaviour persists, it may lead to some disciplinary action or limitation of payment. Doctors employed by the insurance fund or social security agency, or the local medical association may adjudicate on individual cases. Procedures of this kind are extensively used in many Western European countries.

Under accreditation requirements in the United States, hospitals have for many years established tissue committees to review the extent to which normal tissues have been removed, in the attempt to limit unnecessary surgery. In addition hospital utilization committees have been established to examine the appropriateness of admission and of length of stay. While some such committees have had an impact – particularly when or where hospital beds were short – many others have been more form than substance.

A more intensive approach which explores the quality of service more explicitly as well as the cost is to establish quantitative treatment norms for particular diagnoses. Thus, for example, any doctor who keeps a patient with a given diagnosis in hospital for more than a specific number of days may be subject to review for his treatment of that patient. The sanction may be that the insurer refuses to pay for any hospital days held to be excessive. While computers can be programmed to pick out cases which need review on the criteria laid down, and this is by no means inexpensive, the process of examination involves a dummy run afterwards of diagnosis and treatment – 'second-guessing' by professionals. The more these procedures are extended the heavier the cost in terms of manpower.

Under a law passed in 1972 what are called Professional Standards Review Organizations are to be established in the United States by the beginning of 1976 to regulate payments made under the Medicare and Medicaid Programmes. Some 130 organizations will cover the United States manned by local doctors. It will be for local medical societies to establish them to the satisfaction of the Secretary of State. If they fail to do so, other organizations such as state health departments can be invited to establish them. Each area organization will have the task of developing area norms of diagnosis and care for particular conditions. These norms will be reviewed by a national committee. Once the area norms have been developed, they will be used to identify those doctors who have provided care which by these norms appears to be excessive, harmful or of grossly inferior quality. They will then assess the clinical and social situation of the patient and the resources of the institution providing care. The area organization will be able to recommend sanctions – in extreme cases suspension from the programmes and in less extreme cases repayment by the doctor of excessive costs of up to $5000 incurred by the programmes. The American Medical Association is calling for the repeal of this legislation though it had earlier advocated review of this kind, but wanted it to be wholly under the control of the local medical society.[1]

Attempts to prevent excessive costs by gearing the payments which will be made for particular services so that there are disincentives to excessive or unnecessary service can cause unintended distortions of the health care service. As pointed out in Chapter 7, the crude procedure of laying down a standard payment to hospitals per day of care creates an incentive to excessive days of care. Fee schedules for doctors which try and faithfully reflect the time and effort which should be used for every procedure create incentives for the less scrupulous to take advantage of some procedure which they can perform quickly by delegation of the major part of the task to supporting staff or otherwise and perform it in excess. Any attempt to establish relative fees can become rapidly out of date in some respect and some opportunity can be found to abuse it. Attempts to create incentives for efficiency in hospitals have had limited success because only to a limited extent can efficiency be established without taking account of the patients being treated.[2]

At first sight, fee for service payment enables private fee-charging medicine to be readily combined with health insurance without any restriction of clinical freedom. But paradoxically, it is not long before interference with medical practice becomes greater than occurs or needs to occur when doctors are salaried employees in a government service. Doctors are made answerable for each of their acts for which they claim payment. Because there are possibilities for abuse, restrictive and preventive safeguards are established to prevent abuse occurring. The greatest risk is that the values underlying the system of regulation may be inappropriate or positively harmful. For example, at first sight it seems possible to detect unnecessary or inappropriate use of hospital beds. But fear of the regulation system and knowledge of the norms which have been developed may lead doctors to reduce lengths of stay when it is *not* appropriate. The effect may be that some patients are discharged early, cannot find proper care outside hospital and have to be re-admitted later on.

The Regulation of Supply – the Hospital

It is because of the difficulties of regulation by purchase that more and more countries are turning to the regulation of supply. The planning of the education and training of health professions is discussed in Chapter 12. Apart from this the main planning of supply has been devoted to hospitals and to a lesser extent to primary care.

As it has come to be appreciated that hospital beds which are supplied tend to be used, there has been legislation or administrative control by insurers in more and more countries to secure that the number of beds supplied is not in excess of the number 'needed'. Some countries have gone further and planned the hospital system so that there are regional hospitals providing the rarer specialities, district hospitals supplying the more common specialist services and small community hospitals for those who do not need specialist hospital care. This has led on to the planning of establishments for specialist manpower. What is remarkable is how many different countries are verging by different routes to similar solutions.

Hospital planning has been imposed by a variety of different means. One method is for insurers to refuse to pay for care in any new facilities which are built if they consider that facilities are already sufficient. For example, in the United States some Blue Cross plans refuse to pay for care in facilities not approved by the local planning council[3] and from 1972 the capital costs (primarily interest and depreciation) of unapproved facilities need not be paid under Medicare.[4] An alternative approach is to withhold grants for construction. To the extent to which hospitals can raise money by public subscription or can accumulate reserves for construction (which in turn depends on whether depreciation can be charged out to insurers or patients), hospitals may not be dependent on external construction grants and thus can evade any local plans. In France, construction grants from social security agencies have long been used to achieve an element of hospital planning. In the United States the Hill Burton programme[5] was successively used first to increase beds and provide hospitals in rural areas, then from 1965 to develop cheaper facilities for long-stay patients and out-of-hospital facilities but only about a quarter of the beds built in the United States were under the programme. In Sweden where hospitals have been almost entirely developed by local government, central government has used the control of medical establishments to control construction. While a county can build or expand hospitals, it will not secure medical staff without the approval of the national board.[6]

But increasingly control over hospital planning has been exercised directly by special legislation for this purpose, In the United States a network of health planning agencies was established at state and local level under the *Partnership for Health Act* 1966. It had advisory functions but no money to enforce that advice. But more and more States passed certificate-of-need laws under which construction could not take place unless it was approved. Over twenty states had such laws at the time of writing. There has also been a burst of hospital legislation in Western Continental Europe over the past few years (France: 31 December 1970, Netherlands: 25 March 1971, Germany: 29 June 1972). In the Netherlands, a Hospital Planning Council has been established. In Germany, regional plans are prepared jointly by the counties, health insurance agencies and hospital associations. Central and local government grants are only made for approved projects and hospitals cannot include depreciation in the charges for health insurance.[7] France has been divided into twenty-one hospital regions in each of which there is a government-appointed commission to estimate hospital construction requirements and advise the Ministry. No new hospital, public or private, can be built without approval from the Ministry. The Ministry also lays down standards for hospital construction. Regional hospitals for the rarer specialities are planned and there is power to bring together the public and private hospitals in each district into groups with a common management.[8] France is evolving towards the pattern of hospital organization established in Britain in 1948.

Hospital planning is greatly eased when the vast majority of hospitals are owned by government as in Britain from 1948 or Scandinavia where local government is the main owner. When it was found in Sweden that each county was trying to provide facilities for the rarer specialities such as thoracic surgery, neuro-surgery and plastic surgery, regional planning was superimposed on the counties. Eight regional hospital centres have been selected to provide the rarer specialities. The centres were chosen so that they maximized the proportion of the population living within four hours' travelling time and minimized the aggregate travel costs and times for the projected population.[9]

In the U.S.S.R. standards have been developed for the number of hospital beds per 1000 population, for the number of doctors per 10,000 and for the number of medical personnel in different categories, based on studies of morbidity, requests for medical assistance and medical examinations of large samples of the population. From these studies of morbidity, the need for hospital and other care is calculated and adjustments are made for variations in morbidity, age and sex structure and other variables when plans are prepared for particular areas. The hospital bed requirement is calculated on the basis of planned levels of occupancy and planned duration of stay. The medical and other manpower requirement is calculated on the basis of planned work loads and planned hours of work.[10]

Most countries start with an inheritance of plant which had evolved before hospitals were rationally planned and cannot be discarded quickly. They also started with an inheritance of loyalties, traditions and vested interests which cannot be easily overcome. The difficulties are greatest where hospitals are under a variety of different ownerships. Where religious loyalties are strong it is not easy to supersede two hospitals owned by different religious groups with one non-sectarian district hospital – particularly when the hospital helps to finance other activities of the religious group. It is not easy to choose one of several candidates for upgrading to a regional hospital. Countries with a robust tradition of local government do not take kindly to tough hospital planning by central government, even where the populations of the local authorities are too small to provide a comprehensive and efficient hospital system. Where the means and prestige of doctors are bound up with rights in particular hospitals, the planning of hospitals inevitably involves altering the rewards and practices of particular doctors. In such circumstances, the organized profession is likely to be a powerful conservative force, mobilizing public opinion in favour of the status quo.

The Regulation of Supply – Primary Care

As planning has extended over the number, siting and function of hospital beds, it has been increasingly accepted that the number of beds required depends upon the extent of development and coordination of primary care and the organization of it. Thus primary care has been planned in some countries to secure a number of different aims. Not all of these are accepted in every country.

The first is to secure that groups of primary-care doctors work together in cooperation rather than competition to serve the needs of their local community. They do not simply make joint use of premises, share supporting staff and arrange a rota to meet patients' demands arising out of office hours, but work together in planning and operating a comprehensive preventive and treatment service and evaluate their joint work.

The second aim is teamwork with other professionals – pharmacists, home care nurses, public health nurses, social workers and others. Teamwork involves the acceptance that each professional member of the team has skills which contribute to the care of patients and that all skills should be appropriately used and pooled. Doctors working in isolated private practice frequently undertake tasks which other staff can do.[11] Any member of a team may be approached for advice about their health. This raises the controversial question of how far nurses or other trained personnel can and should diagnose and treat.[12] A random control trial in Ontario (Canada) has shown that patients who received most of their care

163

from nurse practitioners had similar health status to those treated by doctors. The quality of care also seemed similar.[13]

The third aim is to secure better coordination not only within the primary care services but with specialist and hospital services and community social services. Coordinated services can prevent unnecessary admission to hospital and facilitate early discharge. And for certain patients services can be developed which provide a higher quality of care in the home than could be provided in any type of institution. In all hospitals there is a risk of cross-infection and admission to hospital may make the patient feel more ill and be more ill than he really is. The artificial contacts of hospital visiting are an inadequate substitute for living in the community – contact with which is seen as part of the quality of care.

The essence of primary care is continuity of relationship so that knowledge is acquired of each patient's medical history, family setting and ideally also of his occupational setting, all of which may be relevant for the care of the patient's health and for helping to assess where that care can most appropriately be provided. The role and training of the primary doctor or general practitioner has been hotly debated over the past few decades. Some have argued that much of what a general practitioner does could be done by someone with less training. This may be true, as the Ontario study mentioned above suggests. But extensive education and training are needed to decide when specialist care is required and from what specialty, to advise on the practicability of care outside hospital and to assess what services are needed and secure that they are provided. In particular a doctor is needed to select and oversee the mobilization of a package of services for care at home. Without authoritative leadership, the alternative of care at home may go by default. Thus general practice needs every bit as much training as any other specialty.

A primary care doctor needs nursing staff to assist him in his consulting room and also to visit his patients in their homes – not just to provide nursing services but to assess when further visits from the doctor may be required and to train relatives to provide simple nursing care when the nurse is not present. Secondly he needs staff to help him with preventive work and find patients who may need services but are not receiving them. Thirdly he needs a supporting staff to contact whatever further services a patient may require on his behalf.

In Britain, Finland and Sweden there has been a rapid development of health centres in which doctors provide a full range of
curative and preventive services and work with other health professionals in premises owned by public authorities. In Finland the
system is most developed and general practitioners who used to be
paid under fee-for-service are now paid by salary though they are
allowed to see private patients after they have done their designated
hours for health insurance. In Sweden the vast majority of doctors
in clinic practice are now salaried. In Britain over half the net
remuneration of general practitioners comes in the form of payments
which are akin to salaries.[14] Moreover home nurses and public
health nurses – paid separately by the health services – increasingly
work from doctors' premises, both those which are owned by the
practitioner and those which are not, and each practitioner can in
addition be reimbursed for two-thirds of the salary of two ancillary
workers.

The provincial government of Manitoba (Canada) is planning 'a
controlled and substantial experiment in community health centres',[15]
and the potentialities of health centres has been stressed in the
Hastings Report[16] for Canada as a whole. Similarly Australia is
making experiments with community health centres.[17] The precise
meaning of the term 'health centre' differs in different countries.
What is important is to resist pressures for more elaborate staffing
and equipment than is really needed. 'Large group practice facilities
which attempt to duplicate the resources of general hospitals
represent a disastrous waste of resources.'[18]

In some countries including Britain thinking has gone still further.
It has become accepted that the use of hospitals depends not only on
action by health-orientated staff but on a whole range of social
services which support the family and provide substitutes for care
by the family. Thus the need for hospital beds depends on what
alternative arrangements are available for the care of the patient.
This depends in part on how far relatives and others are prepared
to care for the sick at home and on the services provided to assist
them to do so. Are doctors, nurses, occupational therapists, physiotherapists and others available to provide services in the home? Are
there staff to help with the cleaning and cooking or can meals be
delivered to the home? Are there neighbours or paid staff available
to look after the patient while relatives go out in the evening or go
away for holidays? Are there nursing homes, hostels or boarding out

arrangements for a patient while relatives are away or unable to provide care?

Much also depends on the suitability of the home for the care of the short-term or long-term sick. Can ground-floor accommodation be made available with bathing and toilet facilities which are convenient? Can the home be adapted by installing hoists, rails and ramps and by widening doorways to take wheel-chairs? Nor is hospital care the only alternative to care at home. People who need care – for example, those who are mentally handicapped or suffering from depression or senility can be boarded out with people paid to look after them in their homes or housed in flatlets or grouped housing where a warden can keep an eye on them and provide support and services. Alternatively they can be cared for in hostels. The hospital is therefore seen as at one extreme end of a variety of care institutions and should be used for tasks which cannot be done elsewhere or which only it can do at reasonable cost.

Much will depend on who pays for what when the choice is made between care at home or care elsewhere and on the incentives for those who decide or influence the decision. Much also will depend on relative costs wherever they fall. Much will depend on the preferences and attitudes of both the patient and the relatives and on who interprets them. But ultimately a choice must be made after assessing the burdens, calculating the costs and weighing up the risks.

Thus it is artificial to draw hard and fast lines between health care and social care. Where social services are well developed problems which would present themselves as sickness problems in primary care may come to be seen as social problems and be taken to the social services. Some people clearly need health services, others only need social services, but many need both. Requirements may often shift radically on a day-to-day basis. Yet in many countries of the world the pattern of services and the financing of services – particularly health insurance – is based on three unstated assumptions. First that health institutions and social services can be clearly delineated. Second that preventive medicine can or should be separated from curative medicine. Third that cure rather than care is the overwhelming need of Western nations. There is an unwillingness to accept that for many the prospects of cure are limited and with an aging population it is the quality of care and support which is the most important requirement for the majority of bed-bound patients, for the chronic sick and the disabled.

The managerial work in primary care, like other managerial work, does not lend itself to fee-for-service payment, for the services which are of critical importance to patient care are communication with others on behalf of the patient – explaining the patient's needs to the occupational therapist or physiotherapist, discussing the case on the telephone with the specialist and explaining why priority should be given in the assignment of domestic help. Whether these tasks are actually done by the doctor himself or by his staff, they are not tasks for which standard payment can satisfactorily be made. Fee-for-service payment encourages the doctor to see his role in terms of tasks which bring reward – the consultation, the diagnostic test, the medical act. The task of arranging for the home care of the patient may be much more time-consuming – time for which a fee schedule cannot appropriately provide.

Moreover the concept of social care does not fit happily with fee-for-service payment. Here the task of the physician is not to deliver procedures but deliver emotional support – to comfort the dying, to prepare women for widowhood, to teach people how to live with a disability, to accept the consequences of aging and to give comfort to distressed relatives. These were tasks which in an earlier age many people looked to the Church to provide, but now many expect these services from their doctor. Is the doctor paid under fee-for-service expected to provide these time-consuming services free and at the sacrifice of time which could be spent in services for which he could readily claim? The fundamental question is whether it is the task of the physician simply to perform medical acts or to deliver comprehensive health care.

Nor does the concept of heading a domiciliary team readily fit with private practice. In many countries home nursing is under-developed and where it exists it is a service wholly separate from the doctor. In the hospital setting the nurse makes it her business to be present when the doctor visits and mutual confidence and effective teamwork are encouraged by these regular meetings. Similarly it is much more satisfactory for home nurses to work with a particular doctor or practice to ease communication and simplify the task of securing that patients who need home nursing help receive it rapidly. But the nurse needs an office from which to work. If she goes on holiday or is sick a replacement needs rapidly to be found.

These problems are more readily solved if both doctor and nurse are part of a wider organization, which provides accommodation and pays for all expenses.

Regulating the Distribution of Manpower

One of the most formidable problems which face virtually every country is to ensure that trained personnel – particularly doctors – are available where they are needed. As pointed out in Chapter 5, one of the disadvantages of fee-for-service payment is that there is little financial incentive for professional personnel to settle in areas where such personnel are most needed. When payment is by salary or capitation, inducements to work in less popular areas can be readily built into the remuneration system, or the number of posts in each area can be regulated. The same effect could, however, be built into a fee-for-service system if payments were made from a total 'pool' based upon the population of each area. Thus doctors would be paid whatever proportion of their standard fees could be financed out of the area pool. But such a system of payment would be unlikely to be regarded as fair.

In Western Europe, a variety of financial inducements have been provided to try and attract doctors to work in less popular areas – particularly rural areas. But in no country have these financial advantages been made large enough to solve the problem. If they were, it would involve a major challenge to the belief that those with the greatest skill and prestige should receive the largest rewards. Provided there are enough doctors, as pointed out in Chapter 5, salaried and capitation systems of payment are likely to secure a more even distribution of doctors than payment by fee-for-service. Under capitation payment, remuneration per doctor will be lower in over-doctored areas than in under-doctored areas. But much depends on the other work which doctors can obtain to supplement capitation payments – work for insurance companies, part-time work in occupational health services as well as private practice. Opportunities for supplementary earnings of this kind are likely to be greater in urban areas. Payment by salary makes it possible to limit the number of posts so that those who cannot obtain a post in the area of their choice must look elsewhere.

In Sweden, the problem of providing services in the more remote rural areas has been eased by giving more extended responsibilities to public health nurses. Norway has been particularly successful in filling medical posts in the thinly populated north. A combination of different measures has been used – financial incentive, a wider job content, opportunities to move to less remote areas after a period of service and the creation of a new medical school. While Sweden has many unfilled medical jobs in remote areas, Norway has almost none.[19]

In Britain modest financial inducements to attract general practitioners to areas where there are not enough are reinforced by a system of negative control: only in exceptional circumstances can a general practitioner set up practice in an area scheduled as 'over-doctored'. The system had some success in the nineteen-fifties when the ratio of practitioners to population was increasing. It had less success in the sixties because the ratio declined. Moreover the areas used for scheduling have been too large. Over-doctored areas include pockets which are, by any standards, short of doctors and under-doctored areas include pockets which are well served. Further it is hard to alter the scheduling of areas after doctors working in those areas have established vested interests in the receipt of extra payments.

In Eastern Europe 'posting' of doctors as well as higher salaries have been used to try and attract doctors to work in under-doctored areas – usually the rural and more remote parts of these countries. This has not been wholly successful. Recently special efforts have been made to recruit staff for professional training from the areas which are under-provided with manpower.[20] The relation between medical education and the distribution of medical manpower both geographically and between specialties is discussed further in Chapter 12.

Budget Control

In view of all the difficulties of finding a way to pay hospitals for their services which limits costs and does not lead to undesirable incentives for the management of the hospital, there are obvious advantages in giving a hospital a budget which cannot be exceeded, except when prices, salaries and wages have risen which justify a supplementary allocation. This places on the hospital the responsibility to provide the best service it can from the money allocated to it. Indeed the budget for each hospital can be derived from a regional budget for all hospitals based on the population served by the region with allowance for the demographic characteristics of that population and any special health needs of the region compared with other regions.

While the cost of each hospital can be contained by giving it a limited budget, there is still a formidable problem of establishing how to allocate fairly a regional budget if hospitals are performing different functions and are of different size. Only if there are fairly large district hospitals providing comprehensive services can the easy solution be adopted of allocating money on the basis of population served. A hospital can curtail its costs not only by becoming more efficient but by treating fewer patients for longer stays, by admitting less severe cases or by treating less intensively. But the key to the efficient use of the hospital may be improvements in out-of-hospital services so that fewer patients need to be referred to it and services are available to give proper care to patients discharged early from it.

Separate budgets for hospital and non-hospital purposes obstruct the process of finding the appropriate balance between hospital and non-hospital services. It is for this, among other reasons, that the British National Health Service was reorganized in April 1974 to provide regional and area budgets out of which comprehensive health services are financed. The idea of creating budgets out of which comprehensive health services should be provided for a given population has gained popularity in the United States under the title 'Health Maintenance Organizations'. For many years what were earlier called group practice organizations (notably Kaiser Permanente) have been shown to provide comprehensive care at lower cost, particularly by making less use of hospital beds. (About 3 per cent of the population of the United States are in plans of this type.)

Hence it is suggested that competing profit and non-profit health maintenance organizations should be established offering services of this kind. If competing organizations were to have their own hospitals in the same area, there would either be an uneconomic duplication of facilities or greater travel costs for hospital users. In so far as H.M.O.s compete this could lead to an undesirable emphasis on amenity and convenience at the expense of economies in those services of the importance of which patients are not aware. In so far as the services of different H.M.O.s are offered at varying prices, the better off may choose the more expensive contracts on the assumption that they *must* be purchasing better services. If they do, this could frustrate the pressures for economy which it is hoped that competition will generate. If organizations are allowed to select their members, premiums will presumably become risk-rated and high-risk users will be forced to pay high premiums or find their health services elsewhere. Competition between organizations could lead to competition for scarce resources, so that the geographical distribution of health services could become worse. This would be more likely to happen if doctors shared all or part of the profits of H.M.O.s. Moreover it would place a heavy strain on medical ethics for groups of doctors to be in the position where every dollar of expenditure they authorized for patients was a dollar deducted from their pay.

Under the Health Maintenance Organization Act 1973, grants will be provided to help establish H.M.O.s which meet certain criteria. To prevent the problems which would arise with risk-rating, to be eligible for grants, H.M.O.s must, subject to defined exceptions, be open to all and enrol a membership which is representative of age, social and income groups. In the attempt to ensure that a quality service is provided, provisions are made for internal and external review and regulation.[21] It is envisaged that H.M.O.s will compete with other insurers for members.

Most of the problems involved in competing H.M.O.s would be avoided if there were only one organization responsible for providing health services for a region of a million or two million people. But there would still be a risk of resources being heavily concentrated in the richer areas and in areas where professional people prefer to practise unless there were manpower ceilings for each region for different categories of scarce personnel. Health insurance can provide money but it cannot ensure that there are doctors, dentists, nurses and other health manpower where that money is being spent.

Where there is one authority with responsibility for health, it is possible to survey the community as a whole and find what needs are unmet or inadequately met and re-allocate resources to meet those needs. It is possible to look at health in its entirety. How do standards of care for the acute sick compare with standards for the chronic sick? Why are there differences in morbidity, infant mortality, maternal mortality and expectation of life in different economic and social groups? What features of the environment are generating ill health? What is the relation between bad housing and health? What occupations are causing hazards to health? Should family planning be promoted to prevent abortion? How can the incidence of venereal disease – second only to respiratory infection in its prevalence among the infectious diseases of the United States – be reduced? How can cigarette smoking be discouraged? How is it possible to cut down the annual toll of road and industrial accidents? Choices may have to be made between free condoms and free coronary care units, between anti-smoking clinics and radical cancer surgery and between high standards of care for those who can appreciate it and technical survival for those who cannot.

Evaluation and Democratic Control

But who are to make these choices? If regional budgeting and regional planning are the future pattern for the organization and financing of health services, the problems of the future are how to establish methods of using these budgets to promote quality of care, to identify and meet health needs in the widest sense, to secure value for money, and to ensure that the bureaucracies that control these budgets are responsive to the wishes of the communities which they are established to serve. In the last analysis whose values should prevail? How can an effective working relationship be established between representatives of patients, representatives of those who bear the costs and health professionals? How can lay representatives be found with the judgment to know where it is proper to overrule professional opinion in establishing broad priorities and when professional opinion should prevail?

At the very least more information is needed about levels of health in different social and occupational groups, the activities of health professionals and the results of these activities. Despite the vast resources devoted to health services, extremely little information is currently available which relates the use of health resources to health benefits in any sense. While some doctor may come to know of a patient's death, disability or recovery, it is not necessarily known to the doctor who took the critical decision in the patient's management. While death and recorded causes of death are carefully registered, this information is not systematically related to past patient management or to the use of health resources on the care of that patient. Rarely is the clinician able to compare his performance with that of his colleagues in a systematic way, standardized for diagnosis, severity, age and other variables. What is needed is a system of information which shows those who take professional decisions, the results of those decisions and the resources used to achieve these results. This information should be available for independent professional review.[22]

Information is needed not only to improve the operation of existing services, but to plan better services for the future. One object of planning is to limit the supply of expensive facilities which are likely to be wasted and to encourage the use of less costly alternatives. A second purpose is to find unmet needs and ensure that they are met. A third purpose of planning is to prevent the under-utilization of scarce skills and expensive equipment.

Health planning can start with studies of the health and social needs of the existing population and how these needs can most appropriately be met. Thus study needs to be made of those needing services which they are not demanding as well as those who are provided with care which is unnecessary or can be provided in an alternative setting. The problem can be broken down into diagnoses for easier handling. What cases need to be admitted to hospital and if admitted how long do they need to stay there? While there have been many studies where hospital doctors have identified those patients who are considered not to need or no longer need hospital care, there have seldom been more careful independent assessments by multi-disciplinary teams. What is needed is imaginative and sympathetic investigation of alternatives to hospital care – not only those that exist in the community and those that might – and experiments with their use.

But any plan needs to be a long-term plan because it takes so long to train manpower and so long to acquire sites and construct large and complex buildings. Thus projections need to be made of social, medical and demographic changes in the population and in its geographical location. But a 'static' survey ignores the dynamics of both health and social care. Current needs are partly determined by the extent to which needs have been met in the past. To an extent which is not precisely known appropriate care given early in the right setting by the right staff can prevent or delay deterioration. What people can do for themselves today depends on what they have been given the opportunities to do in the past. The institution which does not assist those who could get up and about to do so as soon as possible results in more bed-ridden people and more need for nursing care. The institution which provides no occupation, activity or stimulation and cuts residents off from community links may be a cause of mental deterioration. Early efforts at rehabilitation determine long-term care needs. 'The first requirement of a hospital', wrote Miss Nightingale, 'is that it should do the sick no harm.' This cannot be said for every hospital – even those which appear superficially to be providing adequate standards of care.

What are needed are experiments in providing alternative patterns of care and treatments which are monitored over long periods. This is of special importance in evolving patterns of care for long-stay patients – particularly the elderly, the mentally ill and the mentally handicapped. These studies need to be conducted with careful controls if they cannot be conducted with random populations.

What is virtually certain is that any planning norms adopted for the future will prove to be wrong by the time that future comes. There is no way of projecting with any degree of accuracy all the environmental, social and medical changes on which future needs will depend. Thus there must be provision for later adjustments. This can be secured partly by building on hospital and other sites where there is room for extension and designing facilities in a way which makes extension possible. The technique of the rolling plan can be used to revise plans regularly as new information becomes available. Thus each year a new ten-year plan can be drafted. Each year the dates when projects start and the size of manpower training programmes can be reviewed and changed as appropriate.

Conclusion

Thus the supply of health services needs to be planned. It is not enough to attempt to regulate the demands for resources made by doctors after they have been made. Planning needs to extend not only over hospitals and facilities for primary care but over medical and other manpower to staff the services and over all the related facilities for social care.

The quality of planning depends upon the quality of information used for the planning and the skill of the planners. But this in turn depends partly on knowledge of what resources should be used for what purposes and on evaluation of the results. But the best-laid plans can fail to be fulfilled unless those working in the services want to make them work. Thus ultimately what matters is not just the financial incentives operating on those working in health services, but their ethos and their commitment to serve not only individual patients but the health of the community as a whole. This is not true only of doctors, dentists or of administrators and managers, but of nurses, social workers, and paramedical workers as well.

Value for money in health care will not be secured until health professionals see it as part of their responsibility to see that it is. This has major implications for the original education and continuing education of those working in health services. It also has major implications for the selection of those who are educated and trained and for those who provide that education and training. These questions are discussed in Chapter 12.

NOTES

1. See Senate Committee on Finance, *Background Material Relating to Professional Standards Review Organisations*, Washington, D.C., 1974. See also *New England Journal of Medicine*, Vol. 290. No. 3, 1974.

2. See Katherine G. Bauer and P. M. Densen, 'Some Issues in the Incentive Reimbursement Approach to Cost Containment', *Medical Care Review*, Vol. 31, No. 1, January 1974, pp. 79–98. See also *Federal Register*, Vol. 39, No. 16, 23 January 1974, pp. 2693–701.

3. H. E. Klarman, 'Major Public Initiatives in Health Care', *Public Interest*, No. 34, 1973.

4. C. C. Havighurst, 'Regulation of Health Facilities and Services by "Certificate of Need"', *Virginia Law Review*, Vol. 59, 1973, pp. 1143–232.

5. Under the Hospital Survey and Construction Act 1946. See C. C. Havighurst, op. cit.

6. Odin W. Anderson, op. cit., p. 112.

7. S. Eichhorn, 'German Federal Republic', *Health Service Prospects*, Lancet and N.P.H.T., 1973, pp. 84–9.

8. R. F. Bridgman and M. I. Roemer, *Hospital Legislation and Hospital Systems*, Public Health Papers, No. 50, W.H.O., Geneva, 1973. See also P. Cornillot and P. Bonamour, 'France', *Health Service Prospects*, Lancet and N.P.H.T., 1973.

9. S. Ake Lindgren, 'Sweden', *Health Service Prospects*, p. 120. See also V. Navarro, *National and Regional Health Planning in Sweden*, D.H.E.W., 1974.

10. G. A. Popov, *Principles of Health Planning in USSR*, Public Health Papers No. 43, W.H.O., Geneva, 1971.

11. For example, analyses in Germany show that doctors and dentists care for substantially more patients when they are supported by auxiliaries. R. Maxwell, op. cit., p. 24.

12. This is discussed further in Chapter 12 below.

13. W. O. Spitzer and others, 'The Burlington Randomized Trial of the Nurse Practitioner', *New England Journal of Medicine*, 31 January 1974,

pp. 251–6. For the role of feldshers in the organization of health services in the U.S.S.R., see *The Training and Utilization of Feldshers in the USSR*, Public Health Papers, No. 56, W.H.O., Geneva, 1974.

14. See p. 69 above.
15. Government of Manitoba, *White Paper on Health Policy*, July 1972, p. 46.
16. *The Community Health Centre in Canada*, Information Canada, Ottawa, 1972.
17. *The Australian Health Insurance Programme*, Canberra, 1973.
18. R. Maxwell, op. cit., p. 25.
19. ibid., pp. 22–3.
20. *The Selection of Students for Medical Education*, W.H.O. Regional Office for Europe, Copenhagen, 1973.
21. See Marjorie Mueller, 'Health Maintenance Organisation Act of 1973', *Research and Statistics Note*, D.H.E.W., 12 March 1974.
22. See, for example, B. Abel-Smith et al., *Accounting for Health*, K.E.H.F., London, 1973.

CHAPTER 11

Planning in Developing Countries

Developing countries are almost by definition short of the resources which contribute to economic and social development – highly educated manpower, entrepreneurial skill for running large enterprises and funds available for investment. There may also be a shortage of foreign exchange depending on whether crops, minerals or fuels are produced which are particularly sought in world markets. Because levels of living are low, taxable capacity is low, quite apart from the administrative problems of operating complex systems of taxation where the bulk of the population is engaged in peasant farming.

While developing countries share these general characteristics, the extent to which a particular developing country faces each of these problems varies widely. Some developing countries are relatively rich in foreign exchange and some achieve a high level of investment, though much of it is dissipated in luxury residential accommodation. While some have a shortage of young people with the educational attainment expected of those entering higher education, others have a surplus of unemployed graduates – including medical graduates. In some developing countries the population is concentrated in areas with relatively good transport facilities. In others the population is dispersed over vast areas, so that it may take weeks or months to reach remote communities other than by helicopter. Some developing countries have a pleasant climate throughout the year and others are intolerably hot or intolerably cold for long seasons.

The extreme problem facing the health planners in some developing countries can be illustrated by setting out the resources at their disposal. In 1963–4 government health expenditure per head in Indonesia was 20 U.S. cents and in Nigeria, Thailand and Malawi about half a U.S. dollar and in the Sudan about one U.S. dollar.

At about the same period health expenditure in the U.S. was about 200 U.S. dollars.[1] In 1965, Malawi had one doctor per 148,000 population and one nurse per 47,000, Nigeria had one doctor per 50,000 population, the Sudan had one doctor per 29,000 and one nurse per 43,000.[2] Moreover average doctor/patient ratios for a whole country can be misleading. The overall doctor/patient ratio in Ethiopia was one to 65,000 but in the rural areas there were probably five to ten doctors per million population. Half the doctors were in Addis Ababa which in 1965 had only 2·5 per cent of the population.[3] Thailand appears to be better served than most developing countries as in 1965 it had one doctor per 7,600 overall. But there was one doctor per 940 in Bangkok and most of the doctors outside the capital were clustered in provincial capitals. In the truly rural areas there was less than one doctor per 200,000.[4] In Northern Nigeria the ratio was estimated to be one doctor per 140,000.[5] Bombay, Calcutta and New Delhi have doctor/patient ratios around one per 500 while in the rural areas the average is one doctor per 30,000–45,000.[6] This distribution is partly a reflection of the extreme inequality between the living standards of the urban middle class and the rural peasant.

The main resource which developing countries have in common is people. This suggests the need to find labour-intensive ways of doing everything. Where there is a shortage of higher educated manpower, any task which has to be frequently repeated can be delegated to personnel who can be trained to undertake even complex routine tasks. In view of the shortage of taxable capacity and the long-established customs of exchange of labour services, many services can be provided by trained volunteers. It is wrong to start with the Western capitalist assumption that money is the only reward which can be offered for services. In many cultures reciprocal exchange of services is as important as exchange for money, and status is a reward in itself.

As in more developed countries, attitudes and beliefs of the people should be the starting point for any health planning. What are their beliefs about sickness and disease? How do they currently handle ill-health? Which features of their culture are favourable to health and which are unfavourable? What are the habits of personal hygiene? What is the balance of the diet? What foods are excluded from the diet for reasons of taboo? How is water collected and stored and where is human waste disposed? How are children reared and cuts tended? How is mental illness regarded, how far is it tolerated and how is it treated?

In view of the cost of providing health services, the first aim must be to help people look after their own health in so far as this is possible. Hence the importance of health education in its widest sense. The aim must be to improve diet, to create a safer environment with clean water and efficient sewage disposal and to promote personal hygiene. For example, infant mortality is high not simply because of the high incidence of diarrhoeal and airborne diseases, but because children are too mal-nourished to resist disease. Hence the high death-rate from such diseases as tuberculosis and measles as well as the diarrhoeal diseases. Health education should be a part of community development and part of school education. A major part of the health effort should be the responsibility of Ministries other than the Ministry of Health.

Where there are traditional healers, herbalists and practitioners it is important to study the medicine which they practise and how they are rewarded. In many developing countries even relatively poor people spend more on the health services they buy than the government spends on providing them with services.[7] It is a mistake to imagine that all traditional medicine can be ignored or swept away and an alien culture of Western medicine imposed on people with their own deeply held beliefs about the nature of disease and its causes. So much of the effectiveness of all medicine depends upon people believing in it. Traditional healers command the confidence of the population they are serving. This may give them an effectiveness in some areas of medicine which the Western doctor cannot hope to emulate. Moreover, opposition from traditional healers may cause 'Western' health efforts to fail because of lack of cooperation.

A bridge must be built between the old culture and the new and wherever possible a place should be found for the traditional doctor to work in association with the new organized services. He is economic. He operates without costly medical schools and imported drugs and equipment. He needs no electrical equipment and makes no inroads on limited taxable capacity. Most important of all he is in contact with the people and can be a positive or negative force in health education. His remedies are likely to be taken as well as or instead of those provided by the organized health services whatever the strength of the latter. Moreover he can often be trained to include Western remedies as part of his medical practice.

Secondly, any health plan must be designed to use sparingly any resources which are particularly scarce or costly – highly educated manpower, imports or buildings built by foreign contractors. One way of limiting the use of scarce items is to price them well above cost in health budgets and cost calculations. For this reason it may be unwise to exclude health imports from import taxes so that users know that they are using a scarce resource. Moreover local building materials should be used wherever possible. The tall concrete hospitals and medical arts buildings of Western nations are a response to the high costs of labour, land and imported materials. In most developing countries mud, timber and labour are cheap[8] and sites can generally be found at reasonable cost, where buildings can be spread horizontally rather than vertically. This has the great advantage of flexibility for future adaptation when medical techniques alter or standards of care can be improved. Similarly mechanization of the hospital is a further response to high labour costs. In a country with no shortage of cheap labour, many tasks are more economically done by hand than by machine. Moreover sophisticated mechanical equipment needs skilled labour to keep it in repair; such technical skills are particularly rare in developing countries.

Geographical Distribution

A clear decision needs to be taken on how it is intended to distribute health resources before health plans can proceed. Is the aim to spend the same amount on each quarter of a million of the population, whether urban or rural? Or is the aim to provide the same access to services to each quarter million of population, bearing in mind that it will be more costly to provide a service of any level of sophistication to remote rural communities than to areas where population is concentrated, because of the cost of access and transport? Or is the aim to equalize life chances of morbidity and mortality? This may require disproportionately high expenditure on the rural population and on the urban poor and particularly the urban squatter in the shanty towns that surround the cities of Asia and Latin America.

No health plan can be entirely shielded from political considerations. A powerful politician may have promised to secure a hospital for his constituency and he is likely to get it. Any theoretical distributional aim may be modified by short-term political pressures. These are the realities of life in any country. Public opinion may be better mobilized in the cities where more and better hospital facilities may be demanded. All the health planner can do is to point out how few can benefit from an urban hospital and how many less organized and articulate people could gain from the more extensive use of resources to develop services in rural areas.

In a democratic society, governments want to be re-elected and thus adopt policies which they believe will be or will become popular with their electorate. And less democratic governments normally find it more convenient to govern by consent than by force. But the consent they may be seeking is that of the urban middle class and the skilled worker, for policies which favour the wealthy most of all.

Political pressure can create a bias towards health policies which are readily understood and bring easily identifiable results rather than those which are more complex to explain and slower to bring results even if these results will be more lasting. The fact of ill-health is evident for all to see, while the causes of it are much less evident. It is partly for this reason that politicians in many countries are under pressure to provide curative rather than preventive services except where preventive services bring rapid and obvious results. But curative services can be used to build a bridge to the acceptance of personal preventive services. For some preventive health campaigns a rural health infrastructure is essential. But where it exists it is not always used for this purpose.

In many countries a heavy emphasis has been placed on large urban hospitals which are expensive to build and expensive to maintain, and actually serve to a very large extent their local population whatever their theoretical role and purpose. For example, a hospital in Pakistan cost 43·5 million rupees to build while total expenditure for the Rural Health Centre Programme amounted to only 16·5 million rupees.[9] The new 500-bed teaching hospital in Addis Ababa is expected to cost almost as much as the total annual health budget of the country.[10] The 300-bed hospital at Tamale (Ghana) will cost £2·4 million. The running cost is estimated to be £600,000 – more than double the operating budget of the entire Northern Region.[11] For the same cost it would be possible to build 240 Health Centres at West African standards.[12] For the cost of operating the three open-heart surgery units in Bogota, a quarter of the children of that city could be given half a litre of milk per day.[13] Malnutrition, not heart disease, is a major problem in Bogota.

Other governments have consciously sought public co-operation and understanding and built health messages into the process of political education and education in schools. They have made preventive health part of the nationalist message. This appears to have had a major impact in China:

> Cholera and plague were conquered in the first 3 or 4 years after liberation. Flies, rats, bedbugs and mosquitoes were eradicated by a 'people's war' against these pests: every Chinese was asked to swat a few flies every day. This strategy continues, resulting in a practically fly-free country. Health campaigns are propagated by doctors and nurses into popular language. Health education in China is not based on complicated psychologic and sociologic theories as in Western countries, but is part of socialist education in general, stressing everyone's responsibilities with respect to society, family and the individual. There are no rigid regulations from above, but instead information and explanation from below.[14]

The provision of health services can yield political benefits in a country which is torn by sectional feuds and rival racial, tribal and religious loyalties by creating a greater sense of social cohesion. A health service which treats all alike may reduce strife and tension and help to promote national unity. Equal access to services for the sick can provide some compensation for inequalities elsewhere in society. Health services can bring tangible benefits to rural populations which cannot be as rapidly achieved in other sectors of development. A health policy can be a way of providing a share of development for those who often benefit least from economic progress. What is needed is the political will to redistribute resources. In some developing countries, particularly in Latin America, this will is absent.

The decision on how equitably resources should be distributed is of fundamental importance for the planning of manpower training policies because of the crucial problems of access to health services. Some people will travel remarkable distances to obtain health services. Stories abound of the fortitude of sturdy peasants who have walked for days to obtain medical help despite severe injuries. But anecdotes are no substitute for soundly based statistics: 'It was found in Kenya that 40 per cent of the out-patients attending a health centre lived within five miles of it, 30 per cent lived between 5 and

10 miles from it and a further 30 per cent lived more than 10 miles away.'[15] 'In Uganda the average number of out-patients' attendances per person halves for every two miles that people live from a hospital, every one and a half miles from a dispensary, and every mile from an aide post.'[16] 'The better the medicine the further will people be prepared to go for it.'[17]

Those who are least fit to travel use health services least in areas where travel by road is impossible and by air not available. And for many conditions such as cholera or abnormal delivery, the speed at which treatment is provided can be critical. Travel involves costs in absence from work and other activity quite apart from payments for public transport where it is available. Travel costs can be very high when the only practicable way of getting a sick person to a health service is by taxi or hired car. A study of the Metyana Hospital, Uganda showed that the average patient spent 35 U.S. cents in transport to get to the out-patient department to obtain an average of 11 U.S. cents worth of care.[18] The average in-patient spent 1·09 $U.S. in travel. The total expenditure in travel by the patients represented more than half the cost of running the hospital. This calculation takes no account of the loss of working time involved in the visit to the hospital.

More outlets would have substantially reduced the burden of the cost of sickness on the community. If more outlets would have been more costly, then patients would have been financially better off if they had paid a modest charge for their health services and been relieved of the travel cost. It may be more economic to provide mobile services so that the travelling is done by the few providers rather than the large number of users. A mobile service can be most effective when there is an unpaid village worker at each stop to act as the local representative of health services and provide simple care between visits – midwifery, immunization and first aid.[19] This is the logic of the Chinese 'bare-footed' doctor who is given some training and provides such health services as he can on a voluntary basis in his community.

Planning within a Realistic Budget

Planning of services provided by paid staff must start with the money likely to be available and the manpower which can be made available. The starting point for health planning should be economic resources not data on disease. Moreover, what is likely to be available in ten to fifteen years' time, or in the case of university trained staff in thirty years' time, is more relevant to longer-term planning than what is available today, as plans to construct buildings and manpower training policies take time to bring results on a national basis. Somehow some politically approved estimate must be made of the future health budget and of the population which will need to be served out of that budget. Similarly some politically approved estimate must be made of the share of educated manpower which can be allocated to the health sector. Such estimates will need to take into account the health improvements which it would be hoped to secure with extra money, the importance attached to combating any unfavourable health consequences of planned economic developments and any economic benefits expected to flow from health improvements as compared to the gains to be received by directing the money to other sectors of development. This starting point is too often forgotten when health planning is left entirely in the hands of doctors without economic planners working with them.

In Latin America a complex methodology of health planning has been evolved at the Centre of Development Studies – the CENDES method.[20] The method starts from the logic that 'a resource is efficiently used if the benefit obtained from its use is greater than that which would have been obtained if the same resource had been used for something else.' Thus it attempts to relate the benefit of resources used in alternative ways to the benefits in saving deaths and morbidity. The planning objective is to find the combination of resources that will have the greatest impact on health.

The method raises all the problems discussed at the end of Chapter 8. How are lives to be valued? How is morbidity to be related to mortality? Moreover an effective attack on one disease may require an attack on several diseases at the same time. But in addition the method requires knowledge of the effectiveness of all the different forms of intervention and their costs, and knowledge of the incidence of death and morbidity by cause. Even in the most developed countries, much of this information is not available and an enormous costly effort would be needed to make it available in a developing country. While the CENDES method provides a valuable theoretical framework for thinking about the problems of allocating health resources, it cannot produce solutions to the allocation of total resources which can be applied in practice.[21]

Although the data does not exist from which choices can be made among all possible uses of health resources, it is still valuable to piece together such information as is available or can be estimated both about the costs of existing services and about the major health problems which confront a country so that priorities are chosen with the best possible examination of the costs and effects of alternative strategies. Existing expenditure patterns need to be analysed by sources of funds, by geographical allocation of these funds, by social and occupational categories of beneficiary, type of facility and type of health programme (preventive or curative, communicable and other diseases, etc.).[22] There are narrow areas – particularly in the field of communicable diseases – where the effectiveness of intervention is known with reasonable accuracy and cost-effectiveness can be estimated. The priorities which many countries have selected have included malnutrition, family planning, diseases of young children as well as the main communicable diseases. The main measures taken have included immunization, attempts to promote the use of the pill and condom for birth-spacing, attempts to change dietary habits and prevent the decline in breast-feeding and introduce simple sanitation programmes and safer water supplies. Health education has had a key part to play and many programmes to combat communicable diseases have been implemented by personnel with very limited training. But in many countries only a small proportion of health resources has been allocated to programmes of this kind. While lip-service has been paid to these priorities, the bulk of money has been spent on urban hospitals, including teaching hospitals. Between 1963 and 1972, the number of medical schools in Africa south of the Sahara increased from 17 to 31.[23]

Planning must start with the consideration of available resources because a plan which is not realistic for application all over the whole country creates an unintended maldistribution of resources. Developing countries are peppered with the graveyards of earlier, over-ambitious plans. For example, the decision may have been taken to build a demonstration health centre to serve 50,000 population, with three doctors, two midwives, a health visitor, a sanitary inspector and a range of other staff. However desirable such a standard of staffing may be, it simply was not practicable to train the staff and pay them if this plan had been implemented all over the country. Indeed if health services had been provided nationally on that scale half the national income of some countries would have been needed to pay for health services alone, and every student qualified to enter university might have needed to enter medical school. If such a plan has been accepted what often happens is that the first health centre is built but never staffed up to the planned complement, and facilities go unused. Nevertheless that population of 50,000 may still obtain a service costing more than it is possible to provide for any other population of 50,000 in the country for as far as can be seen ahead.

Thus no health plan is of use unless money will be provided to pay all the costs of implementing it on a national basis within a reasonable period of time. A start can be made with a relatively low level of service which can be upgraded later on, if and when resources become available. Secondly, no health plan is realistic unless it is feasible in terms of the availability of the manpower needing training. Thirdly, any plan must be reproducible in a further sense. What can be achieved by a health team led by one outstanding charismatic personality tells us nothing about what the average health team will achieve.

A developing country can afford an unstructured hospital system even less than a richer country. In so far as money can be spared for hospitals, they need to be planned on a regional and district basis so that rarer specialties are only available in regional hospitals. Secondly, the waste of overlapping and duplicated services cannot be afforded. There needs to be one chain of hospitals to serve the whole community and not separate hospitals for different social classes, for different denominational groups, for different occupations or for members of different social security funds.

Starting from manpower and budget ceilings involves tough decisions between alternatives all of which need careful costing. This can be illustrated by setting out some options for local health services in an imaginary country. Let us assume that after allowing for projected running costs of existing regional hospitals, medical schools and the central administration fifteen years ahead the projected health budget allows for 1000 rubars (the local currency) per month to be spent per $\frac{1}{4}$ million population. In the existing budget, 70 per cent of the money goes on staff, and let us assume for the moment that this will still apply under the plan which is selected. (It will be necessary to go back and re-examine all these assumptions at a later stage.) Thus 700 rubars a month is available for salaries of staff to provide health services for each $\frac{1}{4}$ million population. At present, university educated personnel (e.g. doctors or dentists) are paid an average of 100 rubars a month, persons with training following secondary education 30 rubars a month and persons with only primary education 10 rubars a month. Three possible ways of spending the money are shown in Table 3 (There could of course be many more alternatives.)

TABLE 3

Options for Staffing Health Services to Serve 1 million People

	Monthly salary	Options		
		A	B	C
University training	100	7	4	2
Secondary School leaver	30	–	6	6
Primary School leaver	10	–	12	32

Option A is obviously absurd. It cannot make economic sense to have doctors working without anyone to whom they can delegate particular tasks. Most medical services do not need to be provided by doctors – immunization, dressing of wounds, health education, sanitary inspection, obstetrics. Even though some developing countries have general practitioners working without any supporting staff this is equally wasteful. Moreover one doctor per 36,000 persons would leave vast and urgent needs unmet.

Option B looks more promising. At least there are supporting staff working with the doctors. If one decided to station the middle grade of staff at six health centres each with one low-grade worker and supervised by a doctor on alternate days or weeks and the other low grade workers in six dispensaries working alone, each health unit would still be responsible for providing services to over 20,000 people. Option C does at least make it possible to have at least one paid full-time staff member per 10,000 people which is very slender coverage.

Table 3 provides a useful and simple planning tool. Of course, more sophisticated analyses would be needed to allow for staff leave, sickness, refresher courses and the cost of the initial training and to check whether the remaining 30 per cent of the budget is enough to pay for administrative support, equipment and supplies and particularly the transport costs needed for the personnel to perform their allotted tasks in the pattern of health services which is selected. Moreover relative salary levels are not fixed for all time and the proportion of the budget allotted to regional hospitals and central services should also be re-examined particularly as the former provides a service to such a limited urban population. But the essential message is that the size of the budget may well determine what level of staff should be trained if the aim is to bring some service within reach of virtually the whole population.

To those accustomed to the way in which health services are provided in more developed countries it may seem unethical or dangerous to contemplate a health worker with primary education and a short training course who would be expected to provide health services to a population of 10,000 people. The contribution which such a worker could make would depend on the tasks which he is trained to do, on what equipment and medicaments are provided for him to use and on the supervision and further training provided for him. For example, little education is needed to provide immunization services and every society has developed its untrained midwives. None of us would be here if it were impossible for births to take place without the attendance of an obstetrician. Moreover there are many communicable diseases of which the symptoms are readily recognized and for which there are effective cures or courses of treatment. The dangers caused by the application of these remedies in circumstances where they are not justified must be compared with the gains from using them when their use is justified. But if the choice is between one auxiliary per 10,000 and one doctor per 32,000, unmet need is likely to be much greater in the second case simply because of the limit to the number of cases any individual, however well-educated, can see in a day, quite apart from the problems of transport and access.

The work of auxiliaries should not be confined to curative medicine and immunization against infectious diseases. They need to give continuous support to all aspects of environmental sanitation, examine local water supplies and play an active part in health education. They need to give health examinations to infants and children of school age and advise on diet – particularly for young children. These are all tasks for which auxiliaries can be trained. Many countries have long experience of the use of auxiliaries for vaccinations and immunizations. Multi-purpose auxiliaries have been developed in several countries in Africa – not just medical assistants with secondary education but rural medical aids with only primary education before their training. The system has been expanding in Tanzania in recent years. From 1968 Venezuela has developed a programme of simplified medicine provided by medical auxiliaries with four months' training.[24] In the past few years, Iran has begun to train front-line health workers who work in the villages in pairs, one male and one female, to provide preventive services, check on the environment, engage in health education, care for mothers and children and to provide simple curative services linked to the health centre. There are plans to provide a total of 60,000 such workers each to serve an average of 500 people.[25]

The auxiliary worker drawn from the community has advantages over the doctor drawn from another area and isolated from the habits of speech and behaviour of rural people by years of education in an urban setting. The auxiliary worker should be in a better position to understand the real meaning of what is said to him and to find out what other remedies the sick person may be taking and rituals he may be observing in response to the traditional medicine and culture of that community. Moreover he is likely to be content to stay in his community and thus provide continuity of care and come to know and be known by the families he is trying to help. Continuous service from an auxiliary with limited training may be better than service from a constantly changing succession of discontented young and relatively inexperienced doctors required to serve their two years of rural posting before getting on with what they may see as their ultimate career – working in hospital medicine or in urban private practice.

The quality of service provided by auxiliaries of limited education and training can and should be evaluated. How many patients are worse off from being given the wrong treatment or no treatment and with what consequences? How much better a service could have been provided with the resources locally available by a higher trained person? For example, the diagnosis of renal failure is of no value if there is no access to dialysis or transplant facilities. If the district and regional hospitals can only admit a small proportion of those who could benefit from hospital care, it is important that these services should be used to help those who can by some criteria derive the greatest advantage from them. The ascertainment of future cases requiring hospital care does not contribute to the improvement of health unless those cases could obtain greater advantage from the use of resources than those for whom these resources were currently being used. Hospital care should be heavily restricted in the poorer developing countries. Wherever possible patients should be treated while still living at home. This is as important for patients who are mentally ill as for those who are physically ill.

The quality of the work of auxiliaries will depend not only on their original training but on the provision of continuous further training after qualification. It will also depend on the extent to which they are supervised and their work is appreciated by those above them in the chain of command. Thirdly, it will depend on adequate supplies. Just as a doctor needs appropriate equipment and supplies to be effective, so does the auxiliary. It is economically better to have fewer auxiliaries who can be kept fully supplied with medicines and equipment than more auxiliaries who are frequently short of supplies.

The essential principle is that no patient should be treated by a person with greater skill or in facilities of greater sophistication than are needed to provide effective treatment. Dr Maurice King has stated this principle clearly:

> Most patients with the common diseases of developing countries such as kwashiorkor, hookworm infestation, malaria, pneumonia and tuberculosis can be treated effectively from health centres, and for most of them the care provided by the health centre may be as effective as that provided by a district hospital. Similarly, there is a further range of common cases such as most of those due to trauma or the abnormalities of child birth which are likely to be treated nearly if not quite as effectively in a good district hospital as they are in a regional or national one . . . In respect therefore of most cases of these common conditions, there is thus little relationship between the cost and size of a medical unit and its therapeutic efficiency.[26]

It is the common experience of developing countries that whatever services are provided, these services tend to attract more work than they can handle. Moreover when services are provided at different levels of sophistication, the queues at the higher levels are proportionately greater. It does not take long for people to appreciate that a higher quality of service can be provided at a health centre than at a dispensary, at a hospital than at a health centre, and at a regional hospital than at a district hospital. The patient cannot know which conditions require complex facilities and high skill and which do not. Though there may be, in theory, a referral system to ensure that higher levels of care are confined to patients selected for it by lower levels of the service, this can be frustrated by patients going direct to the best-equipped part of the service they can reach. The consequence is vast queues at hospital out-patient departments and in-patient departments of costly regional hospitals filled beyond capacity with patients with relatively simple diseases.

Willingness to queue is not a good criterion of need: those with the greatest need may be the least able to travel. Moreover some queues can be serious health hazards in themselves. It is no remedy to ensure that whether patients go direct to the regional hospital or the local dispensary, the non-referred patient is seen by auxiliaries of the same level of training. It cannot be hidden from patients that a higher proportion of patients are referred to a hospital which is adjacent than to one that is farther away. One possibility is to arrange for cases to be seen initially by less trained staff at a hospital than at a health centre. Another is to charge the full cost to patients who go direct to the hospital and not to charge or charge less when patients use the local facility which they are intended to use. A sterner measure is to stop patients entering the compound of a hospital unless they have evidence that they are referred or come by ambulance as emergencies.

Ideologically it is desirable in all countries for curative and preventive services to be provided by the same health team and for personnel to operate in both areas. But in practice a health worker with both curative and preventive functions is at risk of being so overwhelmed with pressing demands for curative services, that preventive work is indefinitely postponed. Charging for curative services is one way of securing that resources are available for preventive services. But many of those who need health services most may be least able to pay for them. Moreover, those proved to be able to pay may be so few that the cost of administering a system of exemption for those who cannot afford payment may be disproportionate to the amount of money which could be collected.

At first sight it would seem that the more those who can afford to pay for their health services can be made to do so, the more publicly financed services can be made available for those who cannot pay. For example, if the better off can be prevented from using the free services and forced to use private practitioners and pay for their hospital treatment, more of the needs of the poor can be met by the existing free services. But this is not the way it tends to work out in practice. Once the better off go to different and better services, they may resent paying both directly for their own services and indirectly through taxes for the services of poorer people. Their need to purchase their own services has reduced their capacity to pay taxes to finance services for others as well as themselves. Secondly, if the better off use different services, they cease to press for improvements in the basic free services. Thirdly, doctors tend to give more time to private patients. Private practice can seriously restrict the number of doctors willing to work in the organized services. Thus by all these routes less may come to be provided for the poorer section of the population than if all had used the same services. Indeed the poor may be left with a lower standard of service than if the services had continued to be free for all who wished to use them.

In the course of time the better off may find private service so expensive that they demand direct and indirect subsidies towards them. In the case of hospitals, charges for private beds may not be increased in line with rising costs so that the subsidy to a private bed can end up greater than the total cost of a free bed. This has been the case in several countries in Africa and Asia.

The Dangers of Health Insurance and the Growth of the Private Sector

When two or more standards of health services become established, the middle income group will seek admission to the higher level service – at least for the most serious illnesses. As it can involve hardship for them to pay for such services when the need arises, voluntary insurance arrangements are introduced to enable them to pay in advance. It is then not long before there is pressure to extend these arrangements to cover a section of the population by compulsory insurance, for example, government employees and those working for larger employers. In time these arrangements may be extended to cover a high proportion of the urban population.

As shown in Chapter 2, social security may be run by government or by autonomous agencies – in some cases separate agencies for different occupational groups. Responsibility for organizing or supervising social security arrangements is often given to Ministries of Labour rather than Ministries of Health, because of the relation to conditions of employment. This can lead to unfortunate consequences if the government department nominally responsible for health can no longer plan the distribution and organization of health services owing to the growth of separate agencies dedicated to serve the interests of their members irrespective of the consequences for the health services provided for others. In the course of time social security can come to dominate the market for health services and lower the standard of service provided to those who do not have access to it and cannot be provided with access to it. This has been the experience of social security in many countries in Latin America.

The consequences are likely to be most serious when fee-for-service arrangements for payment which originally operated in a relatively small unorganized private sector are used in the compulsory health insurance scheme. The medical profession naturally seeks to retain in health insurance the level of fees which provided doctors with a middle-class level of living from a few private patients even though demand is expanded by health insurance and the payment of bills is guaranteed by the scheme. Private doctors respond to the expanded demand by working longer hours or cutting down on the time given to each patient or delegating tasks to secretarial, nursing and technical staff. Thus private practice becomes much more financially advantageous than work in the government service and doctors leave the government service. Patients are encouraged to use more services or doctors provide more services for which they can charge so that the extra doctors may attain a comparable level of living to those already established. Pressure grows to set aside or build more beds for private patients, better equipped and staffed hospitals; more drugs are prescribed, more pathological tests and X-ray examinations are undertaken: all these extra costs may be covered by raising the health insurance contribution paid by the employee, or employer, or both.

Thus more of the limited health resources of the nation are used for the benefit of the minority covered by health insurance. As it is not practicable to collect compulsory contributions from rural peasants and from small-scale farmers on behalf of their employees and rural earnings are too low for the contributions to be paid, it is impracticable to extend the scheme to cover the rural population. Thus all the forces which make doctors prefer urban practice to rural practice are reinforced by the higher earnings in urban practice. It can then become impossible to find doctors willing to accept posts in rural areas and these posts go unfilled. In the attempt to maintain skeleton curative services, preventive programmes are postponed. Within the health insurance scheme itself, the emphasis is likely to be heavily curative unless strong incentives are built in to encourage personal preventive work (such as immunization). Health priorities are distorted and the major preventive programmes of a collective kind to eradicate or control the main communicable diseases of the rural areas are neglected.

Health insurance may have been originally introduced in the hope that the scheme could eventually be extended to cover the whole population. But once costs become inflated, this becomes impractical. Moreover the costs of the service enjoyed by the urban population may be shifted in part on to the rural population in so far as urban employers raise the prices of their products to cover the cost of the employer's contributions they are required to pay for each employee or taxes are increased to pay for the higher insurance costs of the government service. Some of the goods produced by the urban population will be purchased by the rural population.

In so far as the urban population are paying high premiums for health insurance, their taxable capacity is reduced. It is less possible to require them to pay taxes either to finance rural health services or to finance developments in other fields. In so far as the rural population are paying in higher prices part of the cost of urban health insurance, their taxable capacity is reduced. Thus the money which government might have been able to collect for environmental public health, education and other services and to promote economic growth is mortgaged in advance to pay for curative services for a minority of the population – often including services which are unnecessary, inefficient and ineffective.

These are the dangers of introducing a health insurance scheme before it can be extended to cover the whole population. The risks are greatest when health insurance is allowed to develop outside the control of health departments and without proper safeguards to ensure that the services are provided economically. It is not only inequitable but uneconomic to allow two hospital systems to run parallel – an expensive one for health insurance patients and a poor one for those not covered by health insurance. A country with limited medical manpower cannot afford to lose control of where that medical manpower works and of national priorities in the use of health resources. Thus the levels and systems of remuneration of doctors established in the private sector and in the health insurance sector are as much the concern of government as salaries established in the public service. Having granted doctors monopoly power by registration or licensing, the government must be concerned with how that monopoly power is used. Weakening that monopoly power by flooding the country with medical graduates, if this can be done, is an expensive and ineffective remedy. Many Latin American countries which are generously supplied with doctors have used them to provide costly health insurance schemes for the urban population not better rural health services. They work as surgeons rather than as experts in public health.

The experience of Latin America has important lessons for developing countries in other continents which have not yet started health insurance or started only on a small scale. If it is decided to provide better services for the better off through health insurance, the remuneration provided for doctors working in it must not be more attractive than in government service. This can be best secured by salary or capitation payment. The beds used for hospital insurance patients should be beds in the public hospitals, though a higher level of amenity and greater privacy may be provided for them. Only in this way is it possible to retain control over the planning of national health services.

Conclusion

The conflict between the demands of the more affluent section of the urban population and the needs of the rural population, between private practice and public service, lies at the heart of the problem of health planning in most developing countries. Often the public sector is planned and the private sector is left to develop in response to market forces. But too often these forces frustrate the implementation of plans for the public sector. Only if a country plans the whole of its health services – public and private – will plans have a prospect of success. But the political leadership of few countries is prepared to assume the powers over the private sector which are required. And some lack the will to challenge the enormous inequalities of their societies even in the cause of better health for the majority.

But where there is the will, the method of improving health without making impossible demands on scarce economic resources is increasingly understood. The efficacy of the method has been demonstrated in China – a vast country with poor communications, an enormous population and extremely limited economic resources. The key lies in simple village services provided by people drawn from the village and provided with limited health education.

The contribution to the health of Western nations of their costly and prestigious hospitals has been small compared to the introduction and use of clean water, the safe disposal of excreta, higher standards of personal hygiene and improved nutrition. It does not require five or more years of expensive university education to absorb and teach these messages or start the battle against parasitic diseases with such weapons as are known to be effective. Nor does it require the equipment of the regional hospital. What is required is a leadership which will secure population cooperation. This only emphasizes that health is an integral part of socio-economic development. It is part of what people can do for themselves.

NOTES

1. J. Bryant, *Health and the Developing World*, Cornell U.P., Ithaca, N.Y., 1969, p. 43.

2. ibid., p. 50.

3. O. Gish, *Doctor Migration and World Health*, Occasional Papers on Social Administration, No. 43, Bell, 1971, p. 104.

4. J. Bryant, op. cit., p. 15.

5. M. King, *Medical Care in Developing Countries*, O.U.P., 1966, p. 1.1.

6. O. Gish, op. cit., pp. 73–4.

7. CIBA, *Human Rights in Health*, Amsterdam, p. 7.

8. 'Buildings well constructed in unburnt brick, "pisé de terre", "mud-wattle" or whitewash, or whatever other cheap material is used, and roofed with corrugated sheeting, need not be squalid, provided they are well-planned, properly put together, and kept in good repair.' D. Church, 'The Architecture of Hospitals and Health Centres' in M. King, op. cit., p. 10:6.

9. Gish, op. cit., p. 78.

10. ibid., p. 105.

11. ibid., p. 109.

12. ibid., p. 110.

13. V. Navarro, 'The Under-development of Health or the Health of Under-development', *International Journal of Health Services*, Vol. 4, No. 1, 1974, p. 11.

14. J. H. de Haas and J. H. de Hass-Posthuma, 'Socio-Medical Achievements in the People's Republic of China', *International Journal of Health Services*, Vol. 3, No. 2, Spring 1973, p. 281.

15. M. King, op. cit., p. 2:6.

16. ibid., p. 2:7.

17. ibid., p. 2:3.

18. ibid., pp. 12:7–8.

19. M. King, op. cit., p. 2:3.

20. J. Ahumada et al., *Health Planning Problems of Concept and Method*, Pan-American Health Organisation, Washington, D.C., 1965.

21. For discussion of further problems of using the CENDES method, see H. E. Hilleboe et al., *Approaches to National Health Planning*, Public Health Papers No. 46, W.H.O., Geneva, 1972, Chapter 6.

22. A rudimentary attempt at this is to be found in R. M. Titmuss et al., *The Health Services of Tanganyika*, Pitman, 1964.

23. See *Health Progress in Africa 1968–73*, Regional Office for Africa, W.H.O., 1973.

24. D. Flahaut, 'Front-line Workers', *World Health*, November 1974, p. 30.

25. H. E. Majid Rahnema, 'The Role of Frontline Health Workers', *WHO Chronicle*, Vol. 29, January 1975, p. 9.

26. M. King, op. cit., p. 1:13b.

CHAPTER 12

Education and Training

Plans for education and training should be derived from long-term plans for health service manpower. In turn, plans for health service manpower should be derived from long-term plans for the development of the health services. Thus decisions are needed on what it is planned to accomplish, and where and when it is planned to accomplish it, before it is possible to specify what manpower is needed to do it – how many persons with particular levels of education and specialized skills.

In many countries the health service manpower which has been trained partly determines what health services are provided and where they are provided. Surgery is much more practised in the United States than in Britain, partly because there are more surgeons per head. Some parts of the country have good health services and others poor, partly because health professionals want to practise in some parts and not others. Primary care is underdeveloped because most doctors want to practise as specialists and have been trained as specialists. Standards of public health are poor partly because until recently few doctors have chosen this specialty. In Britain high standards of care are provided for the acute sick and low standards for the aged and mentally ill and handicapped because geriatrics, psychiatry and care of the mentally ill are not popular specialties.

Training and education programmes can involve high costs. For example, in the United States it cost $3 billion dollars in 1972 to educate 300,000 students for eight health professions.[1] Over half this sum was spent on the education of some 10,000 doctors. First there is the cost of the staff, buildings and equipment devoted to the provision of the education and training itself. Second there is the cost of maintaining those being trained or educated while they are not providing services. Some students (for example, nurses) provide apprenticeship services which are of value, while others provide negligible services during their training period. These costs may fall in whole or part on those receiving the education or training or their families or the training body or Ministry concerned. When trainees are required to live away from their families during the training period, costs are higher than when trainees can live with their families. This is one of the considerations which should influence the decision on where training is provided.

The Cost of Medical Education

It is extremely difficult to calculate precisely the cost of medical education. This is partly because most medical teachers are also involved in other activities such as research, the teaching of other health personnel, post-graduate and continuing education for doctors, and the provision of clinical services. A second problem is that a hospital used for teaching normally has higher costs than other hospitals, and it is extremely hard to calculate how far this cost is due to undergraduate medical teaching.

In Table 4 we show for a number of countries estimates of the average annual cost of educating a student until he graduates from

TABLE 4

The Cost of Undergraduate Medical Education

Year of estimate	Location of Medical School	Per capita national income in 1966 U.S. $	Annual cost per student U.S. $	Total cost per graduate U.S. $
–	Colombia (Cali)	256	1 817	24 600
–	Ecuador (Guayaquil)	190	331	2 844
–	Ecuador (Quito)	190	166	1 233
–	El Salvador	241	1950	14 500
1965–66	England (provinces)	1543	3786	24 556
1965–66	England (London 1)	1543	3139	15 683
1965–66	England (London 2)	1543	4001	20 051
–	Jamaica	431	2400	24 000
–	Nigeria (Ibadan)	68	4950	33 600
–	Senegal (Dakar)	183	10500	84 000
1970–71	Sweden	2571	5471	30 091
–	Thailand	112	1618	6 660
–	Uganda (Makerere)	90	3080	26 000
1959–60	U.S.A.	3175	4491	19 630

Source: B. Abel-Smith et al., 'Can we reduce the Cost of Medical Education?', *WHO Chronicle*, Vol. 26, No. 10.

medical school. The earnings foregone while attending school are not included. Part of the wide variations in cost shown in the table may be due simply to the fact that the estimates are not all for the same year; unfortunately, the original sources did not always indicate the years for which the estimates were made. Another possible source of variation is the exchange rate used to convert costs from local currency to U.S. dollars; it is widely accepted that the official rate of exchange may be misleading. Other possible sources of variation are the degree of completeness in reporting and differences in concepts and accounting procedures. No doubt real differences in cost remain, which may be associated in turn with the size and quality of the educational programme and with the care taken to control its cost.[2]

What is remarkable about this table is that the cost per medical graduate appears to be higher in several developing countries than in Britain or the United States. Also remarkable is the vast variation in cost. What is by no means clear is that the more costly medical schools are producing graduates better equipped to undertake the work which will be expected of them.

There are a number of ways by which the cost of medical education can be kept low. First the construction of a purpose-built teaching hospital is often unnecessary. Indeed it can be undesirable if it distorts the geographical distribution of limited medical resources by offering a much higher standard of service to the population in its vicinity than is available elsewhere. In a developing country an urban hospital cannot serve effectively as a national or regional hospital to which the most difficult cases are referred because of the cost and difficulty of travel.[3] Clinical teaching can be done in district hospitals and health centres which are not more elaborate than others provided elsewhere.

The traditional medical school in the more developed countries is built to house separate academic departments each of which may have its own laboratories, lecture rooms, seminar rooms and research facilities, all of which are under-used. The key to designing an economic medical school is to ensure that laboratories are cunningly designed for multi-purpose use and that lecture and seminar rooms and equipment are pooled for joint use by different departments and by students taking different courses. The basic sciences may be taught in the university, so that the laboratories and other facilities can be used by students taking other academic courses. Alternatively purpose-built facilities may be designed for use by all grades of health service staff under training. Laboratories can cost as much as a third of the whole cost of a medical school.

The use of existing medical and other staffs on a part-time basis to do most of the clinical teaching and some of the pre-clinical teaching can reduce running costs and help to ensure that teaching is orientated towards local needs and problems. A wide range of specialized teachers is required if the curriculum is planned on the traditional discipline basis which makes it difficult for students to relate what they have been taught to the actual problems they will confront in medical practice. Thus some new medical schools in developing countries have planned their curriculum on the basis of medical problems and the various subject teachers have shown the application of each discipline to the problem selected for discussion. Curricula designed on this multi-disciplinary basis can be taught with a lower ratio of teachers to students. Schools on these lines are those at Amman, Basra and Beirut. The school at Addis Ababa was originally on this basis.

Standards of provision which may be acceptable in a rich developed country are wasteful if copied in a developing country. For example, the U.S. Public Health Service published in 1961 a report on the minimum costs of a medical school.[4] This report has been frequently used for the quite different purpose of planning medical schools in developing countries. The report allocates one-third of the physical space of the school to research and recommends that a medical library should contain 150,000 volumes and sets of 1,500 periodicals. It has been suggested that a collection of 5,000 volumes and a maximum of 500 periodicals should be sufficient in a developing country for teaching purposes provided students have a sufficient stock of the textbooks which they will use most.[5]

Large though training costs may be, a much larger financial commitment is the provision of remuneration for health personnel after they are qualified and working in the health services. For example, in Britain the average remuneration of a doctor over three years is greater than the average cost of education of a doctor. To train health personnel and then find later on that some cannot find work or are under-employed is to waste the money spent on education and training, whoever paid the cost. It is equally wasteful if they find work by providing unnecessary services. Some Latin American countries (for example, Argentina and Uruguay) have trained such an excess of doctors that some have abandoned medicine and found it more lucrative to work as taxi drivers.

Nor does the cost of making use of a trained person stop with his remuneration. Health personnel cannot use their training effectively unless they have the supporting health resources (buildings, equipment, supplies and supporting staff) to do their work. The fuller the training, the larger resources needed for effective work. For example, in the United Kingdom each year the average general practitioner authorizes prescriptions alone which amount to more in total than his own remuneration and also requests X-rays and pathology tests, home nursing and other services for patients sick at home. The average hospital specialist authorizes expenditure amounting to many times his annual remuneration.

For a thorough economic analysis of the cost of education and training, one has to look not just at the direct costs of training but at what has been lost during the training period. What contribution to production would the trainee have made if he had not been receiving training? Similarly the true economic cost of employing health personnel after training is the contribution they would have made to production if they had entered some other field. Thus, for example, the cost of having doctors or dentists in a developing country may be the loss of prospective business managers or agricultural experts. Where higher education is at an early stage of development these 'opportunity costs' can be very large.

Any plan for education and training must take into account the other needs of the economy. If a disproportionate number of university places in a developing country are devoted to medicine, it is likely that ultimately some of the doctors will not use their medical training. They will become businessmen or take prestigious non-medical jobs in the public service or enter politics. It would be both better and cheaper to allot more places in higher education to subjects which provide a better preparation for business, public administration or politics.

The Loss of Doctors through Migration and Private Practice

The most common waste of a country's money spent on the education and training of health service manpower occurs when doctors, dentists, pharmacists, nurses or other trained personnel emigrate.

The scale of migration of nurses is large but systematic information on net migration is not available. In the case of doctors, the migration from the developing countries to the more developed is one of the tragedies of the post-war world. There has also been large-scale migration between the more developed countries – particularly from Britain to Canada and Australia and from Canada to the U.S.A.

The Mecca for the migrating doctor is the United States. Excluding the United States, China and Eastern Europe, the world's medical schools produce about 40,000 medical graduates a year. The number of doctors taking the American examination for foreign medical graduates (E.C.F.M.G.) in 1969 was 23,000 – over half of them for the first time. About 8,000 candidates passed the examination.[6] There are 63,000 foreign medical graduates in the United States – one-fifth of active doctors, about one-third of hospital interns and residents and a similar proportion of newly licensed doctors.[7] Of those admitted in 1970, 55 per cent came from Asia, 6 per cent from Africa and 5 per cent from South America. The number of foreign-born doctors working in Britain increased by 10,000 between the early 1950s and the late 1960s.[8] Out of the nearly 14,000 foreign-born doctors in Britain at 30 September 1966, about 8,800 came from developing countries, including over 6,000 from the Indian Sub-Continent.[9] Some developing countries have been producing far more doctors than they can absorb. The richer countries have been glad to admit these doctors because they have not produced enough medical graduates of their own. But it amounts to a massive subsidy from the poor countries to the rich. The 63,000 foreign medical graduates in the United States represent an asset which it would cost over $1500 million to produce in the United States.

The number of Indian doctors now working abroad is believed to be 10,000 to 15,000 – about the same number as are serving India's rural population of 450,000,000.[10] The number of Pakistani doctors who left the country between 1962 and 1965 was 55 per cent of the output of Pakistani medical schools;[11] Sinhalese emigrant doctors to Britain in 1966 and 1967 were equivalent to 30 per cent of the output of Sinhalese medical schools.[12] In 1968 the number of Filipino doctors who took one of the United States State Board examinations which provide full registration was one-half of the output of Philippine medical schools in that year.[13] About three-quarters of the output of Thailand's medical schools leave the country upon qualification.[14] In 1969, 850 Iranian doctors took the

E.C.F.M.G. examination compared with an annual output of about 600 graduates from Iranian medical schools.[15] The problem of medical emigration is also serious in Mauritius and the West Indies and becoming serious in some newly independent African countries.

The rewards available to doctors in the more developed countries are far in excess of those available in the developing countries even allowing for the higher cost of living. But the prospect of financial reward is not the only reason for migration. It is a major step to abandon family and friends and country of birth for a foreign land and to risk racial and other discrimination. Emigrating doctors are pushed out by the lack of the job opportunities which they want and attracted by such opportunities elsewhere as well as by the financial rewards.

The doctor who emigrates is a serious loss to the country which trained him as in most countries medical education is heavily subsidized by the government. Moreover the value of a doctor to a society can be much more than the cost of his training, whoever paid the bill. It is true that emigrant doctors tend to send back substantial sums of money to their families. But the education of doctors who emigrate is an expensive way of improving the balance of payments or lightening the burden of over-population.

Not only may doctors go abroad but they may enter private practice and serve only a small section of the population. In developing countries private practitioners make a relatively small contribution to the health of the society and an addition to their ranks can be almost as wasteful of government training costs as emigration. Developing countries which are particularly short of medical manpower often require a period of work in the organized service before a doctor is allowed to enter private practice. One way of combating the growth of private practice is to charge a heavy annual licensing fee to doctors working in this field with the deliberate aim of discouraging private practice.[16]

The emigration of doctors has been facilitated because most developing countries have adopted the medical curricula of more developed countries with little amendment to suit local circumstances. Such curricula are inappropriate for three reasons. First, the pattern of disease is different: the developing countries are still overwhelmed by the communicable diseases and health problems which cause heavy morbidity and mortality in children and young adults while the main health problems of more developed countries afflict the older section of the population – particularly heart disease, cancer and coronaries. Second, and more relevant from an economic point of view, many of the expensive treatments provided in more developed countries – particularly those of uncertain effectiveness – cannot be afforded in developing countries or can only be afforded for very few. Thirdly, the methods of practice need to be simpler as the lavish facilities of more developed countries cannot be afforded. To train a doctor to practise medicine as it is practised in Britain or the United States and then send him to a rural health centre to use a short list of drugs and rudimentary diagnostic equipment is not only wasteful but breeds dissatisfaction. It is not surprising that doctors trained in this way search out opportunities to practise as they were taught, even though this may have little impact on the health problems of their country. Most of the post-graduate education provided in more developed countries is grossly inappropriate for doctors from developing countries.

A similar problem underlies the emigration of doctors trained in Britain. In many British medical schools students became heavily orientated towards hospital medicine and naturally sought to enter a hospital specialty – particularly internal medicine and surgery. When after several years of post-graduate education, they could not find senior jobs in their chosen specialty, many went abroad to countries where they could practise their specialty.[17] Until recently Britain has been producing more hospital specialists than she needs and too few doctors orientated towards general practice. And, as mentioned above, the strong emphasis on hospital medicine in North America is one reason why general practice is a dying specialty.

Each country should decide what jobs need to be done and then train and educate those who are to do them. What grades of health personnel are required with what facilities in what type of setting to provide what type of service? The answer to these questions will depend on the health priorities of each country. If, for example, it were decided in the United States that the key need is good primary care services in deprived urban areas and rural areas, training programmes should be established to provide the teams which will provide this service where it is needed. A corollary may be restriction of entry to over-stocked specialties, such as surgery. A policy of free entry by examination to any specialty can gravely distort a medical care service and seriously inflate its cost, because a specialist can, within limits, create work for himself within his specialty.

Similarly a developing country which has to choose its priorities, whether they are improved nutrition, the acceptance of family planning or the control of communicable disease, should work out and test the most cost-effective programme for achieving these objectives and train the appropriate staff to implement the plan. To achieve many of its objectives a simple infrastructure of health services may be needed. But its orientation and thus its manpower requirement will be a consequence of the chosen priorities.

The Role of other Health Service Staffs

There is nothing sacrosanct about the particular grades of health service manpower which have evolved. Indeed, such terms as doctor, dentist and nurse imply a homogeneity of job content within countries and between countries which simply does not exist. Much of what doctors and dentists do in both developed and developing countries could be done equally well or better by others.

Is a doctor required to take a medical history or can it be done by a nurse or medical secretary using a carefully devised form or questionnaire? A doctor may decide to ask some pertinent further questions when presented with a history recorded by someone else but this would take much less of his time than to take the history himself. How often does the doctor write out or telephone requests which others could make on his behalf? How much administrative work is undertaken by doctors which could be performed as well or better by a purpose-trained administrator? Should the instructions on the home care of a patient be given by a doctor or by a nurse who would provide that care if the patient were in hospital? How much medical as distinct from scientific training is needed to make and interpret pathology tests? Medical knowledge is needed to decide what action the test results indicate, but not necessarily to perform them or interpret them.

The extent to which particular procedures are actually performed by doctors rather than other staff varies according to the customs of the country, the place of practice (in or out of hospital), the remuneration system, staffing ratios and legal provisions. For example, does the doctor or the nurse or some other health worker act as anaesthetist during an operation, deliver a baby, administer an injection, take out stitches or put them in?

The core of the doctor's work is to decide what a patient or community needs. But even in countries where health services are freely available people still manage their own minor illnesses often with help from the local chemist. It is only when illnesses fail to respond to treatment or simply fail to go away that the doctor is consulted. Should a recognized role in the giving of medical advice in all countries be allocated to a grade of personnel with less medical training than a doctor? It may be thought that people would not go to anyone else with their illnesses if a doctor were available. But many people attempt to use chemists for this purpose. When doctors' practices include health visitors, social workers or nurses in Britain, some patients prefer to take many of their problems to them rather than to the doctor though they are free to choose which to consult. Laws regarding the registration or licensing of doctors and their exclusive rights were passed in the West before there were highly trained grades of nurses or of other categories of health personnel. It does not require five or more years of medical education to treat a cut or boil or set a broken arm.

The same is true of dentistry. Most of the dentist's time is spent not in deciding what treatment is needed but in providing it. Normally it is the dentist himself who drills, fills, caps and extracts. In New Zealand, however, most of these tasks are done for children by trained ancillary staff. While extensive knowledge may be needed to decide what needs to be done, the main requirement for the performance of these tasks is manual skill. While nursing staff in hospitals take blood specimens, fit drips and administer injections, drilling teeth is, in many developed countries, the exclusive function of a grade with training equivalent to that of a doctor. Moreover, while hospital nurses administer other injections, local anaesthetics are administered by dentists.

Routine procedures are not necessarily better done by persons with a lengthy professional education. Indeed the reverse may be the case. Where manual skill and conscientious attention to detail are needed, the work may be better performed by those who do it frequently, are unrushed and are not distracted by considering other aspects of patient care. Thus a ward orderly assigned to take temperatures may do it more accurately than a nurse or ward sister who is thinking of all the other tasks which await her attention. The nurse or paramedical worker who takes blood specimens all day will do the job better than the senior pathologist who only does it occasionally for private patients.

In the past few years, there has been growing interest in the more developed countries as well as in the developing countries in using practitioners with lesser training than doctors. This interest has largely arisen because of the difficulty in getting doctors to work in less popular areas and specialties – particularly in general practice. In the United States there has been the additional incentive to find a role for the highly trained and competent military corpsmen returning from the Vietnam War. By 1974, thirty-three states had authorized the functioning of physicians' assistants and seven had authorized nurse practitioners. A report in Canada in 1972 recommended the training of nurse practitioners to meet primary care needs.[18] In many countries there are legal restrictions on what nurses can do. In 1971 nurses in Belgium sent an enquiry to doctors asking whether nurses could properly perform a list of procedures. The reply was that they could and regularly did. It was, however, illegal for nurses to do them.[19] The Ontario study mentioned in Chapter 10 indicates how effectively nurses can operate as practitioners.[20]

While richer countries can afford, but are not necessarily wise to afford, the luxury of using expensive educated staff to undertake tasks which could be undertaken by those with lesser training, a developing country cannot. There should be a greater delegation of tasks to auxiliary grades of health personnel, and a higher proportion of supporting staff should work under the supervision of the doctor or dentist. In practice, however, the reverse is found in many developing countries. It has been suggested that as an optimum there should be $2\frac{1}{2}$ nurses for each doctor.[21] In Egypt, India, Kenya, Pakistan and Turkey there were in the late nineteen-sixties about two doctors to one nurse or midwife.[22] In Latin America and the Caribbean there were three doctors to one nurse but for each nurse there were nearly four nursing auxiliaries.[23] Moreover nurses are heavily concentrated in hospitals rather than in the community.

But even hospitals in developing countries often have fewer nurses, and also fewer technicians and other trained staff per doctor than in more developed countries. This is *prima facie* evidence that earlier training policies have been unbalanced.

Not only do lower levels of staff cost much less to employ after training but the training period is shorter and the cost of training per student/year is much lower. It has been calculated that in Thailand it costs five times more to train a doctor than a nurse and in the United States nearly ten times more. In East Africa two and a half nurses, twenty medical assistants or thirty auxiliary nurses could be trained for the cost of training one doctor. In Columbia, eight nurses or twenty-four auxiliary nurses could be trained for the cost of training one doctor.[24] A training scheme for lower grades can be established much more quickly than for medical students. If it takes one year to establish a two-year course for medical assistants and four years to establish a medical school, a ten-year plan in East Africa would, at current costs, train 700 medical assistants at a total cost of less than a million dollars U.S. In the same period and for the same money it would be possible to build a medical school for a hundred students and pay for the first cohort to complete the first year.[25] Many countries have placed far too much emphasis on the production of doctors and far too little on the recruitment and training of nurses, sanitary inspectors, medical auxiliaries, technicians and other staff with lesser training.

Thus it is extremely difficult to say how many doctors a country 'needs'. Evidence that all needs for health services are not currently being met does not prove that more doctors are required. It may be that the same result could be secured with the same number of doctors, a more efficient deployment of the existing stock and an increase in other grades of staff to whom tasks traditionally performed by doctors could be delegated. This is as true for developed countries as for developing countries. A 'shortage' of doctors may only exist because the legal rights, restrictive practices and customary activities of doctors are regarded as unchangeable.

The Medical Curriculum and the Medical Teacher

Each country should, therefore, consider carefully what precise tasks persons with university education are needed to perform, and design curricula accordingly. The same is true for persons with a lower education. For example, the main objective in Britain is not to try and teach medical students all that is known about medicine but to produce a doctor with 'a knowledge of the medical and behavioural sciences sufficient for him to go forward with medicine as it develops further'.[26] The mention of the behavioural sciences is important. There is some truth in the assertion that 'doctors study medicine which they do not practise and practise social sciences which they have not studied.'[27]

209

In those developing countries where the bulk of the population is rural the functions required of a doctor may be to plan, lead, supervise, evaluate and train rather than undertake medical work himself. He may need to know more about the jobs of other members of his rural health care team than about the work which is performed in the glossy teaching hospitals of the richer countries of the world. For this role, he will need much less knowledge of anatomy and of the basic theoretical medical sciences than a doctor destined to become a hospital specialist in a more developed country but he will need to know much more about preventive, social and community medicine. This does not mean that his education will lack scientific rigour or make fewer intellectual demands. He may be spared the minutiae of anatomy and the more sophisticated biochemistry but he will need expertise in epidemiology and statistics and to be equipped to examine critically the evidence in support of preventive and curative procedures and learn what is known and what is not known about how to prevent and treat the main diseases which he will be combating. He will also need to be equipped to examine the costs of alternative strategies and understand why particular priorities may be established at particular times. Above all else he will need to be trained to seek out the causes of ill-health in the community he is serving, whether they are to be found in culture, diet or environment. His skills will need to be in the planning and control of limited resources and in giving leadership and providing continuing education to the health team he is leading.

One of the major gaps in medical education both in the more developed and in the developing countries is lack of teaching of medical economics. In the developing countries, all doctors play a major part in deciding how medical resources are used at every level of the service. The extent to which the health of the people is improved depends on how efficiently the resources at its disposal are deployed. If a more costly drug is used when a less expensive drug could be equally effective, some patient somewhere is deprived of effective treatment. If a hospital admits a patient unnecessarily or retains that patient longer than is necessary, some other patient is deprived of hospital care. The economical use of medical resources is not just the concern of the government or the administration, it is the concern of every doctor who wants to improve health. Similarly, it is absurd that in more developed countries, doctors who deploy such vast resources are not trained to use them as efficiently as possible. The doctor has a duty to protect his patient's pocket as well as his health, and countries which have conferred clinical freedom on doctors working in social security or health service programmes must be assured that this freedom is used responsibly in economic terms. If it is not, in the long run this freedom may come to be restricted.

Professional education should be much more than the imparting of knowledge and skill. It should impart the attitudes and values of the profession as it should be practised in the particular society. All over the world students tend to absorb the attitudes and values of their principal teachers. In the case of medical students it is usually the clinical teachers who exercise the most influence. If these teachers are only interested in unusual cases, this will rub off on the students. If they are engaged in private practice and their main orientation is towards this, this will also be conveyed to the students. If they denigrate general practice, psychiatry, social medicine, medical administration, this will also be communicated to the students. If they emphasize cure and give little attention to prevention and care, their students will become orientated accordingly. Thus the introduction of new well-endowed departments of social or community medicine into a traditional medical school may have little impact on the orientation of its medical graduates. Only if the most influential teachers favour these subjects and stress their importance are they likely to influence the orientation and interests of the students. If the medical teachers are dedicated to meet the main health needs of the country among the poorer rural population, medical students will become orientated accordingly. Values and a sense of commitment cannot be taught: they are learnt by observing the behaviour and values of those who win respect.

The Location of Training Centres

A large urban hospital is not the best place for teaching health personnel who will be working in a rural setting or perhaps even in an urban setting. The urban teaching hospital tends to orientate medical education towards episodic, curative and mechanistic intervention on a biased selection of hospital patients. The student needs to see the pattern of disease as it actually presents itself in an urban or rural community, observe the functioning of the pattern of health services in which he is being taught to work. If it is planned to change the deployment and organization of health services, the entering student should be trained on the pattern which it is planned to establish, and further education should be provided for those accustomed to different patterns of organization and deployment of personnel.

While the medical student in a developing country may need to visit the large urban hospital to see unusual procedures and diseases, the bulk of his training needs to be in the district. His clinical teachers should be those who are doing the job and he should be conscious of the satisfaction which they derive from doing it well. Similarly in more developed countries experience of good primary care is essential. Only thus can the student learn the importance of managing the home care team – the role of support and care and the relationship between health care and social care.

Traditionally personnel who work in the health services have been trained separately on different courses. There are medical schools, nursing schools and schools for health administration and paramedical staffs. There are not only economies in staffing and accommodation to be gained from training different grades and categories of staff in one complex but advantages for the education and training provided. Indeed some of the teaching should be done together – particularly the teaching of social medicine and of the organization of health services. Health service staff who are intended to work together as a team should in part be trained together as a team. This is important in countries both rich[28] and poor.

Students should be drawn from the communities in which they are intended to work. Those drawn from an urban community are unlikely to be content to live and work in rural areas. Nor would they be as well equipped to understand and interpret the customs and way of life of rural people and to speak their language. Even if a student comes from a rural community but spends several impressionable years at a city university or training school, he is less likely to want to return to a rural setting. Only a small proportion of those trained may be willing to accept the jobs for which they are trained.

Thus, schools for health service staffs should be sited relatively near where health service manpower is needed and the students should be recruited from the local community. This will mean that some of the students will have poorer educational backgrounds than if educational achievement were allowed to determine admission policy. Extra teaching or a longer course may therefore be needed for some students. But this is still likely to be the best and cheapest way of getting staff to work where they are needed. A doctor who is happy to return to the community where he was born and marry into that community is of much more value than a doctor posted for two years to a rural area where his main activity may be to swot for the E.C.F.M.G. examination or for specialist board examinations.

As pointed out in Chapter 10, financial inducements to persuade doctors and other health personnel to work in rural areas or in deprived urban communities are of limited effect. They do not deal with the problem at its roots – the unsuitability of the education provided, the inappropriateness of the place of training and the selection of students on criteria which favour those from the more prosperous section of the community.

Continuing Education

One of the most serious failings of health services all over the world is the relative neglect of continuing education, not only for doctors, but for other personnel working in the health service. Too often it is assumed that all professional personnel can find the time and have the inclination to keep their practice up to date even though only minimal opportunities are provided for them to do so. While some grasp at every opportunity to attend refresher courses, some do not, so that the gap between good modern practice and poor old-fashioned practice continually widens after qualification.

Continuing education is needed partly because of the rapidity of the growth of medical knowledge and techniques. For example, we pointed out in Chapter 6 the rate at which new pharmaceuticals are introduced and the problem of the practising doctor in evaluating new developments and sorting out from the mass of sales promotion which new preparations he should be using for what. The doctor working in a hospital is better placed to check on the merits of new developments from discussion with his clinical colleagues and with the hospital pharmacists. But the doctor in independent practice outside the hospital can easily accept too readily the claims of company representatives. Doctors working in cooperative groups in the community are more likely to keep up to date and there are obvious advantages in pharmacists working as closely with primary-care doctors as with hospital-based doctors.

The system of registration or licensing which confers the right to practise for life without any further education or test of competence is increasingly being questioned. There is a growing demand for attendance at refresher courses or even periodical re-examination to be made a requirement for the continuation of rights to practise.

Continuing education is also needed to facilitate changes in the organization and delivery of health services. For example, doctors who have been trained for independent practice do not readily accept the need to practise as members of a team of professionals and to form cooperative rather than competitive relationships with their colleagues in the same profession. If the key to improving the quality of health services and securing greater value for money lies in better organization and in the participation of all the health professions in the planning of services to achieve desired ends, original education for independent practice needs to be supplemented with education for group and team practice in which the emphasis is on the health of the community rather than the health of the individual.

Conclusion

The whole plan for the training of health personnel should be designed for the pattern of health services which it is planned to establish in the future. Moreover, it is the attitudes, ethics and commitment of those who are trained which will determine how well the best-laid plans will actually function in practice. A key role is played by the doctor. No longer can his work be thought of simply as the provision of medical advice and cures for people who consult him. In every society the doctor controls vast resources and should accept the responsibility as a member of a team for managing patient care and community care in its widest sense. The health of our societies is more than the health of the individuals that compose it.

NOTES

1. Institute of Medicine, *Costs of Education in the Health Professions*, National Academy of Sciences, Washington, D.C., 1974.

2. The annual cost per medical student can be translated into costs per medical graduate by taking two factors into account. The first is the duration of training: the annual cost is multiplied by the number of

years it takes to complete the course. The second factor is the drop-out rate which serves to raise the cost of training a successful graduate. The calculation is complicated by the fact that knowledge of the total drop-out rate for a cohort of medical students is not enough. It is also necessary to know when the wastage takes place. For example, if, of all entering students, the cumulative loss over five years is 25 per cent, and if the entire loss occurs at the final examination, the proportion of all school years wasted is 25 per cent. However, if the attrition proceeds at a uniform rate of 5 per cent per year, the entire loss of school years amounts to only 12·5 per cent.

3. For example, 'about 80 per cent of the patients in the New Mulago Hospital, Uganda's national hospital, come from the neighbouring district of Mengo which contains only 20 per cent of Uganda's people.' M. King, *Medical Care in Developing Countries*, O.U.P., 1966, pp. 2–5.

4. D.H.E.W., *Medical School Facilities*, Washington, D.C., 1961.

5. B. Abel-Smith et al., 'Can we reduce the cost of medical education?', *WHO Chronicle*, Vol. 26, No. 10, p. 449.

6. O. Gish, *Doctor Migration and World Health*, Occasional Papers on Social Administration, No. 43, Bell, 1971, p. 11.

7. T. D. Dublin, 'The Migration of Physicians to the United States', *New England Journal of Medicine*, 20 April 1972, p. 1.

8. Gish, op. cit., p. 26.

9. ibid., p. 32.

10. ibid., p. 73.

11. ibid., p. 77.

12. ibid., p. 82.

13. ibid., p. 93.

14. ibid., p. 95.

15. ibid., p. 99.

16. As suggested in R. M. Titmuss et al., *The Health Services of Tanganyika*, Pitman, 1964, p. 70.

17. See B. Abel-Smith and Kathleen Gales, *British Doctors at Home and Abroad*, Occasional Papers on Social Administration, No. 8, Bell, 1963.

18. Department of National Health and Welfare, *Committee on Nurse Practitioners*, 1972.

19. Ruth Roemer, 'How Five Nations Respond to the Issues', *Hospitals*, Vol. 48, No. 22, 16 November 1974.

20. See pp. 163–4 above.

21. N. R. E. Fendall, 'Primary Medical Care in Developing Countries', *International Journal of Health Services*, Vol. 2, No. 2, May 1972, p. 305.

22. ibid., p. 306.

23. 'The Critical Nursing Situation in Latin America and the Caribbean Area', *Boletin de la Oficiana Sanitaria Panamericana*, Vol. VII, No. 2, 1973, p. 75.

24. J. Bryant, *Health and the Developing World*, Cornell U.P. Ithaca, N.Y., 1969, p. 122.

25. It was roughly estimated that medical schools in Middle Africa were costing U.S. $8,990 per student place. J. Bryant, op. cit., pp. 259–60.

26. *Royal Commission on Medical Education 1965–6,*· Cmnd. 3569, H.M.S.O., 1968, para 200.

27. L. Eigenberg, quoted in *Ned. Tschr* v. *Genseesk* Vol. 118, No. 3, p. 3, 1974.

28. See, for example, Institute of Medicine, *Educating for the Health Teams*, National Academy of Sciences, Washington, D.C., 1972.

CHAPTER 13

Conclusion

In the first two chapters of this book, we showed the somewhat chancy way in which the organization and financing of health services have evolved in different countries. The principal healer, the doctor, emerged from the priestly role he played in a variety of different cultures, and still plays in many primitive societies today, to become torn between the ethical values of professional service and the commercial values of capitalist societies.

How far should he become a capitalist himself, owning his own hospital and diagnostic equipment, selling his own drugs? Should he himself market comprehensive health services – become the owner of a Health Maintenance Organization? This capitalist model is to be found in its most developed, though heavily price-regulated form in Japan. Something approaching it is to be found in parts of France, Latin America, the United States, and elsewhere. Or should he be a public servant operating in a government service, paid a salary like the school teacher, university professor or judge, cooperating with other professionals to serve his local community? The doctor's main worry about this latter role is how far it is possible to combine professional freedom with government service.

Governments have normally intervened first to establish the monopoly rights of the medical profession and secondly to establish hospitals for categories of patients for whom provision clearly had to be made – for the mentally ill, for those with infectious diseases and often also for the poor whose families could not care for them – if provision was not already being made by charity, religious or lay-organizations. But of greater importance for the public health has been the action of governments in the provision of safe water supplies and sanitary disposal. A third stage of development has been the establishment of comprehensive health services for the armed forces and in some countries for wider a range of government employees. But a fourth stage of intervention has been the provision of compulsory health insurance. In Europe this was the extension of arrangements which had evolved on a voluntary basis. But elsewhere compulsory insurance was often introduced with little or no precedent in voluntary action and no prospect of covering more than a limited section of the population.

Compulsory health insurance was introduced for a variety of political reasons including the fact that it was on the whole popular with those brought within the scheme. The poorer knew that the rich had better health and may have attributed this simply to their ability to buy the services of doctors, to pay for the drugs they prescribed and for care in the hospitals to which they were admitted. Politicians may also have attributed their own health simply to their ability to make use of health services whenever they needed them. The doctors working in health insurance and health services provided the largely curative services which they had been trained to provide by the doctors who taught in medical schools – often doctors who practised medicine among the wealthy. These teachers themselves may have come to attribute the health of their patients to their ministrations and forgotten how much was due to the spacious and clean environments in which they lived and the resistance to disease built up by their protein-rich diet.

Some developed countries have substituted planned health services for health insurance services but in many of them the insurance origin is no more than thinly disguised. There remains a conflict between the values which doctors learnt in medical schools and the values of community health improvement for which the health services had been created. It was because the Russians reformed medical education as well as the structure of their health services that practice within their services conformed more to their stated intentions.

When the Europeans took Western health services to the colonies they took the services they needed for themselves – the panoply of hospitals and personal doctors to care for members of the armed forces and the officials who ran the colonies. To an extent which varied according to the colonizing power a start was made later on in trying to improve the environment which was so adverse to the health of the indigenous people. But with colonial freedom came a leadership which often assumed that the key to improved health lay in the facilities which the colonists had provided for themselves.

Thus the provision of curative services was often given priority in countries with inadequate nutrition, with poor water supplies, low standards of personal hygiene and grossly inadequate sanitation. A heavy emphasis was placed on the provision of hospitals in countries where the good done by hospital care could be so rapidly undone when patients were discharged to an unfavourable environment.

In Chapter 3 we explained the rationale for removing the money barrier from health services and in Chapter 4 the peculiarities of the health market. We emphasized two crucial facts. First the consumer cannot assess the quality of what he is receiving. Secondly it is the doctor not the patient who demands and authorizes the use of the bulk of the health resources of a nation.

In Chapter 5, we examined the economic incentives of the doctor under different systems of remuneration. While a fee-for-service system seems at first sight to provide the fairest payment for work done and the most promising setting for the independence of a liberal profession, it can create incentives for excessive intervention and unnecessary services and encourage competition at the expense of cooperation with other health personnel. Moreover, regulations introduced to correct abuses can come to challenge clinical independence. But the alternatives of capitation and salaried payment can also involve abuses, if they are imposed on doctors who are commercially motivated and have opportunities for private practice on the side.

In Chapter 6 we analysed the working of the world pharmaceutical industry. We acknowledged the immense contribution to medical progress which had been made by the large international companies operating under the protection of the patent system. But we drew attention to the need for tough government intervention to regulate the safety and efficiency of what is sold and to control how it is sold. The success of the salesmanship of the manufacturers can place at risk the professional standing of the doctor as well as generate unnecessary costs for health services and health insurance agencies.

In Chapter 7 we analysed the economics of hospitals. We concluded that the supply of hospital beds had to be planned as within limits supply creates demand. But limitation of supply can create bottlenecks and distortions unless doctors are trained and motivated to use what is supplied in the way in which it is intended to be used

and are provided with a full range of alternatives to care in hospital –
day surgery, day hospitals and a full complement of services for
domiciliary health care and social care.

Against this background we discussed health priorities in Chapter
8. We showed that health services were absorbing a continuously
growing proportion of the resources even of the richest countries in
the world. But those countries which spent the most did not necessarily have the highest health standards. We pointed out the need
for the widest possible approach to preventive medicine and the
dilemmas facing richer and poorer societies in restricting individual
liberty and raising other costs in the cause of health improvement.
In the case of developing countries we stressed once again the
importance of nutrition, pure water, sanitation and personal hygiene
in promoting health standards. We explained the underlying difficulties of establishing a health status index from which health priorities
could be derived. We then turned in Chapter 9 to discuss the
relationship between health and economic development. We showed
that health services could contribute to economic development and
economic development to improvement in health status. We
described attempts to measure the economic effects of health services. But we stressed that the underlying purpose of health services
was to provide better health not economic growth.

We turned in Chapters 10 and 11 to discuss the implications of
this analysis for health planning in countries at different levels of
development and in Chapter 12 for the education and training of
health service manpower. Planning is necessary because both
experience and theory have shown that leaving the private market
to respond to money-backed demand results in maldistribution of
resources, risks for the quality of some services, the provision of
excessive, unnecessary and ineffective services, an inflation of costs
and a general distortion of health priorities in societies at all levels
of development. Spending more on health services does not necessarily generate better health for the country as a whole.

The recognition that the important causes of ill-health lie in how
people live and in the environment in which they live leads to two
conclusions. First, some countries are over-investing in the provision
of health services compared to other methods of social investment to
improve health. Secondly, much of what is currently spent is not
spent efficiently even for the achievement of the somewhat limited
objectives of current services. Already there are several countries in

which the working population is working nearly a month in the year just to pay for health services. Soon it may be five weeks a year and if present trends continue it will not be long before five weeks becomes six. Will there come a time when the working population says, 'So much is enough'? How long will it be before the working population demands hard evidence that it is really getting value for each day devoted to working to pay for health services? How much is spent to establish a diagnosis which if established could not lead to effective treatment? How much is spent in costly efforts to save life which had only a remote prospect of being successful and no prospect of achieving anything approaching recovery? How much is spent in postponing death by days or weeks without providing an extension of conscious life or the prospect of doing so? As Dr Mahler, Director General of W.H.O. said recently:

> . . . the major – and most expensive – part of medical technology as applied today appears to be more for the satisfaction of the health professionals than for the benefit of the consumers of health care.[1]

These questions bring us face to face with the difficult ethical dilemmas of medical practice. What is health improvement? And how is it to be assessed by those who have to take these difficult decisions? How much discomfort should be imposed on the patient with what prospect of health improvement? How much should be spent with what chances of extending what is little more than technical survival?

Attention has become increasingly focused on these fundamental ethical problems, partly because of the extension of medical technology and partly because of the cost of this extension. Before there are pressures to limit clinical freedom, because our societies are unwilling to incur the economic costs which that freedom is imposing, the health sector has a duty to satisfy the public that it is achieving a tolerable level of efficiency in the use of resources – that resources are only used in the provision of services when they can be effective and that effective services are provided at the lowest cost consistent with acceptable standards of care.

This cannot be achieved without planning and skilled management. The key lies in coordination and cooperation between the health professionals and skilled managers, and an effective dialogue with community representatives. This requires a unified structure of services at the national, regional and local level. But, last but not least, it requires health professionals who are committed and trained to work within such a system and who can see beyond the health needs of the individual patient to the wider health needs of the whole community.

NOTES

1. H. Mahler, 'New Possibilities for WHO', *WHO Chronicle*, Vol. 29, February 1975, p. 43.

Index

Addis Ababa, 178, 181, 201
Africa: auxiliary health workers, 188, 209; medical schools, 185; migration of doctors, 203, 204; mission hospitals, 102; private beds in hospitals, 192
Alberta, 19, 22, 93
Alsace, 18
American Medical Association (AMA), 10, 22, 91, 159; Council on Drugs, 86
American Pharmaceutical Association, 93
Amman, 201
anaesthetics, development of, 1
apothecaries, 5
Arab Kingdom and early development of hospitals, 3
Argentina; doctors, 50, 201–2; hospitals, 23; voluntary health insurance, 9
asepsis, 1
Asia: breast feeding, 139; migration of doctors, 203; mission hospitals, 102; private beds in hospitals, 192
attitudes to medical care, 26–7
Australia: community health centres, 165; compulsory health insurance, 22; drugs, 92, 94; health expenditure, 122; hospital service, 19, 22; reimbursement to patient scheme, 18, 60; voluntary health insurance, 8
Austria: doctors, payment of, 14–15, 64; health insurance, 8, 14

auxiliary health workers, 107, 187–90, 207–9
Axnick, N. W. 149

Bangkok, 178
Barlow, R., 151
Basra, 201
Belgium: compulsory health insurance, 16, 65; doctors, payment of, 64; drugs, 86; midwifery, 6, nurses, 208
Bellevue Hospital, 4
Beirut, 201
Berki, S. E., 109
birth control, 127, 150–1
Blue Cross, 20–1, 39, 161
Blue Shield, 60
Bogota, 181
Bombay, 178
brand names (pharmaceuticals), 80, 81, 92, 93, 97
Brazil, 9
Britain: appliances, 95; attitude to medical care, 26; British Medical Association, 6, 8, 15, 54; care institutions, variety of, 166; Code of Marketing Practice (pharmaceuticals), 91; compulsory health insurance, 15, 16; dental service, 158; doctors, distribution of, 169; doctors, payment of, 60, 68, 69–70, 71–2, 73, 116, 201; drugs, 77, 86, 87, 92, 95; education, medical, 209; friendly societies, 9–10, 15; general practitioners, 15, 25, 67–8, 116; health centres,

Britain—*centd*
165; health expenditure, 122, 123, 125; home care services, 112, 165–6; home nursing, 6; hospital service, 4, 19, 20, 25, 72, 104, 109, 116, 117, 162; in-patients, length of stay, 104, 112; manpower, 198; Medicines Commission 93; migration of doctors, 205; Midwives Registration Act 1902, 6; Minister of Health, 25; mortality rates and health expenditure, 125; National Health Service, 4, 24–5, 60, 72, 86, 89, 95, 158, 170; pharmaceutical industry, 83, 91; preventive medicine, 149; private medicine, 60, 71–2; referral system, 67–8; role of care, 131; Royal Commission (on health insurance), 20; Sainsbury Committee, 83–4, 86, 89, 91, 92, 93, 95; sick absence in working population, 144; specialists, 25, 60, 68; voluntary health insurance, 8, 9–10; voluntary hospitals, 19, 20, 25, 104; V.P.R.S., 95

British Columbia, 19, 22, 209
British Medical Association, 6, 8, 15, 54
budget control, 169–72
Buenos Aires, 50
Burma, 22

Calcutta, 179
California, 54, 63
Canada: compulsory health insurance, 22, 43; doctors, payment of, 19, 60; Hastings Report, 165; health expenditure, 122; hospital admissions, 116; hospital insurance, 20; nurse practitioners, 208; Pharmaceutical Act 1972, 93; pharmaceutical industry, 89, 92; Restrictive Trade Practices Commission, 92
capitation system of payment for doctors, 67–71, 219

care, role of, 130–1
Caribbean, 208
Ceylon, 149, 151, 203
Chain, 79
chemist, role of, 207
child mortality, 140–1
Chile, 17, 22, 25–6
China: 'bare-footed' doctor, 183; health education, 182; health services, 196
chloramphenicol, 86
cholera, 2, 3, 33, 148, 150
chronic sick, 35, 38, 43
Columbia, 87, 199–200
collective goods, 33
community health service, 221–2, 214
compulsory health insurance, 8, 13–29, 218
consumer (of health services): lack of knowledge, 41–2, 56, 219; limitations of choice, 34–6, 45–9; *see also* patients
Cordoba, 50
'cordon sanitaire', 128
costs: medical education, 198–202, 208–9; of health services increasing, 220–1; of ill-health, 143–51; preventive medicine, 149
curative medicine, 129–30, 191
curriculum, for medical studies, 201, 204–5, 209–11
Czechoslovakia, 6

de Gaulle, 60
democratic control, of health services, 172–4
Denmark: doctors, payment of, 15, 16; drugs, 95; hospital service, 3, 19
diseases of industrial societies, 139
developing countries: auxiliary medical workers, 187–9; 208–9; birth control, 150–1; birth-rate, 142–3; culture of, 178–9; distribution of resources, 180–3; economic costs of ill-health, 144;

developing countries—*contd*
education, medical, 200, 209, 210; health education,179; health status indices, 136; hospital services, 102–3, 115, 186; malnutrition, 132–3; migration of doctors, 202–6; mortality rates, 132; needs of, compared with more developed countries, 200–1, 204–5; pharmaceuticals, 94, 96–7; planning health services, 177–96; traditional healers, 179

doctors: and pharmaceuticals, 78, 81, 82, 90, 92, 97; as members of health team, 73, 163, 214; as purchasing agents, 51–5, 219; capitation system of payment, 8, 67–71; conflict of interests, 52–3, 155; costing of health services, lack of knowledge of, 54, 81, 92; dispensary, 6; earnings related to supply, 50; education of, 56, 198–214; ethical code, 53, 217; fee-for-service payment, 53, 58, 59–67; in service training and study, need for, 49, 83, 90–1, 97, 213; migration of, 202–6; monopoly powers of, 50–1, 156, 195, 217; offering health insurance, 37–8; owning hospital or pharmacy, 53, 155; patient ratios, 178; role of, 2–3, 11, 55, 217; salary, payment by, 8, 71–3; training, 49–50; 198–214

drugs: advertising, 82, 83, 84, 90, 91, 92, 96, 97; and doctors, 78, 81, 82, 85, 90, 92, 97; brand names, 80, 81, 82, 92, 93; chemists and drug substitution, 93; control, 94, 95; effectiveness, 90; Food and Drug Administration (U.S.), 86, 90, 94; generic prescribing, 97; -induced illness, 82, 127; multi-national drug companies, 80, 87–8, 96; new, 82–3, 87; non-prescription drug sales, 77; number of prescriptions, 77; on free list, 94, 95;

patents, 80, 81, 92, 96, 97, 156, 219; pricing of, 80–1, 87, 88; profits of drug companies, 87–9, 92–5, 156; safety, 79–80, 90, 219, sales representatives for drug companies, 83, 84, 91, 97

E.C.F.M.G., 203, 213
economic costs of ill-health, 143–8
economic development and health, 138–51, 220
Ecuador, 199–200
education: health, 129, 179, 182, 185, 188; in-service training and study, 49, 83, 90–1, 97, 213–14; medical, 78, 131–2, 140, 175, 187–90, 198–214, 220
Egypt, 50, 208
El Salvador, 199–200
employers, and voluntary health insurance, 39–40
England, cost of medical education, 199–200
environment, factor in health, 126–7, 132
'ethical' pharmaceuticals, 77–8
ethics of medical profession, 53, 56, 58, 66, 72, 73, 74, 175, 211, 217
Ethiopia, 178
Europe: and health services in colonies, 7, 218–19; attitude to medical care, 26; Eastern, 50, 81, 111, 169; nineteenth-century development in medicine and health services, 1–6, 8–10; origins of health insurance, 22, 23, 27; Southern, 72; Western, 1, 16, 17, 19, 115, 158, 161, 168; *see also* under names of countries
euthanasia, 141
evaluation of health services, 172–4
external benefits, 33, 41

families, social costs of ill-health, 146
fee-for-services payment, 52–3, 58, 59–67, 70, 159–60, 219

Feldstein, M.S., 109, 117
Finland, 18, 165
First National City Bank of New York, 88
Fleming, 79
Flexner report (U.S.), 50
Florey, 79
Food and Drug Administration (U.S.), 86, 90, 91, 94
France: alcohol-related disease, 127; attitude to medical care, 26; doctor, role of, 217; doctor-owned hospitals, 23, 101; doctors, payment of, 18, 61, 64, 66; drugs, 86, 92; French Revolution, 3; health expenditure, 122, 123, 124–5; hospital service, 20, 22, 23, 161, 162; in-patient, length of stay, 115; mortality rates and health expenditure, 124–5; number of drug prescriptions, 77; reimbursement to patient system, 23, 60–1; voluntary health insurance, 8
free health service, 41, 46–7

general practitioner, 5, 16, 164
generic prescribing, 97
Germany: compulsory health insurance, 13–15, 16, 59; doctors, payment of, 14–15, 18, 61, 62–3, 64, 66, 67; drugs, 86; health expenditure, 122, 124–5; hospital services, 20, 101, 161–2; industrial health insurance, 13; in-patients, length of stay, 115; mortality rates and health expenditure, 124–5; sick funds and regulation of purchase, 157; voluntary health insurance, 8, 9, 16
Ghana, 181
Glaser, W. A., 63
government, costs of ill-health, 146

Hastings Report (Canada), 165
health and economic development, 138–51

health centres, 165
health education, 179, 182, 185, 188
health expenditure, trends in, 121–5
Health Maintenance Organization (U.S.), 217
health profession, regulation of, 49–51
health insurance: compulsory, 13–29; private, 38–9; voluntary, 1–11
health services: and redistribution of income, 40–2; and social investment, 220; and social services, 154–5, 164, 166; as a right, 42–3; as investment in people, 140–3; as necessity, 40–2; increase in expenditure, 121–5; justification of free, 32–4; mobile, 183; objectives, 126; political advantages of, 182; priorities in, 121–36
health status index, 133–6, 220
Holland: attitude to medical care, 26; compulsory health insurance, 16, 60; doctors, distribution of, 69; doctors, payment of, 68, 69, 70; hospitals, 20; in-patients, modified fee-for-service, 16; see also Netherlands
home care, 102, 111, 112, 115, 164
Hong Kong, 148
hospitals: alternatives to, 173, 220; budget, 169–70; construction of, 101–2; demand and supply of hospital beds, 102, 117–18, 155, 160; development of, 1, 3–5, 7, 217; economics of scale in, 106–10, 111, 118; efficient use of, 101–18; health insurance and, 22–4; in-patients length of stay, 111–15, 160; isolation, 3; large, 108; non-profit, 102, 103; out-of-hospital services, development of, 5–7; payment per day of care, 159; planning of service, 105, 111, 118, 160–3, 186; prestige,

hospitals—*contd*
103–4; regulation of supply, 160–3; siting of, 110–11; small, 109–10; social costs of, 108; teaching, 4, 211; under-used, 102–3; unnecessary admissions, 115–17
hypochondria, 46, 47

ill-health, causes of, 126–7
import restrictions on pharmaceuticals, 80
India: auxiliary medical workers, 208; hospital service, 3, 7–8, 22; migration of doctors, 203; preventive medicine, 149
Indonesia, 177
Iran, 189, 203–4
Ireland, 87
Israel, 10, 27, 72
Italy: compulsory health insurance, 15, 16; doctors, payment of, 68, 69; drugs, 81; economic effects of ill-health, 148; hospital service, 5, 23; INAM, 69

Jamaica, 199–200
Japan: compulsory health insurance, 16–17; doctor-owned hospitals 53, 101; doctors, payment of, 66; doctors selling pharmaceuticals, 17, 53; hospital service, 23; role of doctor, 17, 217
Jenner, 1

Kaiser Permanente, 170
Kenya, 139, 182, 208
King, Dr Maurice, 190
Kupat Holim (Israel), 10, 27

Latin America: attitude to medical care, 26; auxiliary medical workers, 208; Centre of Development Studies (CENDES), 184; distribution of resources, 182; doctor, role of, 71–2; hospital supply, 195, 201–2, 203; doctors, payment of, 71–2; hospital service, 3, 7, 102; occupational health services, 7; reimbursement to patient scheme, 18; social security, 24, 27, 193; voluntary health insurance, 9
Lee, Dr Philip, 88
life expectation, effects of increase in, 142–3
Lloyd George, 15
Lorraine, 18

Mahler, Dr H., 221
malaria, 33, 147, 149–50, 151
Malawi, 177, 178
Mali, 148
Manitoba, 93, 94, 165
Manpower, 156, 168–9, 198, 205, 206–9
Mauritius, 204
Maxwell, Robert, 124
mechanization in medical procedures, 107
Medicaid, (U.S.), 23, 27, 66, 94–5, 159
medical associations, and role of doctor, 11
medical journals, 82, 84, 85, 91, 95, 96
medical market, 45–57, 155, 219
medical schools, 200–1
medical teaching staff, 201
medical technology, 35–6, 37, 106–7
Medicare (U.S.), 19, 21, 23, 27, 43, 66, 94, 131, 157, 159, 161
Medicines Commission (Britain), 93
Metyana Hospital (Uganda), 183
Mexico, 7, 23
Middle East, 72
midwifery, development of, 6–7
migration of doctors, 202–6
mission hospitals, 8
modern medicine, development of, 1–3
money barrier, to use of health services, 32–44, 147, 155, 219
monopoly powers of doctors, 50–1, 156, 195, 217

mortality rates and health expenditure, 124–5
multi-national drug companies, 87–8, 96

Nassau, Duchy of, 6
national health services, beginnings of, 13–29
Netherlands: compulsory health insurance, 16, 65; doctors, payment of, 63, 64, 68; drugs, 77, 86; health expenditure, 122, 123, 125, 158; Hospital Planning Council, 161; hospital service, 161; midwifery, development of, 6; mortality rates and health expenditure, 125
New Delhi, 178
Newfoundland, 19
New York City, 10; State, 104, 117
New Zealand: auxiliary medical workers, 207; doctors, payment of, 18–19; drugs, 94, 95; health expenditure, 122; New Zealand Medical Association, 18–19; voluntary health insurance, 8
Nigeria: doctor/patient ratios, 178; health expenditure, 177; medical education, cost of, 199–200
Nightingale, Florence, 174
Norway: compulsory health insurance, 15; doctors, 6, 15; drugs, 94; hospitals, development of, 3; medical staff, distribution, 169
nursing staff, 164, 165, 167–8

occupational insurance schemes, 43
Ontario, 19, 93, 163–4, 208

Pakistan: auxiliary medical workers, 208; migration of doctors, 203; Rural Health Centre Programme, 181
patents, drug, 80, 81, 92, 96, 97, 156, 219; non-patent market, 81
patients: and lack of knowledge, 47, 48–9, 53, 70, 130, 155; /doctor relationship, 47; length of stay in hospital, 104, 112–14, 118, social costs of in-patients, 117; see also consumer
payment of doctors, 58–74, 165
Peru, 7, 23
pharmaceutical industry, 17, 77–98, 155, 156, 219; see also drugs, patents
Philippines, 203
placebos, 47, 52, 80, 90
planning health services, 220, 221; in developing countries, 177–96; in more developed countries, 154–75
Poland, 6, 24
Pole, J. D., 149
polyclinics, 6, 10
'poor law' development, 5
Poor Relief (Ireland) Act 1851, 6
population growth, 123–4
Portugal, 3, 7, 26
preventive medicine, 33, 126–9, 146–51, 166, 181, 191, 194
primary care, 163–8
priorities in health services, 121–36
private medicine, 5, 6, 51–2, 58–9, 62, 71–2, 101–2, 156, 163, 167–8, 191–2, 192–5, 202–6
Professional Standards Review Organizations (U.S.), 159
Prussia, 6, 13–14
public health, 6, 217

Rafferty, J. A., 117
referral system for levels of health care, 191
regulation of health services, 157, 160–8, 190–1
reimbursement to patients system, 17–19
research, 34, 79, 131, 140
Roemer, Milton, 117
Roosevelt, 21
rural/urban health services, 178, 180, 193–4, 195

Sainsbury Committee (Britain), 83–4, 86, 89, 91, 92, 93, 95
salaried system of payment for doctors, 71–2, 74, 219
Saskatchewan, 19, 22, 94
Scandinavia: hospital service, 3–4, 24, 162; voluntary health insurance, 8
Scotland, 112
Seattle, 10
Senegal, 149, 199–200
smallpox, 1, 3, 33, 148
social care, 167, 170, 212
social security, 16, 40, 41, 43, 193–4
Somers, Professor, 105
Spain: attitude to medical care, 26; compulsory health insurance, 16; doctors, payment of, 68; hospital service, 3, 7, 23; ill-health, economic effects, 148; voluntary health insurance, 9
Spencer, D. J., 149
substitution, drug, 93, 156
Sudan, 177, 178
Sweden: doctors, payment of, 61, 63, 64, 66, 71–2; drugs, 77–8, 86; health centres, 165; health expenditure, 122, 123, 124–5; hospital service, 3–4, 5, 19, 112, 116, 161, 162; medical education, 199–200; mortality rates and health expenditure, 125; nursing service, 168–9; reimbursement to patent system, 18, 60, 61; voluntary health insurance, 8
Switzerland: doctors, payment of, 6, 18, 64, 66; reimbursement to patient system, 18, 60; voluntary health insurance, 8

Tamale, 181
Tanzania, 189
Task Force on Prescription (U.S.), 88, 89, 92, 93
teaching hospitals, 4, 211
Thailand: doctor/patient ratio, education, medical, 199–200,

208; health expenditure, 177; migration of doctors, 203
traditional healers, 179
Truman, President, 21
Tunisia, 22
Turkey, 208

Uganda, 183, 199–200
Upper Volta, 148
urban/rural health services, 178, 180, 193–4, 195
Uruguay, 9, 201–2
U.S.: American Medical Association (AMA), 10, 21, 86, 91, 159; American Pharmaceutical Association, 93; attitude to medical care, 26–7; auxiliary medical workers, 208; Bellevue Hospital, 4; Blue Cross, 20–1, 39, 161; Blue Shield, 60; compulsory health insurance, 21–2; consumer cooperatives, 10; County Medical Societies, 10; Department of Health, Education and Welfare, 122; doctor, role of, 217; doctors, payment of, 18, 58, 63, 66, drugs, 77–8, 80, 82, 83, 85, 86, 87, 92, 93, 96; education, medical, 50, 51, 198, 199–200, 209; Flexner report, 50; Food and Drug Administration, 86, 90, 91, 94; health expenditure, 121–2, 123, 124–5, 178; Health Maintenance Organization Act 1973, 171; Health Maintenance Organizations (HMOs), 38, 170–1; Hill Burton programme, 161; hospital insurance, 20–1; hospital service, 4–5, 22, 101, 102, 103–5, 109, 116, 117, 161; hospital utilization committees, 158; in-patients, length of stay, 104, 112; ill-health, economic effects, 143, 144, 150; manpower planning, 198; Medicaid, 23, 27, 66, 94–5, 159; Medicare, 19, 21, 23, 27, 43, 60, 66, 94, 131, 157, 159, 161; midwifery, development of, 7;

U.S.—*contd*
modern medicine, development of, 1, 2; monopoly powers of doctors, 51; mortality rates and health expenditure, 125; National Academy of Sciences, 86; negligence suits, 54; 'New Deal' social security legislation, 21; New York, 10, 104; New York State, 104, 117; Partnership for Health Act 1966, 161; pharmacists, 78; prescriptions, numbers of, 77; preventive medicine, 146, 148, 149; Professional Standards Review Organizations 159; Public Health Service, 201; surgeons, 74; Task Force on Prescription Drugs, 88, 89, 92, 93; tissue committees, 158; voluntary health insurance, 10, 26
U.S.S.R.: doctors, payment of, 71–2, 73; education, medical, 218; hospital planning, 162; manpower planning, 50; national health service, 24; polyclinics, 17; rural medical service in nineteenth century, 6

Veblen, 103
Venezuela, 23, 189
Vietnam, 96
voluntary health insurance, 8–10, 18, 36–40, 42–3
voluntary hospitals, 4–5

Washington D.C., 10
Weisbrod, B.A., 149
West Indies, 204
World Health Organization (W.H.O.), 1, 80, 97, 148, 221
World Medical Association, 18